Statistics for the Behavioural Sciences

To Sandra

Contents

Preface   xi
Acknowledgements   xiv

1 Introduction and basic concepts   1
Why is statistics useful in the behavioural sciences? 1
Measurement scales 6
Descriptive and inferential statistics 9
What is an experiment? 10

2 Descriptive statistics   14
Organising raw data 14
Frequency distributions and histograms 14
Grouped data 15
Stem-and-leaf diagrams 17
Summarising data 20
Measures of central tendency: mode, median, and mean 21
Advantages and disadvantages of mode, median, and mean 23
A useful digression on the Σ notation 26
Measures of dispersion (or variability) 27
*Further on the mean, variance, and standard deviation of
    frequency distributions 33*
*How to calculate the combined mean and the combined variance
    of several samples 35*
Properties of estimators 36
Mean and variance of linearly transformed data 38

3 Introduction to probability   42
Why are some notions of probability useful? 42
Some preliminary definitions and the concept of probability 43
Venn diagrams and probability 44
The addition rule and the multiplication rule of probability 47
Probability trees 49
Conditional probability 50
Independence and conditional probability 53
Bayes's theorem 54

4   Probability distributions and the binomial distribution   57

Introduction 57
Probability distributions 58
Calculating the mean (μ) of a probability distribution 60
Calculating the variance (σ^2) and the standard deviation (σ)
  of a probability distribution 62
Orderings (or permutations) 63
Combinations 66
The binomial distribution 66
Mean and variance of the binomial distribution 70
How to use the binomial distribution in testing hypotheses 70
The sign test 75
Further on the binomial distribution and its use in hypothesis testing 76

5   Continuous random variables and the normal distribution   78

Introduction 78
Continuous random variables and their distribution 78
The normal distribution 81
The standard normal distribution 84
Hypothesis testing and the normal distribution 87
Type I and Type II errors 89
One-tailed and two-tailed statistical tests 93
Using the normal distribution as an approximation of the
  binomial distribution 95

6   The chi-square distribution and the analysis of categorical data   100

Introduction 100
The chi-square (χ^2) distribution 100
The Pearson's chi-square test 101
The Pearson's χ^2 goodness of fit test 103
Further on the goodness of fit test 107
Assumptions underlying the use of Pearson's χ^2 test 108
Pearson's χ^2 test and the analysis of 2×2 contingency tables 110
Further on the degrees of freedom and the calculation of the expected
  frequencies for any contingency table 113
The analysis of $R \times C$ contingency tables 114
One- and two-tailed tests 115
How to measure the strength of the association between variables
  in a contingency table 116
A fundamental conceptual equation in data analysis: Magnitude of a
  significance test = Size of the effect × Size of the study 119
An important note on the inclusion of nonoccurrences
  in contingency tables 120

7   Statistical tests on proportions   123

Introduction 123
Statistical tests on the proportion of successes in a sample 123

Confidence intervals for population proportions 124
Statistical tests on the difference between the proportions of successes
  from two independent samples 127
Confidence intervals for the difference between two independent
  population proportions 129
Statistical tests on the difference between nonindependent proportions
  of successes (McNemar test) 130

8   Sampling distribution of the mean and its use in hypothesis testing   134
Introduction 134
The sampling distribution of the mean and the Central Limit
  Theorem 134
Testing hypotheses about means when σ is known 136
Testing hypotheses about means when σ is unknown: the Student's
  t-distribution and the one-sample t-test 137
Two-sided confidence intervals for a population mean 141

9   Comparing a pair of means: the matched- and the independent-samples
     ***t*-test**   146
Introduction 146
The matched-samples t-test 146
Confidence intervals for a population mean 149
Counterbalancing 150
The sampling distribution of the difference between pairs of means and
  the independent-samples t-test 151
An application of the independent-samples t-test 155
Confidence intervals for the difference between two population means 157
The robustness of the independent-samples t-test 158
Ceiling and floor effects 162
Matched-samples or independent-samples t-test: which of these two tests
  should be used? 164
A fundamental conceptual equation in data analysis: Magnitude of a
  significance test = Size of the effect × Size of the study 165

10   Nonparametric statistical tests   168
Introduction 168
The Wilcoxon matched-pairs signed-ranks test 168
The Wilcoxon rank-sum test 172

11   Correlation   176
Introduction 176
Linear relationships between two continuous variables 176
More on linear relationships between two variables 178
The covariance between two variables 181
The Pearson product-moment correlation coefficient r 183
Hypothesis testing on the Pearson correlation coefficient r 184
Confidence intervals for the Pearson correlation coefficient 185

Testing the significance of the difference between two independent
   Pearson correlation coefficients r *187*
Testing the significance of the difference between two nonindependent
   Pearson correlation coefficients r *188*
Partial correlation 190
Factors affecting the Pearson correlation coefficient r *192*
The point biserial correlation r_{pb} *194*
The Spearman Rank correlation coefficient 198
Kendall's coefficient of concordance W *200*

12 Regression   202
Introduction 202
The regression line 202
Linear regression and correlation 207
Hypothesis testing on the slope b *207*
Confidence intervals for the population regression slope β *209*
Further on the relationship between linear regression and Pearson's r:
   r^2 *as a measure of effect size 210*
Further on the error of prediction 211
Why the term regression? 212

13 Introduction to power analysis   214
Introduction 214
Effect size and power 215
Factors affecting the power of a statistical test 215
Power calculations for the one-sample t-*test 219*
Power calculations for the independent-samples t-*test 222*
Power calculations for the matched-samples t-*test 223*
Power calculation for correlation coefficients 225
Power calculation for the difference between two independent
   Pearson's correlation coefficients r *227*
Power calculation for a single proportion 228
Power calculation for the difference between two independent
   proportions 229

Appendix   231
References   238
Index   239

Preface

Personal computers that are fully loaded with the latest software packages that allow us to perform more or less complicated statistical analyses are readily available. Hence, it has become "easier" for a user to enter a set of data into a computer and obtain the correct answer. However, this process is not as straightforward as it may appear.

In order to feed the computer with all your data and obtain the right answer, you first need to know what you want to do with your data and what it is the most appropriate way to analyse them. If you do not have a clear understanding of the rationale that underlies each statistical procedure you need to use, then is very likely you will have a poor understanding of the output obtained from any statistical package (even when the output may contain the right answer!). Given these premises, the approach taken in this book has been to introduce and explain statistical concepts and the application of statistical techniques in a clear and detailed manner. It is fundamental to understand why and how specific statistical analyses should be performed. A good understanding of statistics is preferable to learning a set of procedures by rote, or to learning how to press the right button on the computer. Furthermore, notice that without a relatively good understanding of the process of statistical hypothesis testing, most of the articles published in psychology journals will be almost incomprehensible.

In a nutshell, the main aim of this book is to help the reader understand the basic concepts of statistics. This book provides full and exclusive coverage of the material usually taught in first year statistics courses which are part of undergraduate degree schemes in the behavioural sciences. It provides a clear, step-by-step introduction to basic statistical techniques with plenty of examples, each discussed in depth, based on psychology studies which utilise the statistical techniques described. The presentation of these techniques aims to provide a conceptual understanding of the basic concepts of elementary statistics. The book is written in such a way that fundamental concepts, e.g., the logic of statistical inference, are often recapitulated and repeated several times in different contexts, thus providing an adequate basis for an in-depth understanding and retention of key statistical concepts. Given the introductory emphasis adopted here, more advanced statistical techniques such as Analysis of Variance, Multiple Regression, and Multivariate Methods are not covered in this textbook.

It may be surprising that after having mentioned the use of statistical packages in carrying out statistical analyses no commitment to any particular statistical package has been made in this book. This unbiased approach has been chosen because it does not force instructors into using any, maybe unwanted, specific statistical package. Learning how to use a statistical package is easier than learning statistics. This statement has not been made to scare the reader, but just to warn that learning statistics is a challenging but also a rewarding experience. If you find some concepts difficult to grasp immediately, *do not worry*, since this feeling is quite common (I have experienced it on a fairly regular basis!). Just read the relevant section(s) more than once. On the other hand, learning to use a statistical package is relatively easy but not necessarily very rewarding: It is enough to consult its manual.

The textbook is composed of 13 chapters. Chapter 1 is introductory. It provides a convincing argument, using a simple example, as to why some statistical knowledge is useful to students in the behavioural sciences. Furthermore, some basic concepts of statistics and research methodology are presented. Chapter 2 describes the main statistical techniques employed to summarise and describe sets of data. You will notice that a few mathematical formulae are given. Mathematical formulae cannot be avoided in statistics, and a minimal knowledge of basic algebra will help to understand them. Some formulae will appear more complicated than other, but in all cases appropriate steps have been taken to make these formulae easy to understand. Chapter 3 introduces some concepts of probability. Since most of the book describes inferential statistics techniques (alternatively called statistical hypothesis testing techniques), and given that the decision process performed in statistical inference is based on the probability of obtaining a set of data assuming that certain conditions are true, Chapter 3 describes some important concepts of probability which are relevant to clearly understanding the process of statistical inference.

Chapters 4 and 5 introduce the concept of probability distributions and their use in the process of statistical hypothesis testing. The appropriate application of this process to sets of data is paramount to answer questions of the type: "Is a particular type of therapy effective?" or "Is intentional learning more effective than incidental learning?". Chapter 4 mainly concentrates on probability distributions of discrete variables, in particular the binomial distribution, while Chapter 5 is mainly devoted to probability distributions of continuous variables, in particular to the normal distribution. Both chapters give examples of the application of probability distributions in the process of statistical hypothesis testing. Moreover, Chapter 5 describes the types of errors that can occur in this process.

Chapter 6 describes the use of the Pearson's chi-square test in the analysis of categorical data. This chapter also introduces the concept of effect size and the use of indexes of effect size to express the strength of the relationships between variables. Chapter 7 is dedicated to the process of statistical inference on proportions. This chapter describes the necessary tools to answer questions of the type: "If in a random *sample* of 2000 UK voters you find that 32 per cent vote Labour, what is the proportion of people in the whole *population* of UK voters that vote Labour?".

Chapters 8 and 9 are devoted to the process of statistical hypothesis testing on the mean or pairs of means (i.e., z and t tests). The central limit theorem and the concept of sampling distribution of the mean are also presented. Great emphasis is not only given to the classic binary decision strategy involved in the process of hypothesis testing (i.e., can I reject the null hypothesis?), but also to the calculation of confidence intervals. This process uses sampled data to estimate ranges of values that have a relatively high probability to include the unknown true population mean (you will learn reading this book that inferential statistics is used to estimate population parameters while working on the data collected from relatively small samples). Chapter 10 is dedicated to the nonparametric equivalents of the independent-samples and of the matched-samples t-tests.

Chapter 11 describes how to calculate the strength of the linear relationship between two continuous variables (i.e., the Pearson's index of correlation r). It also describes the process to calculate indexes to measure the correlation between variables where at least one variable is not measured on a continuous scale. In some cases researchers may not only be interested in assessing the strength of the linear relationship between two continuous variables, but they may also be interested in predicting the values of one variable on the basis of their knowledge of a second variable. This can be obtained by calculating the simple linear regression equation as described in Chapter 12. Finally, Chapter 13 provides an introduction to power analysis for most of the statistical tests described in the text. One of the aims of power analysis is to provide researchers with tools aimed to reduce, when planning a research, the risk of failing to reject a null hypothesis when this should in fact be rejected.

If one looks at the table of contents it can be observed that the above description provides only a brief summary of the contents of this book. In fact, each chapter contains more material than that described above. Overall, some of the details and some of the material presented may be outside the scope of a standard first year statistics course which is part of undergraduate degree schemes in the behavioural sciences. But this book could also be useful for "eager" undergraduates who would like to broaden their knowledge of statistics, or also to postgraduate students looking to "brush up" on the basics. In saying this, the relative modularity of the textbook is such that it allows instructors to easily select those sections that are more suitable for the requirements of the course they teach. For example, if Chapter 7 would not be considered strictly relevant to a specific course, its omission will not affect the understanding of the remaining part of the book. Similarly, some sections within the various chapters can be omitted without jeopardising the understanding of later sections.

Finally, since most of the book is dedicated to hypothesis testing using inferential statistics techniques, the figure below provides a decision tree to select the statistical test more appropriate for the data to be analysed.

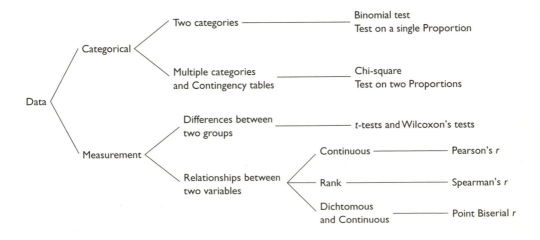

Acknowledgements

I would like to thank the people who have read various versions of this manuscript and made suggestions and corrections. These include Thom Baguley, David Clark-Carter, Naz Derakshan, Val Cronin, and Linda Murdoch. I am very grateful for all the help that I have received from the named sources and others, although, of course, any remaining errors are the author's alone.

Chapter 1

Introduction and basic concepts

Why is statistics useful in the behavioural sciences?

To say the least, it is quite common that a large number of students starting an undergraduate degree in psychology are not enthusiastic about having to study statistics and research methodology. It is highly possible that this lack of enthusiasm originates, at least in part, from the unappreciation of the relevance that statistics plays in the scientific understanding of human behaviour. The aim of this introduction is to provide a convincing argument, using a simple example, as to why some statistical knowledge is useful to students in the behavioural sciences.

Simple example of statistical testing

While revising for the end of year exams a university student notices that the material is better remembered when some classical music is played in the background, while less information seems retained when no background music is played. This observation is used by this student as a basis to support their theory that listening to classical music while studying facilitates the memorisation of the exam material, and as a consequence they suggest their classmates use the same strategy when revising. If you were one of the classmates would you be so impressed by your friend's theory that you would follow their suggestion? Probably not, but why not?

One objection that could be raised is that classical music may work for your friend, but its effect may not generalise to other people. After all, not everybody likes classical music; so there is the possibility that some students may find this music interferes with their studying. Therefore, in order to see if the effect of listening to classical music on memory for exam material is not specific to your friend, a relatively large number of students should be tested. A second objection refers to the way in which the zassessment of the two methods of study was made. More precisely what kind of evidence was used to claim that the music method led to better retention than the no music method? It is likely that your classmate had a feeling that they remembered more information after listening to classical music, but no formal assessment was made. However, it would be appropriate to have a more accurate way of measuring the amount of information retained under the two study conditions. Basically, it is important to obtain some sort of measurement of the phenomenon under investigation.

Overall it appears that the theory suggesting that listening to classical music while studying helps memorisation could potentially be correct, but the types of evidence used to support this theory are not compelling. Hence, more people should be tested, and a clear way to measure the amount of information retained is to assess if the effect of listening to classical music while studying leads to an increment in the amount of information memorised compared to a condition where no music is played.

Thus, let us imagine implementing a study to provide a better evaluation of what we could name the "classical music theory". As remarked above, to have a clearer assessment of the effect of classical music on memory for exam material, we will need to test a sizeable number of people (how large this number should be is discussed in Chapter 13). At this point a further decision needs to be made. Should the same group of people be tested in both study conditions (i.e., with and without exposure to classical music)? Or should two different groups of people be used so that, within each group, subjects are tested in only one of the two conditions? These two approaches have both advantages and disadvantages that will be discussed later in the book. For the moment, and without questioning why, we use the second approach. Therefore one group of students will be given some material to study for a given amount of time during which classical music will be played in the background. A second group will receive the same material to be studied in the same amount of time, but no music will be played in the background. If classical music is beneficial we should find that the group exposed to classical music will retain more information than the group not exposed to music while studying.

Before discussing how we can measure memory for the material studied, some issues about the selection of the subjects participating in the study need to be addressed. Participants should be allocated to each of the two groups in a way that no bias is introduced in the evaluation of the two study techniques. Assuming, for simplicity, that 30 university students participate in the study, it would be inappropriate, for example, for the best students to be allocated to the music condition while the poorest students are allocated to the no music condition. Under these circumstances it is likely that the classical music group would remember more information than the no classical music group simply because the students in the music group are more capable, and not because of the music factor. A study like this would lack *internal validity*; i.e., its results do not represent what we think they should represent. A way to circumvent the above problem would be to randomly allocate the participating students to the two conditions of the study, and, possibly, to have the same number of students in each group. In doing this, roughly the same number of able and poor students should, in principle, be included in each group so that these individual differences should be comparable between the two groups, and, therefore, students' ability should not bias the result of the study. Random allocation is fundamental because it reduces the risk that there is a confound between students' ability and the conditions of the study (e.g., that the better students are selectively allocated to the classical music group).

Before discussing how to measure students' memory for the exam material, a further digression on the selection of the subjects taking part in the study is in order. We said earlier that 30 university students should be selected to take part in the study. Thus we study a sample, and not the entire population of university students, because it would be unrealistic, very costly and time consuming to test the entire population. However, we would like the results obtained with the selected sample to generalise to the entire relevant population. In order to generalise the results of our study to the entire population of university students, our selected sample should accurately reflect the characteristics of the entire population. If this occurs, it is then said that the study conducted has *external validity*. However, if a sample is biased, then the results obtained are biased too, thus these cannot be generalised to the entire population being studied. If, for example, all of our selected students are very able and all likely to obtain "A" marks in their exams, we will have a biased sample because only a small percentage of students perform so well. The optimal way to obtain an unbiased sample is to draw a random sample from the entire population (using procedures similar to those used in the National Lottery draw). In this way every member of the population has equal probability of being included in the sample, thus the sample obtained should accurately reflect the characteristics of the population of university students. However, random sampling from the entire population is not practically possible in most real research. Nevertheless, it is important that samples are reasonably representative of the populations we want to generalise to (for more details on sampling procedures see Upton & Cook, 1997). Obviously, the extent to which the sample obtained is not representative of the entire relevant population leads to a limitation in the generalisation of the results that can be obtained in a study. For example if we study how families with a monthly income up to £1000, per capita, spend their money, we may have difficulty in generalising the results to the population of families with a monthly income up to £3000 per capita.

Summarising, to test any psychological theory or hypothesis we need to study and measure some behaviour in a sample of subjects, and in doing this we aim to draw conclusions on the entire population from which the sample is taken. Therefore, while studying the behaviour of a relatively small sample we want to be able to generalise the results obtained to the entire relevant population. As an addendum it should be said that populations are not necessarily finite. A population could be the collection of a potentially infinite number of items (e.g., the set of all possible e-mails that people could potentially write). In this case it would be impossible to list all the elements in the population.

Let us now consider how we can measure the retention of the studied material. For example each group of 15 students have to study a prose passage for one hour, the content of which is comparable to exam material, where 60 important pieces of information are highlighted. Remember that we sampled 30 students; 15 to be exposed to classical music while studying and 15 not exposed to any background music. A convenient index, but not necessarily the best one to measure the retention of the to-be-learned information, is the number of key pieces of information correctly recalled 24 hours after the study phase. Hence the relevant information we will obtain is going to be the number of key pieces of information retrieved by each student, and this measure will be used to decide if students retain more information when they listen to classical music while studying, compared to a no background music condition.

A reasonable approach to decide on the above matter would be to suggest that classical music is beneficial if the students in the "classical music" group recalled more units of information than the students in the "no music" group. Unfortunately, at first, the obtained data will only be an unorganised set of 15 memory scores for each of the two groups of students who participated in the study, and no useful information is likely to be extracted from these numbers without further manipulations. Some order needs to be imposed on these data to be able to decide which of the two groups of students recalled more information. For example, as a first step, the performance of the students in each group could be rank ordered. This would permit the inspection of the memory scores for each group, ordered from the lowest to the highest. A useful piece of information is also the average number of items recalled in each group (see Table 1.1a). A quick glance at the rank ordered data seems to suggest that more items are recalled in the classical music group (i.e., for almost any rank more items are recalled in the classical music than in the no music group). Moreover, on average, more items are recalled in the classical music group. It seems, therefore, that we could answer the original question and conclude that, when classical music is played while studying, more information about exam material is remembered compared to a condition when no background music is played.

Table 1.1 Fictitious data on the effect of listening to classical music while studying on the retention of the material to be learned. In Table 1.1a data are ordered within each studying condition (where I corresponds to the rank of the lowest scoring student and XV to the highest). In Table 1.1b data are ordered irrespective of the studying condition

Table 1.1a

Group	Rank within each group and score	Average score
	I II III IV V VI VII VIII IX X XI XII XIII XIV XV	
A (with classical music)	28 30 33 35 36 38 39 40 42 44 45 45 48 49 50	40.1
B (with no music)	25 28 32 34 35 37 38 40 40 42 43 43 44 45 47	38.2

This conclusion may, however, be premature. In fact, various reasons suggest that the type of inference used above to decide on the memory effect of classical music is incorrect. First of all, taking a closer look at the rank ordered data might indicate that the performances in the two groups are comparable. Apart from a small number of relatively extreme scores, which appear to be larger in the classical music group, the majority of scores are comparable in the two groups (see Table 1.1b where all the scores are ordered from the smallest to the largest).

Table 1.1b

Group	Score									
A (with classical music)	28 30	33	35 36		38 39 40	42		44 45 45		48 49 50
B (with no music)	25 28		32 34 35	37 38	40 40 42 43 43 44 45		47			

The second important point to make is that, despite the average memory scores being numerically different, this difference could have occurred simply by chance and not because the two groups in the study were treated differently. To illustrate this concept, imagine that 30 more students are randomly sampled from the same population of university students, and that these students are randomly assigned to two groups. These are conveniently labelled Group A and Group B. However, unlike the previous study, both groups are now asked to commit to memory the relevant material while there is *no* music in the background *for either group*. Table 1.2 displays the rank ordered performances of the two groups. There are some noticeable similarities between the data displayed in Table 1.1a and in Table 1.2. The most striking features are that

Table 1.2 Hypothetical replication of the study of the effect of listening to classical music on learning, where no music is played at all

Group	Rank within each group and score	Average score
	I II III IV V VI VII VIII IX X XI XII XIII XIV XV	
A	28 29 33 35 37 38 39 40 42 43 44 46 48 49 52	40.2
B	27 28 32 33 35 37 39 40 41 42 43 44 46 48 49	38.9

in both tables the average performance of Group A is numerically larger than the performance of Group B, and that the average performance of the A groups is almost identical in the two tables. Thus the results obtained in the second study are very similar to those previously found despite no classical music ever being played in the background. Therefore these results cast some doubt on the validity of the previous conclusion regarding the effectiveness of background classical music in improving students' memory for exam material.

How then is it possible to obtain a set of results like those just described? As previously mentioned, we assumed that the students taking part in both studies were randomly sampled from the population of university students, and that they were further randomly allocated to the A and B music groups. This process is fair since, in principle, it avoids introducing bias in the allocation of students to different groups. It is, however, important to keep in mind that students differ along several dimensions, as for example in their abilities to memorise. It then follows that, when students are randomly assigned to different groups, random variations in the average characteristics of the students in these different groups are bound to happen. Thus these random differences can influence memory performance even if the two groups are treated in the same way (i.e., no music is played during learning). As a consequence, what may have happened is that the two groups obtained different average memory scores simply by chance, despite all selected students being randomly sampled from the population of university students, and despite the students being randomly allocated to different groups. Students are not identical, so despite being randomly allocated, small differences in the recall abilities of different groups may have occurred by chance. In the second study, where both groups of students were treated in the same way, the small difference in the average scores must have occurred by chance. Given that the results in the second study are very similar to those obtained in the first study, it could well be that the numerical advantage in the average memory score obtained in the first study by the "real" classical music group had nothing to do with the effect of music, but simply reflected the fact that the average performances of random samples drawn from a given population differ by chance.

The above reasoning points out the need for an appropriate methodology to decide if classical music played in the background does indeed improve memory for exam information, or if the average numerical advantage shown by students exposed to classical music in the first study simply reflected random variations which occur naturally among samples of students randomly allocated from the population of university students. Inferential statistics techniques aim to provide an answer to these types of question. A large part of this book is dedicated to describing some of these techniques. Furthermore, notice that the process of statistical inference is a probabilistic one.

Therefore, a chapter of this book will be dedicated to the description of some basic concepts of probability theory.

This introduction has gone a long way towards showing how various approaches, which can be classified within the field of statistics, are essential in the behavioural sciences. We started with a fairly simple, and admittedly quite naive psychological theory. We then showed that to test this theory some measurement of the phenomenon under investigation was required, and that a relatively large sample of people needed to be tested under different study conditions. We discussed some implications involved in assigning subjects to study conditions, and the need to provide some preliminary description of the collected data. We then demonstrated the need for inferential statistics techniques to evaluate the plausibility of a psychological theory using the data collected in an empirical study. Finally, notice that the example above indicated the need for a quite sophisticated approach to empirically test a question that appeared potentially interesting (i.e., the effect of music on retention). Research questions often arise to shed light on an interesting phenomenon. It is important to keep in mind that in this process an attempt should be made to provide a theoretical understanding of the phenomenon. It then follows that research should be conducted to test theoretically relevant questions, so that the outcome of the research either supports or disconfirms specific theoretical explanations of a given phenomenon. The remainder of this chapter will expand on some issues related to measurement in psychology, on the distinction between descriptive and inferential statistics, and on the distinction between experiments and other less controlled ways to test psychological theories.

The "classical music" study has demonstrated the relevant role of statistics in providing a scientific understanding of human behaviour. Some statistical knowledge is fundamental to anybody who intends to carry out an empirical study. Moreover, degree courses in psychology and social sciences often require students to carry out empirical research in the final year. Some statistical knowledge is also essential to understand the large majority of published journal articles, which will, very likely, be included in some reading lists for the courses you will undertake. Most of these articles will describe some empirical study and will report the statistical analyses conducted on the gathered data. If you ignore the statistical procedures used by the authors it is very likely that your level of understanding of the study will be very limited. Finally, several different statistical techniques, more or less complex, are commonly used in all areas of psychology. Therefore if, for example, you intend to become a clinical psychologist, and you think that statistics is not relevant to your future career, then go to any university library and spend an hour browsing through the content and the structure of the studies published either in the *Journal of Abnormal Psychology* or in the *Journal of Consulting and Clinical Psychology*, both leading journals in the field. I am convinced that after this brief experience you will change your mind.

Measurement scales

A variable refers to a property of events, objects or people that can take a value (i.e., that can be measured). An example of a variable is how fast a sprinter reacts to the starter's gunshot. The value of this variable could be, for example, the time it takes the sprinter to move the first foot away from the starting blocks. In the example described earlier the measured variable was the number of key pieces of information recalled one day after learning the exam material. Variables can either be discrete or continuous.

Discrete variables assume only numerical values that we can make a list of (i.e., discrete data). In the exam example, the number of items that could be recalled varied between the integers 0 and 60; thus, this variable was discrete (as a reminder, integers are whole number—not fractional numbers—that can be positive, negative, or zero). Other examples of discrete variables are the number of correct responses in a trivia game (this variable can take as a value any integer between zero and the total number of questions being answered during the game), or the number of heads that can occur in tossing a fair coin ten times (the values that can be taken by this variable are 0, 1, 2, . . . , 10). Usually discrete variables can only take a limited number of values.

In the case of a continuous variable it is not possible to make a list of all possible values that this can take (i.e., continuous data). The sprinter's reaction time is a continuous variable since it can take, in principle, any value (e.g., 127.329167 . . . milliseconds). Physical quantities like weight and speed are other examples of continuous variables. It is however relevant to notice that although some variables are continuous, they are recorded as discrete. This is often due to limitations in the precision of the instruments of measurement. For example, sprinters' reaction times are usually reported to the nearest millisecond.

From the above definitions of discrete and continuous variables it seems that the only type of data that can be collected are quantitative (i.e., those collected using some sort of instrument of measurement). In fact, data can also be qualitative (alternatively named as categorical). Events, objects and people can be classified into different categories, and frequency counts can be made of the number of elements classified in each category. For example, the patients admitted in a psychiatric ward every year can be classified according to their diagnosis (e.g., schizophrenia, depression, personality disorder, etc.), and a frequency count can be made of the patients admitted every year with a specific diagnosis (e.g., 33 patients received a diagnosis of schizophrenia, 25 of depression, 15 of personality disorder, etc.).

Overall, then, when talking about variables, it is implied that some sort of measurement is made. Measurements can be made along different scales. These are called nominal, ordinal, interval and ratio scales and they have different mathematical properties.

At the level of *nominal* scales, numbers are used to classify events in different categories. Numbers are simply labels for categories. In the classical music example, students were assigned to two groups named "A (with classical music)" and "B (with no music)". Alternatively the classical music group could have been named "1" and the no music group "0". In this context 0 and 1 are simply labels for the different groups. Similarly, each diagnostic category previously mentioned could simply be indicated with a number (e.g., "0" = Schizophrenia, "1" = Depression, "2" = Personality Disorder, etc.).

At the level of *ordinal* scales, numbers are used to order events, objects and people along a continuum. For example, a particular person can rank order a series of ten paintings in terms of pleasantness. The painting that receives a score of "1" is considered a more pleasant painting than the painting that receives a score of "2" and so on until the tenth painting. However, this type of scale does not allow us to state that the difference in pleasantness between the paintings ranked first and third is the same as the one between the paintings ranked fifth and seventh. The numbers used in ordinal scales do not contain this type of information, which, instead, is available at the level of interval scales.

With *interval* scales not only is the ordering of the events being measured represented, but the relative distance of these events along the scale is also represented. A classical example of an interval scale is the Celsius scale of temperature. A difference in temperature between −5° and 0° is equivalent to a difference between 5° and 10°, and to a difference between 10° and 15°. It is, however, important to notice that a 5° temperature is not half as hot as a 10° temperature. The reason being that the scale does not have an absolute zero point that corresponds to the absence of the event being measured (e.g., try to think what temperature would be five times as hot as minus 5°; you will find no answer to questions of this type). Zero degrees Celsius corresponds to the temperature at which water freezes. It does not represent the absence of temperature.

When a scale has an absolute zero this is called a *ratio* scale. Ratio scales include the properties of the previous scales. Moreover it is meaningful to make statements about ratios between measurements. Given that zero time corresponds to the absence of the phenomenon, it is possible to say, in physical terms, that an interval of 200 milliseconds is twice as long as an interval of 100 milliseconds (or equivalently that the 100 milliseconds interval is half as long as the 200 milliseconds interval). Ratio scales are not common in psychology since it is difficult to establish the absence of a psychological phenomenon. For example, a score of zero obtained in a computer literacy test does not necessarily mean that the person who obtained that score does not know anything about computers. It could simply mean that the test used is not sensitive enough to discriminate among people who know very little about computers. Possibly, with a more sensitive test, the score obtained could have been greater than zero. An example of measurement at the level of ratio scale in psychology is the use of reaction times since a time of zero corresponds to the absence of the phenomenon.

Measurement scales are considered by some authors to be extremely important with respect to the type of statistical analysis that can be performed on a set of collected data (e.g., Miller, 1974). Thus, according to this position, it is possible to calculate means and standard deviations (we will describe these concepts in Chapter 2) only with data that are at least at the level of the interval scale. The reason being that, in order to calculate means and standard deviations, it is necessary to add and divide sets of numbers, and that these operations make sense when numbers represent units which are constant in size (this property does not belong to nominal and ordinal scales). On the other hand other authors are less stringent on the need to tie the statistical treatment of data to the type of scale at which the data have been collected. For example, Howell (1997, referring to Lord, 1953) indicated that statistical tests make use of numbers without any consideration about the events to which these numbers refer; thus, any mathematical operation can be carried out on numbers irrespective of the underlying type of measurement scale. However, he stressed that, when interpreting the results of any statistical analysis, it is important to keep in mind the characteristics of the underlying psychological variable that is measured with a particular scale. An example should clarify this point. Imagine that the Spielberger anxiety inventory is administered to three people to measure their levels of anxiety as a personality trait. This questionnaire is made up of 20 questions asking how people generally feel (e.g.,

"I feel nervous and restless", "I worry too much over something that really does not matter", etc.), and for each item it is possible to answer one of the following: "almost never", "sometimes", "often", "almost always" (corresponding to a score of 1, 2, 3 and 4 respectively) (Spielberger, Gorsuch, Lushene, Vagg, & Jacobs, 1983). The score that can be obtained by an individual in this test varies from 20 to 80, where higher scores indicate increased levels of trait anxiety. Let us assume that the trait anxiety scores in the three individuals are 32, 44, and 56. The measurement scale used may appear to be an interval one. However, when interpreting these results, it would not be feasible to conclude that there is a constant increment in the level of trait anxiety across the three subjects. After all, for example, the difference in the underlying levels of anxiety between the responses "almost never" and "sometimes" may not be identical to the difference between responding "sometimes" and "often". Although in principle these differences are numerically identical (i.e., 1), the differences in the levels of the underlying anxiety corresponding to these numerical differences may not be constant. Therefore, in this case, it would be more appropriate to suggest that there is an ordinal increment in the levels of trait anxiety among the three people.

In psychology several types of data seem, prima facie, to be collected using some type of interval scale. These are, for example, general and more specific measures of intellectual abilities like Intelligent Quotient (IQ) scores or Memory Quotient scores. It is however questionable, for reasons similar to those raised in the case of the measurement of trait anxiety just discussed, that a difference in IQ scores between 80 and 90 is identical, with respect to the underlying variable measured (i.e., general intellectual ability), to a difference between 90 and 100. Numerically, the difference between these IQ scores is constant; however, when interpreting the results, it would be more appropriate simply to suggest that a person with an IQ of 90 is less intellectually able than a person with a score of 100, and that a person with a score of 80 is less intellectually able than a person with an IQ of 90. In summary, it seems reasonable to suggest that any statistical manipulation can, in principle, be applied to numbers irrespective of the apparent scale used to measure the phenomenon under investigation. However, to avoid reaching unrealistic conclusions, it is fundamental to keep in mind the characteristics of the psychological variable(s) we are studying when interpreting any empirical result.

Descriptive and inferential statistics

In the classical music example previously described, some data were collected from various samples of students. As stated, these data originally appeared as unorganised and were not particularly useful unless some organisation was imposed. Thus, in general, a first step to be taken when raw data are collected is to provide some useful description of these data. Earlier we decided that it was useful to rank the data collected within each of the two groups (i.e., the "A (with classical music)" and the "B (with no music)"), and to calculate their respective averages. In doing this we applied some numerical manipulations that can be classified under the umbrella of descriptive statistics. This is the branch of statistics that deals with those numerical manipulations that can be used to describe and summarise data sets. The main aim of descriptive statistics techniques is to extract useful information from unorganised data. These techniques can be applied to data obtained either from samples or from the entire relevant population.

It is useful to remember than when a descriptive index, as for example an average, is obtained from a sample, this index is called a *statistic*. On the other hand when an index is calculated on the entire population this is called a *parameter*. Chapter 2 describes some of the most common techniques to summarise and describe data.

Working with samples is useful if, as previously mentioned, we can infer something about the entire population. Populations may be limited in size as, for example, when the population of reference consists of all first year students enrolled in the Psychology BSc at the University of Essex in the academic year 1999–2000. However (and this occurs in the vast majority of cases), if the population of reference is extremely large, for example, the population of all first year university students in the UK who, in the academic year 1999–2000 took psychology as a major subject, it is necessary to work with samples which should be representative of the relevant population. This is necessary so that researchers can infer the characteristics of the population of reference from the sample they are working with. *Inferential statistics* provides those techniques that allow us to infer the characteristics of a population from sample data (i.e., while working on sample statistics we want to provide estimates of the size of the relevant parameters in the population of reference). Since most sections of this book will describe various inferential statistical techniques, the above issue will be dealt with at length in the following chapters.

What is an experiment?

Let us again consider the previously described fictitious empirical study to assess if classical music played in the background could improve memory for exam material. In that study a random sample of university students was taken. A random half of the sampled students was assigned to the "with classical music" condition, while the remaining random half of the students was assigned to the "with no music" condition. It was said that if classical music had a beneficial effect on memory for exam material, then the students who learned while classical music was played should have remembered more information than the students in the no music condition. A fundamental characteristic of this study was that the learning conditions were under the control of the researcher conducting the study, and that the only difference between the two groups of students was, in principle, in the different conditions under which the exam material was studied. In these circumstances if, for example, it is established that the students in the classical music condition retrieve more information than those in the no music condition, it is then possible to claim that background classical music is the *cause* of improved memory for exam material.

An empirical study with the above characteristics is called an experiment. What is under the control of the experimenter and leads to changes in the observed behaviour is usually called the *independent variable*. Changes in the level of the independent variable correspond to changes in the measured behaviour (i.e., *dependent variable*). In the experiment just described the dependent variable was the number of key pieces of information recalled, while the independent variable was the type of learning condition to which the students were randomly assigned. Thus the independent variable had two levels or conditions (i.e., "with classical music" vs "with no music"). In the above example the "no music" condition acted as a control condition, while the "classical music" condition acted as the experimental condition. The control condition should provide a suitable standard to assess the effect of the manipulation of interest. In the previous example, this was the effect of the presence of classical music over no music. In general, experiments are used to test psychological theories, which, in turn, should make clear predictions. Usually these predictions indicate that changes in the levels of the independent variable should correspond to specific changes in the dependent variable being measured. The number of levels of the independent variable does not need to be restricted to two, as in the example above. This number usually depends on the aim of the experiment and the specific predictions arising from the theory being tested.

Let us now consider a different example of an empirical study aimed to assess the effect of trait anxiety (i.e., the independent variable) on the speed of correct responses in a target selection task (i.e., the dependent variable). Here subjects observe on a screen a series of letters presented in sequence and their task is to press a button, as quickly as possible, only when either letter "X" or letter "Y" appears on the screen. Two groups of participants are selected according to their levels of trait anxiety. Those in the low trait anxiety group have a score between 20 and 35 in the Spielberger trait anxiety inventory, while the subjects in the high trait anxiety group have a score larger than 45 in the same inventory. If, after an appropriate statistical test, it turns out that less anxious individuals are faster in responding to the target than high trait anxiety individuals, would it then be possible to conclude that low trait anxiety is the cause of faster reaction times? The answer is no. Why?

The main difference between the above study and the experiment using classical music is that, in the classical music experiment, participants were randomly assigned to the conditions of the study. These were deliberately manipulated by the experimenter to provide a test of some specific hypothesis, while all the other aspects of the experiment were left constant. In the case of the effect of anxiety on reaction time, no experimental condition has been deliberately manipulated by the experimenter. Here the levels of the independent variable (trait anxiety) were associated with some subjects' characteristics that could not be manipulated by the experimenter. As a consequence it is possible only to infer that there is a relationship between anxiety and reaction times, but not that high levels of trait anxiety cause an increment in reaction times. If, for example, high trait anxiety individuals cannot sustain their attention for long while performing a task, then their performance may suffer. In this case anxiety would not be the cause of the differences in reaction time between the low and high trait anxiety groups. A third variable, e.g., differences in the ability to sustain attention which is associated with both anxiety and speed of responding, could be the real underlying cause of the variation in the reaction times. In summary, whenever the levels of the independent variable are not deliberately manipulated by the experimenter, it is always possible that another uncontrolled variable may be the cause of the relationship observed between the independent and the dependent variable. Other examples of variables that cannot be deliberately manipulated by the experimenter are for example: age, IQ, sex, socio-economic status, health status, and personality. Therefore, empirical studies involving these types of variables should be more appropriately called either correlational or observational studies, rather than experiments, since the researchers do not directly control the studied variables (nor can they assign subjects to the conditions of the study randomly). Correlational studies are common in psychology. The important thing to keep in mind, both when conducting such studies and when reading journal articles based on correlational research, is that no causal statement on the effect of the studied variables can be made without other evidence.

From the above argument it appears that, when it is not possible for a researcher to deliberately manipulate the levels of the independent variable, it is not possible to make causal inferences on the effect that the independent variable exerts on the dependent variable. However, it is important to notice that, while deliberate control can be exerted on the levels of the independent variable, not everything that occurs during an experiment can be strictly controlled. It is, therefore, important to take care of what can be called irrelevant variables. These are variables that, despite not being manipulated by the experimenter, may still bias the outcome of an experiment. To avoid (or minimise) any bias, it is essential that these irrelevant variables have no systematic effect on the outcome of an experiment. What are these irrelevant variables? An important type of irrelevant variable refers to the individual differences of the subjects taking part in an experiment. When describing the classical music study it was said that the outcome of the experiment would have been biased if, for example, all poor students had been allocated to the no music group and the good students to the classical music group. If this had happened, the irrelevant variable that could be named "individual differences among students", would have been confounded with the independent variable studied. Therefore if classical music had led to better recollection of the studied material, it would have been unclear if the improved performance was due to the manipulated variable, or to the fact that the more capable students were assigned to the classical music group. As stated above, the random allocation of subjects to conditions, should, in principle, prevent the occurrence of any systematic bias in favour of any experimental condition.

Other types of irrelevant variable refer to the context, used in a wide sense, in which an experiment is conducted. Consider an example where subjects have to perform a reaction time task similar to the one described earlier. Now there are two levels of the independent variable which are under the control of the experimenter (easy vs difficult selection conditions) and the experiment is conducted either in a room with a temperature of 13° Celsius, or in another room with a temperature of 21° Celsius. It is known that faster reactions are more likely to occur in the warmer environment. Therefore if testing in the easy condition occurs more often in the warmer room than in the colder room, and the opposite occurs in the difficult condition, then any reaction time advantage for the easy condition over the difficult condition can be due either to the experimental manipulation (easy vs difficult selection) and/or to the warmer temperature of the room more often used for testing subjects in the easy condition. Again, the best solution would be to randomise the assignment of subjects to rooms, or alternatively, in this case, making sure that a random half of the subjects, in each of the selection condition groups, are tested in one room and the other half in the remaining room.

Irrelevant variables are in general those factors that are not directly manipulated by the experimenter, but that may, nevertheless, if not taken care of, bias the results of the experiment. Other types of irrelevant variables are, for example, testing different subjects at different times of the day, or the different moods in which the experimenter may be when testing different subjects, or even differences in accuracy over time of the instrument used to measure the dependent variable. In general little control can be exerted on these variables. The best approach to deal with these irrelevant variables is to randomly assign subjects to the various conditions of the study. In this way it is unlikely that any systematic bias will occur and, therefore, that the effect of the relevant variable is confounded with the effect of any irrelevant variable.

Some basic concepts of statistics and research methodology have been introduced in this first chapter. These concepts will be recapitulated in different parts of the book and several examples will illustrate how they are applied in the statistical analyses of the kinds of data collected in behavioural science research. The next chapter will describe some of the most common and useful statistical techniques used to organise and describe sets of data.

Chapter 2

Descriptive statistics

Organising raw data

When data are collected, they can initially look quite messy and unorganised, and hence difficult to interpret. As indicated in the previous chapter, some order needs to be imposed on raw data if we want to extract useful information from them. Several techniques are available to display data in a concise way and to organise them in a clear manner. Some of the most common and useful techniques for plotting data will be described in this chapter.

Frequency distributions and histograms

First let us consider some hypothetical data collected in a naming task. A sample of 40 4-year-old children are presented with a series of 50 pictures depicting everyday objects. Their task is to name the objects represented in each picture, and the number of correctly named pictures is recorded for each child. The raw data are presented in Table 2.1. A useful way to organise these data would be to record the frequency of occurrence of each score in the data-set. In a frequency distribution table the scores are usually ranked from the lowest to the highest, and the number of occurrences of each score is given. Table 2.1 also includes the frequencies of the observed scores obtained by the sample of 4-year-old children in the naming task. The cumulative frequency and the percentage cumulative frequency of the scores are also given. The cumulative frequency of the scores is useful since it reveals the number of observations falling at or below (or above) a given score. The percentage cumulative frequency of the scores is also useful since it can be used to obtain the percentage of observations falling at or below a given score.

From the frequency distribution table it can be easily seen what are the lowest and the highest naming scores (i.e., 12 and 42 respectively), and what is the most common score (i.e., 26). Using the cumulative frequency column it can be seen that 10 children could name 21 pictures or less. From the percentage cumulative frequency column it can be observed that a score of up to and including 21 was obtained by 25 per cent of the children assessed.

Frequency distributions can be plotted in a pictorial format called a histogram or bar chart. In the naming data case, the number of the named pictures is marked along the horizontal axis. The height of the vertical bars indicates the frequency of occurrence of each naming score (see Figure 2.1). Figure 2.2 displays the cumulative frequency distribution of the data presented in Table 2.1.

Table 2.1 Hypothetical raw data on the number of pictures named in a sample of 40 4-year-old children. Their frequency distribution is also provided

Raw data

30	26	25	12	17	21	42	25	21	30	21
26	26	36	33	22	24	22	26	17	25	26
32	33	18	17	18	40	30	29	35	38	24
24	25	27	28	27	28	13				

Frequency distribution table

Score	Frequency	Cumulative frequency	Percentage cumulative frequency
12	1	1	2.5
13	1	2	5.0
14	0	2	5.0
15	0	2	5.0
16	0	2	5.0
17	3	5	12.5
18	2	7	17.5
19	0	7	17.5
20	0	7	17.5
21	3	10	25.0
22	2	12	30.0
23	0	12	30.0
24	3	15	37.5
25	4	19	47.5
26	5	24	60.0
27	2	26	65.0
28	2	28	70.0
29	1	29	72.5
30	3	32	80.0
31	0	32	80.0
32	1	33	82.5
33	2	35	87.5
34	0	35	87.5
35	1	36	90.0
36	1	37	92.5
37	0	37	92.5
38	1	38	95.0
39	0	38	95.0
40	1	39	97.5
41	0	39	97.5
42	1	40	100.0
Total	40	40	

Grouped data

In the naming data there were some scores with a frequency of zero and several other scores with frequencies no higher than two. Moreover, given that the naming scores obtained ranged from 12 to 42, it followed that the frequency table used to describe these data was quite large, thus it did not provide a very neat and compact way to organise the data (i.e., the data in the table look quite spread out, and the histogram

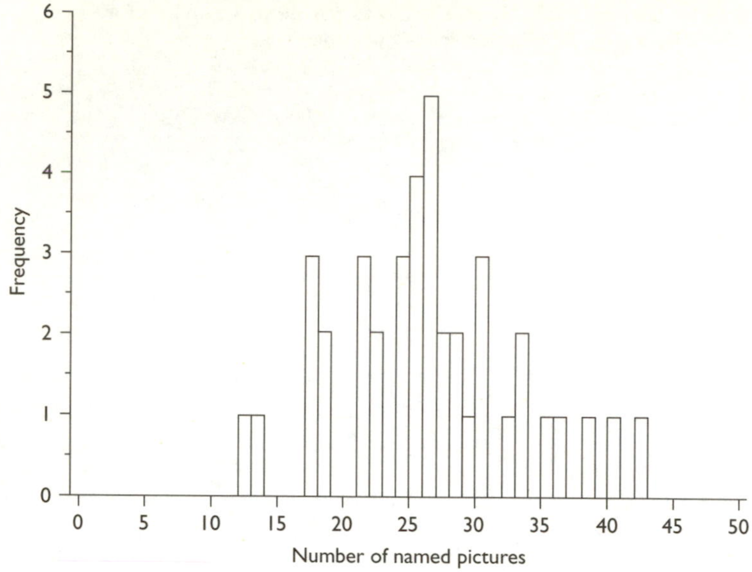

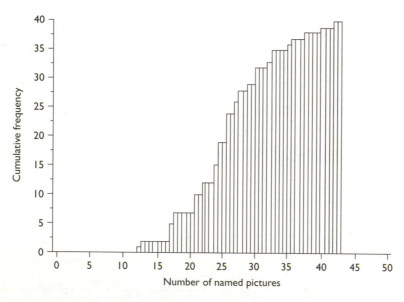

Figure 2.1 Histogram displaying the data from Table 2.1.

Figure 2.2 Cumulative frequency histogram of the data in Table 2.1.

looks like a broken comb). In general, when data are dispersed, a more manageable way to organise the data can be achieved by grouping them. It is quite common, when data are grouped, to use about 7 to 15 intervals. When the naming data are grouped using intervals (or equivalently, classes) of 5 units, we obtain seven intervals. Comparing Table 2.1 and Table 2.2 it appears that the grouped frequency table provides a

Table 2.2 Grouped frequency table of data in Table 2.1

Interval	Middle point	Frequency	Cumulative frequency	Percentage cumulative frequency
9.5–14.5	12	2	2	5.0
14.5–19.5	17	5	7	17.5
19.5–24.5	22	8	15	37.5
24.5–29.5	27	14	29	72.5
29.5–34.5	32	6	35	87.5
34.5–39.5	37	3	38	95.0
39.5–44.5	42	2	40	100.0
Total	40	40		

more compact and clearer description of the data. However, clarity comes with a cost. Since only the total number of observations in each interval is reported in grouped frequency tables, individual observations are lost.

In the grouped frequency table, the true lower and upper limits are, in the case of the first interval, 9.5 and 14.5. For the second interval these are 14.5 and 19.5, etc. This means that scores equal to or greater than 9.5 and smaller than 14.5 are included in the first interval, and that scores equal to or greater than 14.5 and smaller than 19.5 are included in the second interval, etc. A more formal way to describe these intervals could be achieved in the following manner: let us call X the variable being measured, then the expression $9.5 \leq x < 14.5$ indicates all possible values that the variable X can have in order to be included in the first interval. For the second interval we have $14.5 \leq x < 19.5$, etc. True limits are expressed to the first decimal place of the unit of measurement used. This is done because data, especially when these are continuous, are usually rounded to the nearest integer. In the naming data example the measurement was expressed in terms of the number of pictures named, thus in the interval $9.5 \leq x < 14.5$ the occurrences of the values 10, 11, 12, 13 and 14 would be reported. Figure 2.3 displays the frequency distribution and the cumulative frequency distribution of the grouped data. Bars are centred at the middle point of each interval. Middle points are calculated as the average of the upper and lower limit of each interval. Frequency polygons are a further way to display the distribution of grouped data (a frequency polygon of the grouped data in Table 2.2 is shown in Figure 2.3). Frequency polygons can be constructed, provided the intervals used to group the data are of equal size, by joining the middle point of each interval. To obtain a closed shape two extreme classes with zero frequency are also joined.

Stem-and-leaf diagrams

Both of the above approaches to organising data have their pros and cons. Frequency tables and frequency histograms, while representing each individual observation, may not provide a compact description of the data. On the other hand, while grouped frequency tables and grouped frequency histograms provide a compact description of the data, individual observations are lost. Stem-and-leaf diagrams avoid the disadvantages of the above methods.

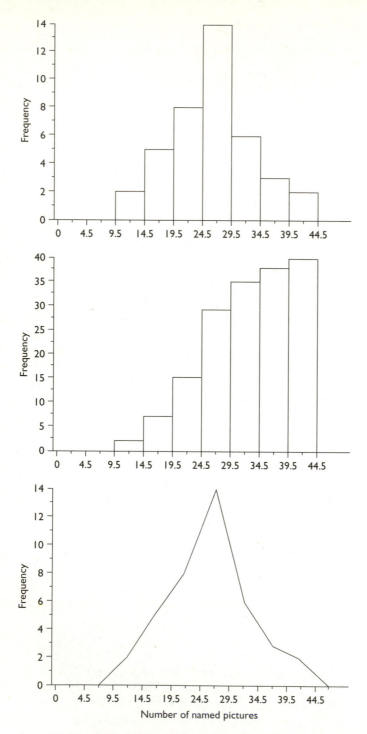

Figure 2.3 Frequency distribution, cumulative frequency distribution and frequency polygon of the grouped data in Table 2.2.

Table 2.3 End-of-year exam marks obtained by a sample of 60 students who regularly attended an introductory biology course (at least 80 per cent of the course)

Raw data

38	39	40	41	43	45	47	47	48	48	49
50	50	51	51	51	52	53	54	54	55	55
55	55	56	56	56	57	59	59	60	60	60
61	61	61	62	62	63	63	63	64	65	65
66	66	67	68	70	70	71	72	73	75	75
75	78	80	83	85

Stem-and-leaf diagram of the end-of-year exam data

Stem	Leaf
3	89
4	013577889
5	0011123445555666799
6	000111223334556678
7	001235558
8	035

Consider the hypothetical set of marks obtained at the end-of-year exam in an introductory course in biology from a sample of 60 university students who regularly attended the course (at least 80 per cent of the course). The data, ordered from the lowest to the highest, are presented in Table 2.3. These are also presented using the stem-and-leaf diagram. In this type of diagram each observed mark is displayed as a leaf stemming from the most significant digit or stem (in this particular case stems are "tens" and leaves are "units"). For example a mark of 60 is displayed using the stem "6" and the leaf "0". For those cases where more than one student obtained the same exam mark, multiple identical leaves are used. Thus, given that three students obtained a mark of 60, this is represented in the diagram by attaching three "0" leaves to the "6" stem. From the stem-and-leaf display of the exam results it immediately appears that the majority of the marks awarded were in the 50s and 60s bands, while fewer students obtained very high or very low marks.

Stem-and-leaf diagrams are also useful to compare two distributions. Consider, for example, that we also know the results obtained in the end-of-year exam in the above biology course by another sample of 60 students who did not attend the course regularly (i.e., less than 50 per cent of the course). Table 2.4 displays, side-by-side around the stem, the distributions of the exam marks obtained by the students who regularly attended the biology course and of those who did not attend the course regularly. From the diagram it appears that, for the students who did not attend the lectures regularly, a large proportion of the exam marks tended to be in the 40s, 50s and 60s. A visual comparison of the two distributions of marks seems to suggest that regular attendance at lectures is associated with higher exam marks, while poor attendance is associated with lower marks. However, as said in the first chapter, inferential statistics techniques are necessary to substantiate this type of claim.

In some cases, especially when a large number of "leaves" is attached to single "stems", it may be useful to split the stems to increase their number, and obtain a

Table 2.4 Stem-and-leaf diagram of the end-of-year exam results for the group of students who regularly attended and for the group of students who did not regularly attend the introductory biology course

Poor attendance		Regular attendance
8877643	3	89
9877665544210	4	013577889
98887766544443322100	5	00111234455556666799
8776654432100	6	0001111223334556678
654320	7	001235558
I	8	035

Table 2.5 Stem-and-leaf diagram, using split stems, of the end-of-year exam results for the group of students who regularly attended and of the group of students who did not regularly attend the introductory biology course

Poor attendance		Regular attendance
43	3	
88776	3x	89
44210	4	013
98776655	4x	577889
44443322100	5	001112344
988877665	5x	5555666799
4432100	6	000111223334
877665	6x	556678
4320	7	00123
65	7x	5558
I	8	03
	8x	5

more efficient and finer graded data summary. Table 2.5 provides a stem-and-leaf diagram of the exam results using two stems for each of the "tens". The units 0, 1, 2, 3 and 4, are attached to stems without the letter "x", while the "leaves" corresponding to the units 5, 6, 7, 8 and 9 are attached to the stems with the letter "x". Finally, stem-and-leaf displays can be applied to both discrete and continuous data. However, the latter type of data have to be treated as being discrete (e.g., 564.5347 . . . milliseconds when rounded to the nearest millisecond is recorded as 565).

Summarising data

The techniques previously described are useful to organise raw data so that it is possible to display their distribution. It would be useful, in conjunction with these techniques, to obtain some numerical indices that summarise the most useful information in a set of data. The rest of this chapter will focus on two types of index: those that provide a measure of the central tendency of a distribution (i.e., measures of location), and those that provide a measure of the spread of a distribution (i.e., measures of dispersion or of variability).

Measures of central tendency: mode, median, and mean

The mode

The mode is the most common value that occurs in a set of discrete data. In the naming task data (see Table 2.1) the mode was 26 since this was the score that occurred most often. If there are two most common values which occur with equal (or almost equal) frequency in a distribution of discrete data, then there are two modes, and the distribution is called bimodal. For example, imagine that a new type of cola drink is tasted by a sample of 30 people, and everyone rates how much they like it on a five-point scale (1 = not at all, 3 = neutral, 5 = very much). The results are presented in Figure 2.4. The distribution of these data is bimodal since there are two ratings (i.e., 1 and 5) which are the most common and which were chosen by the same number of people (i.e., 9).

Notice that when the data are continuous the mode does not really exist. Consider the case in which the variable measured is the weight of a sample of people who have been treated for anorexia nervosa. If the weight has been measured with extreme accuracy, let us say to the milligram, it is extremely unlikely that two people in the sample will have exactly the same weight. In the case of continuous data, as in the measurement of weight, the data can be grouped into classes of weights. For example, calling the variable weight W, then the first class would include all the weights in the interval 49.5 kg $\leq w <$ 54.5 kg. The second class would include the weights in the interval 54.5 kg $\leq w <$ 59.5 kg, etc. The class that includes the largest number of people's weight is the modal class. Similarly, for grouped discrete data there is no mode but a modal class (for the naming data in Table 2.2 the modal class corresponds to the interval 24.5–29.5).

The median

When data are ordered from the smallest to the largest, the value that divides the distribution into two equally sized sets is called the median. The median is thus the

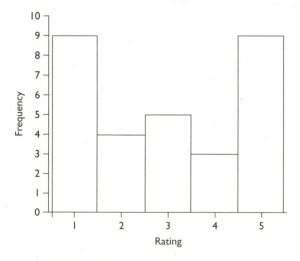

Figure 2.4 Bimodal distribution: rating of a new cola by a sample of 30 people.

middle point of a distribution. For the naming data in Table 2.1 the median is 26. In general, if the number of observations (i.e., n) in a distribution is even, then the median corresponds to the value of the average of the $\left(\dfrac{n}{2}\right)$th and the $\left(\dfrac{n}{2}+1\right)$th ordered observations. This is the way in which the median was calculated for the naming data in Table 2.1 (i.e., the average of the scores of the 20th and the 21st ranked observations). On the other hand, if the number of observations in a distribution is odd, then the median corresponds to the value of the $\left(\dfrac{n+1}{2}\right)$th ordered observation. For example the median of the following set of data:

21   24   33   42   93

corresponds to 33.

   Notice that for grouped frequency data, the calculation of the median is a bit more complicated since this needs to be estimated by interpolation. Now the median corresponds to the value of either the $\left(\dfrac{n}{2}\right)$th or the $\left(\dfrac{n+1}{2}\right)$th ordered observation depending on n being even or odd. The $\left(\dfrac{n}{2}\right)$th, or the $\left(\dfrac{n+1}{2}\right)$th, ordered observation is used to identify the interval within which the median is located. In the grouped naming data (Table 2.2) the sample size is 40, so the median corresponds to the 20th ordered value. This is located within the interval 24.5–29.5 where there are 14 observations (i.e., between the 15th and the 29th ordered observations in the cumulative frequency distribution). The next step is to estimate the value of the 20th ordered observation. This is obtained in the following way:

$$24.5 + \frac{20-15}{29-15} \times (29.5 - 24.5) = 26.29 \text{ (to 2 d.p.)}$$

where 24.5 is the upper limit of the interval immediately below the one where the median is located; $(20 - 15)$ is the difference between the rank of the median and the total number of observations in the cumulative frequency distribution up to, but not including, the interval where the median is located; $(29 - 15)$ is the difference between the total number of observations in the cumulative frequency distribution including the interval where the median is located, and the total number of observations in the cumulative frequency distribution up to, but not including, the interval where the median is located; $(29.5 - 24.5)$ are the boundaries of the interval where the median is located. Thus, rounding the result, the median obtained is 26. Notice that, when working with grouped data, the individual observations are lost, thus the median obtained could differ slightly from the one calculated using all the individual observations. In some cases only grouped data may be available, so it is not possible to calculate the median using all the individual observations. It is important to keep in mind that the loss of precision in calculating the median from grouped data is small, so this process has a minimal impact on the way the data are summarised.

The mean

This is the most frequently used measure of central tendency for both discrete and continuous data. It is calculated as the sum of all observed scores divided by the total number of observations. If a set of data is made up of n observed values (with the values denoted as x_1, x_2, x_3, ..., x_n), then the mean of a sample of observations is denoted as $\bar{x}$ and is given by:

$$\bar{x} = \frac{(x_1 + x_2 + x_3 + \ldots + x_n)}{n}.$$

In general, the sum of n scores is usually denoted by the Greek letter sigma (in upper case): Σ. Thus the formula for the sample mean is simplified as:

$$\bar{x} = \frac{\Sigma x}{n}.$$

When this formula is applied to calculate the mean exam mark obtained by the sample of 60 biology students whose marks are reported in Table 2.3 we obtain:

$$\bar{x} = \frac{(38 + 39 + 40 + \ldots + 85)}{60} = \frac{3558}{60} = 59.3.$$

Notice that the mean does not necessarily correspond to any of the values used to compute it. In the above example the average mark obtained is 59.3, but none of the students obtained this mark.

In the first chapter we introduced the distinction between statistics and parameters, where statistics refer to indices obtained from samples, while parameters are indices calculated from the entire population. Further on this distinction, it is conventional to denote *sample* statistics with *Latin* letters, while *Greek* letters are used for population *parameters*. The sample mean, as calculated above, is denoted by $\bar{x}$. On the other hand, the population mean is denoted by the Greek letter μ (pronounced "mew"). The formula to calculate μ is identical to that used to calculate $\bar{x}$. Finally, unlike the mode and the median, the mean summarises all the data used to calculate it. If a value in a distribution changes then this change will affect the mean, while the median and the mode may remain unchanged.

Advantages and disadvantages of mode, median, and mean

None of the above measures of central tendency is perfect. Thus, in order to select the most appropriate index to summarise a specific set of data, it is useful to know the strengths and weaknesses of the mode, median and mean.

The main advantage of the *mode*, unlike the median and the mean, is that it is applicable to nominal data. For example, if in a survey a sample of people is asked to choose their preferred shoe colour, then the mode may be a useful indicator for shoe-shop owners about the kinds of shoe colour they should stock the most. In this case it is meaningless to calculate either the mean or the median shoe colour. Another advantage of the mode, unlike the mean, is that it is unaffected by extreme scores. For example, the mode of the following sets of data is always 2 (set A: 1, 2, 2, 2, 3, 4, 6, 7, 9; set B: 1, 2, 2, 2, 3, 4, 6, 70, 126), while the means of the two sets differ considerably, 4 and 24, respectively.

One of the disadvantages of the mode is that, as we saw earlier, it may not be unique in a set of data as in the bimodal distribution of Figure 2.4. A further disadvantage of the mode, or more precisely of the modal class, is that the modal class of a set of data may vary depending on the size of the chosen class intervals. Finally, since the mode is not defined using an equation, it cannot be manipulated using the rules of algebra.

The main advantage of the *median* is that like the mode, but unlike the mean, it is not affected by extreme scores. The median of both set A and set B is 3, while their means are 4 and 24, respectively. This resistance to the influence of extreme scores makes the median a useful summary of central tendency for some specific sets of data. For example, in collecting reaction time data in a task where subjects are asked to respond as quickly as possible to the appearance of a particular letter on the computer screen, it is quite common for each subject to have some reaction times that are extremely slow. These slow reactions are often due to errors in trying to press the right button, or to some nonrelevant factors momentarily affecting the subject's attention (e.g., sneezing). If these extreme observations are just spurious, then the median, by being resistant to the influence of these extreme observations, is a useful index to summarise each subject's performance. The main disadvantage of the median is that it may not correspond to any observed value (e.g., for the data-set: 3, 5, 6, 11; the median is 5.5). In addition the median is quite variable across different samples of the same size drawn from a given population (this point will be illustrated later in the chapter). A further limitation is that the median cannot be manipulated algebraically. There is no equation that defines the median. Remember, the median is just the score that divides an ordered distribution of values into two equal groups.

The *mean* is the most commonly used index of central tendency. A reason for this is that it can be entered into an equation and be manipulated using the rules of algebra. This is because, unlike the mode and the median, there is, as we saw earlier, an equation to define the mean. Another advantage of the sample mean (i.e., $\bar{x}$) is that it is more useful than the median to estimate the population mean (i.e., μ). This issue will be addressed later in the chapter. The main disadvantages of the mean are that it is influenced, as seen above, by extreme scores, and that it may not exist in the set of data from which it has been calculated.

Further on the mode, median, and mean

It is useful to see where the mode, median, and mean are positioned depending on the shape of the frequency distribution. If the distribution of scores is symmetrical (see Figure 2.5a) then the mode, median, and mean have about the same value. On the other hand if the distribution has a long tail to the left (i.e., it is negatively skewed), then the median tends to be positioned to the left of the mode and the mean to the left of the median (see Figure 2.5b). If, however, the distribution has a long tail to the right

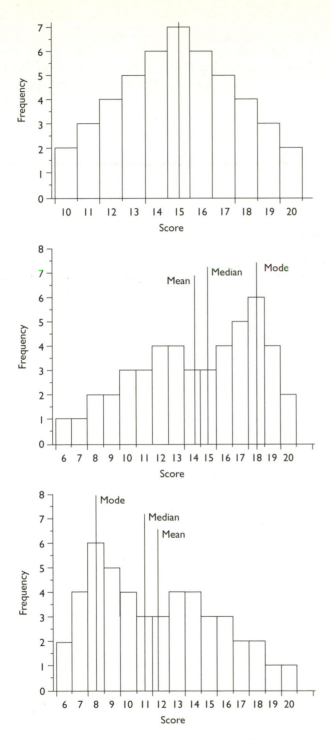

Figure 2.5 (a) Symmetrical frequency distribution;
(b) Negatively skewed frequency distribution;
(c) Positively skewed frequency distribution.

(i.e., it is positively skewed), then the median tends to be positioned to the right of the mode, and the mean is positioned to the right of the median (see Figure 2.5c).

As we saw earlier a distribution can be bimodal. This is one of the cases in which the mean is not a useful index to summarise the data. The reason is that the mean is likely to lie midway between the two peaks in the distribution of scores. In this case the mean identifies a value whose surroundings are poorly represented in the distribution.

Finally, the above descriptions and characteristics of frequency distributions also apply to continuous data. In particular, in the case of continuous data, if a distribution is symmetrical with a bell shape it is called a normal distribution. The normal distribution curve, its properties and its uses will be considered in Chapter 5.

A useful digression on the Σ notation

In order to calculate the mean, it is necessary to sum up the values of each observation and to divide this sum by the number of observations. As we saw earlier the Σ notation is used to indicate the sum of a given number of values. Since it is quite common in statistics to add different values, it is useful to briefly describe how the Σ operator works, and to provide some useful manipulations involving this operator.

In the case of the sample mean it was said that this is given by:

$$\bar{x} = \frac{\Sigma x}{n}.$$

This is actually shorthand for: $\bar{x} = \dfrac{\sum\limits_{i=1}^{n} x_n}{n}$

where $\sum\limits_{i=1}^{n} x_n$ stands for the sum of all n values that the variable X takes, starting at $i = 1(x_1)$ and going up to $i = n(x_n)$, i.e., $x_1 + x_2 + x_3 + \ldots + x_n$. In general, if there is no loss of clarity, the subscripts are not reported.

Here are some useful rules that apply to the summation operator:

$$\Sigma(x \pm y) = \Sigma x \pm \Sigma y$$

$$\Sigma cx = c \Sigma x$$

where c represents any constant (i.e., a number that does not change its value, unlike a variable whose value changes),

$$\sum_{i=1}^{n} c = nc$$

where n is the number of values being summed, and

$$\Sigma(x \pm c) = \Sigma x \pm \Sigma c = \Sigma x \pm nc.$$

Measures of dispersion (or variability)

Measures of central tendency, on their own, provide an insufficient summary of a set of data. Distributions may have, for example, the same mean and median, but the spread of the data may differ substantially between data-sets. For example, consider these distributions:

A) −12, −8, −4, 0, 4, 8, 12
B) −60, −40, −20, 0, 20, 40, 60
C) −120, −80, −40, 0, 40, 80, 120
D) −60, −40, −20, 0, 1, 1, 118

Although the median and the mean are the same in the four distributions (i.e., 0), the data are relatively compact around the mean in distribution A, while their spread around the mean is more pronounced in distributions B, C and D. Therefore, to have an accurate summary of a distribution of data, measures of central tendency need to be complemented by measures of dispersions of the data. The description of some of the most common indices of dispersion follows.

The range and the interquartile range

The *range* is a measure of the distance between the lowest and the highest value in a distribution. Considering the four distributions given above, the ranges are 24, 120, 240 and 178 for distributions A, B, C and D, respectively. A limitation of the range is that it is severely influenced by extreme values, so that it may provide a distorted picture of the spread of the data. Consider, for example, the range of distributions B and D. The range of D is almost 50 per cent greater than the range of B; however, more data are closer to the mean in distribution D than in B.

The *interquartile range* is the range of the middle 50 per cent of the distribution, so it is less influenced by extreme values than the range. It is calculated by taking the difference between the 75th and the 25th percentile of a distribution, or equivalently the difference between the third quartile and the first quartile (percentiles subdivide the distribution into hundredths; quartiles subdivide a distribution into quarters). Considering again the data in Table 2.1 the interquartile range is 9 (i.e., 30 − 21; these are the values corresponding to the 75th and the 25th percentile, respectively).

The boxplot

Boxplots (or box-and-whisker plots) make use of the interquartile range and the median to display, in a compact way, a set of data. As in the case of the stem-and-leaf displays, boxplots are useful to visually compare two distributions. Figure 2.6 displays, side by side, the boxplots of the end-of-year exam marks obtained by students who had either high or low attendance at lectures (see Table 2.4 for the individual marks). The edges of each box correspond to the values of the first quartile (Q1) and third quartile (Q3). The line within the edges of each box is the median. The length of each whisker extending outside each box is given by taking 1.5 times the interquartile range (i.e. (Q3 − Q1) × 1.5). For low-attendance students the median is 54 and the

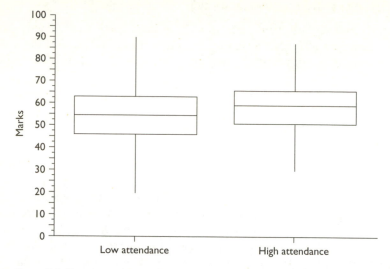

Figure 2.6 Boxplots of the exam results from Table 2.4.

edges of the box correspond to 46 and 63.25; thus, the length of each whisker is 25.875. For high-attendance students the median is 59.5 and the edges of the box correspond to 51 and 66, thus the length of each whisker is 22.5. If outliers are presents (i.e., unusually extreme values), these would be individually indicated either by stars or crosses positioned either above or below the end of the whiskers. The presence of outliers should alert the researcher that, possibly, some error occurred when the data were entered in the package used to analyse the data. Alternatively, outliers may be genuine. In this case it is important to try to understand their origin. This is not always an easy task since the nature of the outliers often depends on the specific nature of the experimental/observational design used to collect the data. More will be said about outliers in Chapter 11. Finally, as a cautionary note, keep in mind that when using a statistical package to obtain boxplot displays there may be differences between statistical packages in the way they define the elements of the boxplot.

Average deviations and the variance

Given the limitations of the range it would be useful to obtain a more suitable index of dispersion. In particular, it would be useful for the mean of the data to be used in calculating this index of dispersion. The reason is that the mean can be manipulated algebraically, so it can be integrated into different equations.

The *average deviation from the mean* may appear, prima facie, to be a good index of variability in a distribution of data. This is defined as:

$$\frac{\Sigma(x - \bar{x})}{n}$$

where

$$\Sigma(x - \bar{x}) = (x_1 - \bar{x}) + (x_2 - \bar{x}) + \ldots + (x_n - \bar{x}).$$

However, the sum of the differences between each observed value and the mean is equal to zero. Applying the summation rules earlier described we obtain:

$$\Sigma(x - \bar{x}) = \Sigma x - \Sigma \bar{x} = \Sigma x - n\bar{x}$$

but

$$\frac{\Sigma x}{n} = \bar{x}, \text{ so } \Sigma x = n\bar{x}.$$

Thus,

$$\Sigma(x - \bar{x}) = n\bar{x} - n\bar{x} = 0$$

and therefore

$$\frac{\Sigma(x - \bar{x})}{n} = 0.$$

Thus, the average deviation from the mean cannot be used as an index of dispersion.

A possible alternative index is the *absolute average deviation from the mean*. The formula to calculate this index is similar to the one for the average deviation:

$$\frac{\Sigma |x - \bar{x}|}{n}$$

where the only difference is that the sum of the absolute differences from the mean is averaged. Absolute deviation scores are the deviation scores with the sign removed (i.e., negative scores are taken as positive and the vertical lines are conventional to show this). This index is simple to calculate but, given that algebraic manipulations of absolute numbers are inconvenient, this index is not used in statistics.

An alternative to the above indices, and commonly used as a measure of dispersion is the *variance*. In order to calculate the variance, instead of working with sums of deviations from the mean, we work using the sum of squared deviations from the mean (often simply called the *sum of squares*):

$$\Sigma(x - \bar{x})^2 = (x_1 - \bar{x})^2 + (x_2 - \bar{x})^2 + \ldots + (x_n - \bar{x})^2.$$

The sum of a set of squared values is always positive, thus the problem encountered when working with the sum of deviations from the mean is avoided. The variance is defined as the average of the squared deviations from the mean; thus, in principle, the formula to calculate the variance should be:

$$\frac{\Sigma(x - \bar{x})^2}{n}.$$

However, this formula has limited application since it can only be used to calculate the variance of a sample of data drawn from a given population. Unfortunately, it is not useful for estimating the *variance of the population* from which the sample has been drawn, because it provides, on average, too small an estimate. In general, as explained in Chapter 1, we are not interested in statistics *per se* (i.e., in indices reflecting characteristics of a sample), but we *are* interested in obtaining estimates of the population parameters while working with sample data. Therefore, a more appropriate formula is required to estimate the population variance using sample data. The population variance estimated from sample data is usually labelled as s^2 and is defined as:

$$s^2 = \frac{\Sigma(x - \bar{x})^2}{n - 1}$$

where n is the number of observations in the sample, and $\bar{x}$ is the sample mean (we will see later why having $n - 1$ instead of n as the denominator provides a better estimate of the population variance). For completeness the population variance calculated from the entire population is denoted as σ^2 (sigma squared) and it is given by:

$$\sigma^2 = \frac{\Sigma(x - \mu)^2}{n}$$

where n is the number of all the values in a population and μ is the mean of the population. (You will also meet this as $\text{VAR}(X) = \sigma^2 = \frac{\Sigma(x - \mu)^2}{n}$)

The formula given above to calculate s^2 is the defining formula, but it is not very practical in use. If s^2 needs to be calculated on a relatively large set of data a more practical, and equivalent, formula is the following:

$$s^2 = \frac{\Sigma x^2 - \frac{(\Sigma x)^2}{n}}{n - 1}$$

where $\Sigma(x - \bar{x})^2$, also called the *sum of squares*, has been replaced by $\Sigma x^2 - \frac{(\Sigma x)^2}{n}$. The reasoning is as follows:

$$\Sigma(x - \bar{x})^2 = \Sigma(x^2 + \bar{x}^2 - 2x\bar{x}) \qquad \text{(multiplying out the brackets)}$$

$$= \Sigma x^2 + \Sigma \bar{x}^2 - \Sigma 2x\bar{x} \qquad \text{(the } \Sigma \text{ operator is distributed)}$$

$$= \Sigma x^2 + n\bar{x}^2 - 2\bar{x}\Sigma x \qquad \text{(applying the rules for summation and remembering that } \bar{x} \text{ is a constant)}$$

$$= \Sigma x^2 + n\left(\frac{\Sigma x}{n}\right)^2 - 2\frac{\Sigma x}{n} \times \Sigma x \quad \text{since } \bar{x} = \frac{\Sigma x}{n}$$

$$= \Sigma x^2 + \frac{(\Sigma x)^2}{n} - 2\frac{(\Sigma x)^2}{n}$$

$$= \Sigma x^2 - \frac{(\Sigma x)^2}{n}.$$

An alternative formula for s^2, since $\dfrac{(\Sigma x)^2}{n} = n\bar{x}^2$, is the following:

$$s^2 = \frac{\Sigma x^2 - n\bar{x}^2}{n - 1}.$$

Let us calculate s^2 from data-set A (i.e., 6, 7, 8, 9, 10) and data-set B (i.e., 2, 4, 8, 12, 14).

For set A

$$s^2 = \frac{\Sigma x^2 - \dfrac{(\Sigma x)^2}{n}}{n - 1} = \frac{(36 + 49 + 64 + 81 + 100) - \dfrac{40^2}{5}}{4} = 2.5.$$

For set B

$$s^2 = \frac{(4 + 16 + 64 + 144 + 196) - \dfrac{40^2}{5}}{4} = 26.$$

Both sets have the same mean (i.e., 8), however set B has a larger spread than set A. This is captured by the difference in the obtained s^2.

Notice that the variance is very sensitive to the influence of extreme scores. The further away a score is from the mean, the more it contributes to inflating the variance. As an example, consider a set of 11 scores ranging from −10 to 10 with their mean equal to zero. The contribution of a score of 1 to s^2 is $\dfrac{(1 - 0)^2}{10} = 0.1$, while the contribution of a score of 10 to s^2 is $\dfrac{(10 - 0)^2}{10} = 10$. Although these scores deviate 1 unit and 10 units from the mean, their contribution to the estimated population variance is 0.1 unit and 10 units, respectively. Finally, an important tip to remember is that *if*, in calculating sums of squares or variances, these turn out to be *negative*, then you have certainly made a computational *error*. Sums of squares and variances are always positive. This is because squared numbers are always positive. A further thing to remember is that the quantities Σx^2 and $(\Sigma x)^2$ are almost never identical. Take for example the values 3 and 4. For these values we have that:

$$\Sigma x^2 = (3^2 + 4^2) = 25$$

while

$$(\Sigma x)^2 = (3 + 4)^2 = 7^2 = 49.$$

The standard deviation

A limitation of the variance as an index of variability is that it is not expressed in the same units as the observed variable (because differences from the mean are squared).

A way around this problem is to take the positive square root of the variance. This is called the standard deviation. In this way the variability in the data is measured in the same units as the variable being measured. The standard deviation of the population estimated using sample data is called s (sometimes SD), and it is given by:

$$s = \sqrt{\frac{\Sigma(x - \bar{x})^2}{n - 1}}$$

or equivalently,

$$s = \sqrt{\frac{\Sigma x^2 - \frac{(\Sigma x)^2}{n}}{n - 1}}$$

where n is the number of observations in the sample, and $\bar{x}$ is the sample mean.

For completeness the population standard deviation calculated on the data from the entire population is denoted as σ (sigma) and it is given by:

$$\sigma = \sqrt{\frac{\Sigma(x - \mu)^2}{n}}$$

where n is the number of all the observations in a population and μ is the mean of the population.

For simplicity, given that it is common to work using sample data, from now on we will only use the terms standard deviation and variance; so we will drop the words "of the population estimated from sample data". Remember that these terms will always refer, unless otherwise clearly specified, to estimates of the relevant population parameters.

When the above formula is applied to calculate the standard deviation (s) of the exam marks obtained by the sample of 60 biology students whose marks are reported in Table 2.3 we find that $s = 11.03$ and $s^2 = 121.71$ (rounding to the second decimal place; however, in order to avoid inaccurate calculations, remember to always use several decimal places during any computation). As an exercise try to calculate, using both the defining and the more practical formulae, the variance and the standard deviation of the exam data from the biology students who did not regularly attend to the lectures (see Table 2.4; the correct values are $s = 11.60$ and $s^2 = 134.55$, to 2 d.p.).

Finally, provided that the distribution of the sampled data is reasonably symmetrical and reasonably bell shaped, then approximately two-thirds of the observations lie within one standard deviation below the mean and one standard deviation above the mean; while about 95 per cent of the observations lie within ±2 SD from the mean (a comprehensive discussion about this issue will be provided in Chapter 5). These approximations are useful to check if the standard deviation has been calculated correctly. For example, for the data in Table 2.3 where the mean is 59.3 and the standard deviation is 11.03, 40 out of 60 observations lie between 48.27 and 70.33 (i.e., ±1 SD from the mean); while only two observations are outside ±2 SD from the mean.

Further on the mean, variance, and standard deviation of frequency distributions

At the beginning of this chapter the frequency distribution of data from a picture-naming task was reported (Table 2.1). When we know that each score x_i occurs with frequency f_i, there is also an alternative formula for calculating the mean of a frequency distribution. This alternative formula is based on the fact that the sum of the frequencies at which each score occurs is equal to the total number of observations; thus, the mean is given by:

$$\bar{x} = \frac{\sum\limits_{i=1}^{m} f_i x_i}{\sum\limits_{i=1}^{m} f_i}$$

where the numerator is the sum of the products of each observed value (i.e., x_i) multiplied by its frequency (i.e., f_i), for each of the m values of x, and the denominator is the sum of the frequencies of each observed value, i.e., n. This formula will turn out to be useful when, in Chapter 4, we calculate the mean of probability distributions.

Consider the case where 40 subjects are asked to rate, using a five-point scale (1 = very easy, 5 = very difficult), the perceived difficulty of a problem-solving task. Let us assume that the results obtained are those in Table 2.6. Then the mean rating is:

$$\bar{x} = \frac{(4 \times 1) + (7 \times 2) + (8 \times 3) + (12 \times 4) + (9 \times 5)}{4 + 7 + 8 + 12 + 9}$$

$$= \frac{4 + 14 + 24 + 48 + 45}{40} = \frac{135}{40} = 3.375.$$

The computational formula to calculate the variance of a frequency distribution is given by:

$$s^2 = \frac{\sum\limits_{i=1}^{m} f_i x_i^2 - \dfrac{\left(\sum\limits_{i=1}^{m} f_i x_i\right)^2}{n}}{n-1}$$

and the standard deviation is given by:

$$s = \sqrt{\frac{\sum\limits_{i=1}^{m} f_i x_i^2 - \dfrac{\left(\sum\limits_{i=1}^{m} f_i x_i\right)^2}{n}}{n-1}}.$$

Table 2.6 Frequency distribution of the rating of the perceived difficulty of a problem-solving task in a sample of 40 subjects

Rating (x_i)	1	2	3	4	5
Frequency (f_i)	4	7	8	12	9

Thus, the estimated variance of the subjective ratings in Table 2.6 is:

$$s^2 = \frac{(4 \times 1^2) + (7 \times 2^2) + (8 \times 3^2) + (12 \times 4^2) + (9 \times 5^2) - \frac{[(4 \times 1) + (7 \times 2) + (8 \times 3) + (12 \times 4) + (9 \times 5)]^2}{40}}{40 - 1}$$

$$= \frac{521 - \frac{18225}{40}}{39} = 1.676 \quad \text{(to three decimal places)},$$

while the standard deviation is:

$$s = \sqrt{\frac{521 - \frac{18225}{40}}{39}} = 1.295 \text{ (to 3 d.p.)}.$$

As discussed above (pages 15–17), it is often the case that data in frequency distributions are grouped. If you need to calculate the mean of grouped data, like those presented in Table 2.2, then the formula to be used is the same as the one just described for frequency distributions. However, instead of multiplying each observed value (i.e., x_i) by its frequency of occurrence (i.e., f_i), the middle point of each interval is multiplied by the frequency of the observed values within each interval. When data are grouped the individual observations are lost and, therefore, the calculated mean may not exactly correspond to the actual mean of the data-set. The mean of the grouped data in Table 2.2, calculated using the formula for grouped data is then:

$$\bar{x} = \frac{(2 \times 12) + (5 \times 17) + (8 \times 22) + (14 \times 27) + (6 \times 32) + (3 \times 37) + (2 \times 42)}{2 + 5 + 8 + 14 + 6 + 3 + 2}$$

$$= \frac{1050}{40} = 26.25$$

while the mean calculated using all the individual observations (see Table 2.1) is 25.975. If you have both grouped and individual values for a set of data, it is more appropriate to calculate the mean using individual data. However, in some cases you may only access grouped data; consequently, the above formula is the only way to obtain an estimate of the actual mean of the data.

A similar problem occurs in calculating the variance and the standard deviation from grouped frequency tables. The formulae to be used are the same as those used for frequency distributions. However the x_i are now the middle points of each interval, and the f_i are the frequencies of occurrences of the values within each interval. Applying the appropriate formulae to the data in Table 2.2, the variance is:

$$s^2 = \frac{(2 \times 12^2) + (5 \times 17^2) + (8 \times 22^2) + (14 \times 27^2) + (6 \times 32^2) + (3 \times 37^2) + (2 \times 42^2) - \dfrac{1050^2}{40}}{40 - 1}$$

$$= \frac{29590 - 27562.5}{39} = 51.987 \text{ (to 3 d.p.),}$$

while the standard deviation (i.e., s) is:

$$s = \sqrt{\frac{29590 - 27562.5}{39}} = 7.210 \text{ (to 3 d.p.).}$$

Notice that the variance and the standard deviation, when calculated using all the individual observations, are 47.102 and 6.863, respectively.

How to calculate the combined mean and the combined variance of several samples

In some cases the only data available may be the variance and the mean obtained in several independent samples (this usually indicates that different subjects were tested in the different samples), and from these data it is useful to obtain the overall mean and variance of the combined samples. First, we show the formulae that generalise the calculations to any k number of samples, then an example using two samples will be provided.

The formula to calculate the mean of k combined samples is given by:

$$\bar{x} = \frac{\displaystyle\sum_{i=1}^{k} n_i \bar{x}_i}{N}$$

where n_i is the number of observations in each of the k samples, $\bar{x}_i$ is the mean of each of the k samples, and $N = \sum n_i$, i.e., the total number of observations in the combined samples.

The formula to calculate the variance (i.e., s^2) of k combined samples is given by:

$$s^2 = \frac{\left(\displaystyle\sum_{i=1}^{k} (n_i - 1)s_i^2 + \sum_{i=1}^{k} n_i \bar{x}_i^2 \right) - \dfrac{\left(\displaystyle\sum_{i=1}^{k} n_i \bar{x}_i \right)^2}{N}}{N - 1}$$

where s_i^2 is the variance of each of the k samples, $\bar{x}_i$ is the mean of each of the k samples, and $N = \sum n_i$. This formula looks quite messy, but it is simply the standard formula for s^2 in disguise (i.e., $s^2 = \dfrac{\sum x^2 - \dfrac{(\sum x)^2}{n}}{n - 1}$). In fact, the quantity in the first set of brackets, calculated taking into account all the values of x in the k samples, gives the usual $\sum x^2$. It is obtained from the equation shown in the previous section,

$s^2 = \dfrac{\sum x^2 - n\bar{x}^2}{n-1}$, which, after some rearranging, becomes $(n-1)s^2 + n\bar{x}^2 = \sum x^2$. The quantity in the second bracket corresponds to $(\sum x)$ calculated taking into account all the values of x in the k samples.

Applying the above formulae to the two samples of the end-of-year exam marks for the biology students shown in Table 2.4, the combined mean is:

$$\bar{x} = \frac{\displaystyle\sum_{i=1}^{k} n_i \bar{x}_i}{N} = \frac{(60 \times 59.3) + (60 \times 54.7)}{120} = 57.0,$$

while for the combined variance we obtain:

$$s^2 = \frac{\left(\displaystyle\sum_{i=1}^{k}(n_i - 1)s_i^2 + \sum_{i=1}^{k} n_i \bar{x}_i^2\right) - \dfrac{\left(\displaystyle\sum_{i=1}^{k} n_i \bar{x}_i\right)^2}{N}}{N-1}$$

$$= \frac{\{[(59 \times 121.71) + (59 \times 134.55)] + [(60 \times 59.3^2) + (60 \times 54.7^2)]\}}{119}$$

$$- \frac{\dfrac{[(60 \times 59.3) + (60 \times 54.7)]^2}{120}}{119} = 132.39 \text{ (to 2 d.p.)},$$

where 59.3 and 54.7 are the mean exam scores in the samples of good and poor lecture attenders; 121.71 and 134.55 their respective variances, and 60 was the size of each sample. For convenience we displayed only two decimal places in the formula; however, the computations were carried out with twelve decimal places to obtain a precise estimate of the variance. Finally the standard deviation can simply be obtained by taking the square root of the variance (i.e., $s = 11.51$, to 2 d.p.).

Properties of estimators

We have stressed that it is normal practice to work with samples in order to obtain estimates of the population parameters. Therefore, since the statistics obtained from samples are only estimates of the corresponding population parameters, it would be useful to know how well each statistic estimates the corresponding parameter. In doing this we will concentrate on the most commonly used estimators of central tendency (i.e. $\bar{x}$, to estimate μ), and of variability (i.e. s^2, to estimate σ^2; remember that the properties of the standard deviation are the same as those of the variance).

A good estimator should be calculated making use of all the data in a sample. If this occurs, the statistic is said to be *sufficient*. Both $\bar{x}$ and s^2 are *sufficient* statistics because they are calculated making use of all the data in a sample. Other statistics like the mode and the range, for example, are not sufficient since they are not obtained using all the data in a sample.

An estimator is said to be *efficient* if its sample statistic clusters closely to the value of the population parameter. For example, if all possible samples of n observations are drawn from a population with $\mu = 10$, their sample means, i.e. $\bar{x}_i$, will cluster closely around 10. On the other hand, the sample medians will cluster less closely around 10 than the sample mean. Thus the sample mean is more efficient than the sample median as an estimator of μ. Both $\bar{x}$ and s^2 are the most efficient statistics to estimate μ and σ^2, respectively.

An estimator is said to be *unbiased* if its long-term average (or alternatively its *expected value*), calculated over a very large number of samples drawn from the same population, corresponds to the population parameter it intends to estimate. Both $\bar{x}$ and s^2 are unbiased estimates of μ and σ^2, respectively. What it is meant by long-term average? Imagine, for example, that we draw 10 samples of 100 observations each, from a population with $\mu = 50$, and we calculate their means. If we then calculate the mean of these sample means we should obtain a value very close to 50 (i.e., the population mean). If we draw 100 samples from the same population and we carry out the same procedure, then the mean of these sample means will be even closer to μ. If the same procedure is performed on a larger number of samples from the same population, the mean of these sets of sample means will be even closer to μ. If this process is pushed to the limit and all possible samples of 100 observations are taken from the population, then the mean of all possible sample means will be equal to μ. This limiting value of the sample mean is its long-term average (or expected value). We will now use an example to illustrate the concept of an unbiased estimator.

Imagine that the entire population of an island consists of three castaways, whose heights are 160, 165 and 170 cm, respectively. Thus $\mu = 165$ and $\sigma^2 = 16.667$. The total number of different samples of two observations that can be drawn from this population is nine (when order is considered relevant). These nine samples are obtained with random sampling, and replacement, from the population. One castaway is randomly drawn and his/her height is recorded, then the drawn castaway is replaced in the population and another selection is made. Therefore the same height can be sampled twice to form a sample of two observations. When replacement is allowed, the sampled observations are independent. This means that the first draw does not affect the probability of selection in the second draw (if the first observation is not "put back" in the population, then the probability of drawing any of the remaining observations is higher than the probability of drawing the first, i.e., $\frac{1}{2}$ instead of $\frac{1}{3}$). The nine different samples of two observations with their means and variances calculated using both the formula that provides an unbiased estimate of the population variance (i.e., $s^2 = \dfrac{\Sigma(x - \bar{x})^2}{n - 1}$) and the formula that provides a biased estimate of the population variance (i.e., $\dfrac{\Sigma(x - \bar{x})^2}{n}$ which for convenience we name Biased-var) are:

160, 160 ($\bar{x} = 160.0$, $s^2 = 0$, Biased-var $= 0$);
165, 165 ($\bar{x} = 165.0$, $s^2 = 0$, Biased-var $= 0$);
170, 170 ($\bar{x} = 170.0$, $s^2 = 0$, Biased-var $= 0$);
160, 165 ($\bar{x} = 162.5$, $s^2 = 12.5$, Biased-var $= 6.25$);
160, 170 ($\bar{x} = 165.0$, $s^2 = 50.0$, Biased-var $= 25.0$);
165, 170 ($\bar{x} = 167.5$, $s^2 = 12.5$, Biased-var $= 6.25$);
165, 160 ($\bar{x} = 162.5$, $s^2 = 12.5$, Biased-var $= 6.25$);
170, 160 ($\bar{x} = 165.0$, $s^2 = 50.0$, Biased-var $= 25.0$);
170, 165 ($\bar{x} = 167.5$, $s^2 = 12.5$, Biased-var $= 6.25$).

As you can see each sample mean is fairly close, if not identical, to the population mean. Moreover, when the mean of the possible sample means from the population of castaways is calculated, we obtain the value of the population mean $\mu = 165$. Thus the expected value of the sample mean is the population mean.

The same applies to the variance, but only when this is calculated dividing the sum of squares obtained on the sampled data by $n - 1$ (i.e., when s^2 is calculated). The average s^2 is equal to the variance of the population of castaways' heights (i.e., 16.667, to 3 d.p.). If the variance of each sample is calculated dividing the sum of squares by n instead of $n - 1$, then the average of these variances is smaller than the population variance (i.e., 9.17 instead of 16.667). Thus the above example demonstrates that to obtain an unbiased estimate of the population variance from sample data, it is necessary to divide the sums of squares by $n - 1$ (i.e., the formula to calculate s^2).

Why is it necessary to divide the sample sum of squares by $n - 1$ to obtain an unbiased estimate of the population variance? As a reminder, the formulae to calculate σ^2 and s^2 differ, not only in their denominators (i.e., n and $n - 1$), but also in the mean used to calculate the sum of squares. In the case of σ^2 the sum of squares is calculated as $\Sigma(x - \mu)^2$, where the population mean is known, while in the case of s^2 each sampled observation is subtracted from the sample mean (i.e., $\Sigma(x - \bar{x})^2$), which is used as an estimate of the unknown μ. When μ has been estimated using $\bar{x}$, the latter is fixed, thus, to estimate the variance, there are now only $n - 1$ sample observations free to vary. In other words, if the average of a sample of n observations is fixed, then we are free to chose any set of $n - 1$ observations we want. However, in order to obtain the fixed mean, the last nth observation cannot be chosen. For example, assume that the mean of 5 observations is fixed and it is 10. Then it is possible to select any set of 4 observations, as for example the set {8, 9, 10, 11}. However, given this set of values, the only way to obtain a mean of 10 is by having the fifth observation equal to 12 (similarly, if the set {2, 8, 10, 16} is chosen, the only way to obtain a mean of 10 is by selecting 14 as the fifth observation). We are not *free* to select the fifth value, therefore we say there are only 4 degrees of *freedom*. The above restriction is reflected in the denominator where the sum of squares is averaged by taking into account only the total number of values free to vary (i.e., the degrees of freedoms are $n - 1$). The concept of degrees of freedom will be further elaborated later in the book.

Mean and variance of linearly transformed data

In some cases a set of data needs to be transformed. For example, all the original data need to be shifted by a constant amount. One instance of this type of transformation is when the mean of a data-set is subtracted from each score. In doing this the data are centred around a new mean (i.e., zero). In this type of transformation a constant value is added (or subtracted) to each of the observed scores. What is the effect of this process on the mean and the variance of the original set of data? In the case of the mean, when a constant is added to each value, the increment of each score corresponds to the added constant, thus the mean of the new data (i.e., $\bar{y}$) is given by the mean of the old data (i.e., $\bar{x}$) plus the constant (i.e., a). More formally, when the new score y is:

$$y = a + x$$

then

$$\bar{y} = \frac{\Sigma y}{n} = \frac{\Sigma(a + x)}{n} = \frac{\Sigma a + \Sigma x}{n} = \frac{na + \Sigma x}{n} = \frac{na}{n} + \frac{\Sigma x}{n} = a + \bar{x}.$$

For example, if we add a constant $a = 5$ to the data-set {5, 7, 9} having a mean of 7, then the mean of the new data-set {10, 12, 14} is given by:

$$\bar{y} = a + \bar{x} = 5 + 7 = 12.$$

In the case of the variance, when a constant a is added to each of the original xs, the variance of the new set of data is the same as the old set. Intuitively, if every value is shifted by a constant, then the distance of each individual score from the mean has not been affected, therefore the sum of squares and the variance are not affected. More formally, if

$$y = a + x$$

then

$$(y - \bar{y}) = (a + x) - (a + \bar{x}) = (x - \bar{x})$$

therefore

$$s^2 = \frac{\Sigma(y - \bar{y})^2}{n - 1} = \frac{\Sigma(x - \bar{x})^2}{n - 1}.$$

Hence, for both {5, 7, 9} and the new data-set obtained by adding $a = 5$ to the old set, i.e., {10, 12, 14}, the variance is: $s^2 = \dfrac{(-2)^2 + 0^2 + 2^2}{2} = 4$

Often, in order to change scale, each original value is multiplied by a constant b. In this case, the mean of the new data is obtained by multiplying the mean of the old data by the constant. More formally if:

$$y = b \times x$$

then

$$\bar{y} = \frac{\Sigma(bx)}{n} = \frac{b\Sigma x}{n} = b\bar{x}.$$

If we multiply each observation of the set {5, 7, 9} by $b = 3$, we obtain the new data-set {15, 21, 27}. The mean of the new set is then obtained as: $\bar{y} = b\bar{x} = 3 \times 7 = 21$.

When each of the original values is multiplied by a constant, the variance of the new set of data is given by multiplying the variance of the original set of data by the square of the constant. More formally if

$$y = b \times x$$

then

$$(y - \bar{y}) = (b \times x) - (b \times \bar{x}) = b \times (x - \bar{x}).$$

After squaring each term we obtain

$$(y - \bar{y})^2 = [b \times (x - \bar{x})]^2 = b^2 \times (x - \bar{x})^2,$$

and therefore

$$\Sigma(y - \bar{y})^2 = \Sigma[b \times (x - \bar{x})]^2 = b^2 \times \Sigma(x - \bar{x})^2.$$

Dividing each term by $n - 1$ we obtain:

$$s^2 = \frac{\Sigma(y - \bar{y})^2}{n - 1} = b^2 \times \frac{\Sigma(x - \bar{x})^2}{n - 1},$$

that is,

$$s_y^2 = b^2 \times s_x^2$$

where s_y^2 is the variance of the transformed scores, and s_x^2 is the variance of the original scores. Thus, if we multiply each observation of the set $\{5, 7, 9\}$ by $b = 3$, we obtain the new data-set $\{15, 21, 27\}$. The variance of the old data-set is $s_x^2 = \dfrac{(-2)^2 + 0^2 + 2^2}{2} = 4$ and the variance of the new set is then: $s_y^2 = b^2 \times s_x^2 = 3^2 \times 4 = 36$.

In general, if a linear transformation is performed on a set of data (i.e., $y = a + bx$), then the mean of the new data is given by:

$$\bar{y} = a + b\bar{x},$$

the variance by:

$$s_y^2 = b^2 \times s_x^2,$$

and the standard deviation by:

$$s_y = b \times s_x.$$

Thus, if the old set is $\{5, 7, 9\}$ with $\bar{x} = 7$ and $s_x^2 = 4$, and we apply the linear transformation $y = 5 + 3x$, then the new set is $\{20, 26, 32\}$. The mean of the new set is given by:

$$\bar{y} = a + b\bar{x} = 5 + 3 \times 7 = 26,$$

the variance is: $s_y^2 = b^2 \times s_x^2 = 3^2 \times 4 = 36$, and the standard deviation is:

$$s_y = b \times s_x = 3 \times 2 = 6.$$

A very useful type of transformation is the standardisation. Standardisation is achieved by subtracting the mean of a set of data from each observation in the set (i.e., centring the data around zero), and then dividing this difference by the standard deviation of the set of data. More formally, the new standardised score y is given by:

$$y = \frac{x - \bar{x}}{s_x}$$

The mean of standardised data is zero, and their standard deviation is 1. Thus if we standardise the data-set $\{5, 7, 9\}$ having $\bar{x} = 7$ and $s_x = \sqrt{s_x^2} = 2$, we obtain the values:

$$y_1 = \frac{5 - 7}{2} = -1, \quad y_2 = \frac{7 - 7}{2} = 0, \quad y_3 = \frac{9 - 7}{2} = 1;$$

i.e., $\{-1, 0, 1\}$ with $\bar{x} = 0$ and $s_x = s_x^2 = 1$.

Standardised scores are often useful to work with since they allow the comparison of common units (i.e., standard deviation units) obtained from different scales. For example, if in two different attitude tests a student obtains scores of 75 and 54, it is difficult to appreciate in which test the student performed better. On the other hand, assuming that it is known, after extensive use of these tests with several people, that the first test has a mean of 65 and a standard deviation of 10, and the second test has a mean of 40 and a standard deviation of 7, we can then calculate the standardised scores obtained in the two tests by our student. These standardised scores are for the first and second tests, 1 and 2, respectively. Thus it appears that, in the first test, our student obtained a score about 1 SD above the mean, while in the second test the performance was 2 SD above the mean. Although the score obtained in the first test was numerically higher than the score obtained in the second test, when these scores are standardised, it appears that the student performed better in the second test. More will be said about standardised scores in Chapter 5 when the standard normal distribution will be presented.

Finally, only a limited number of possible data transformations have been presented in this section. In general, several different types of transformations can be performed on any set of data by simply applying some specific function to the data, e.g., $y = \sqrt{x}$. As we will see in the following chapters, to correctly apply inferential statistics techniques, distributions of observations need to have specific characteristics. Data transformations can sometimes be performed on "rogue" data so that these can be made amenable to specific statistical analyses (for further details on transformations see e.g., Howell, 1997).

Chapter 3

Introduction to probability

Why are some notions of probability useful?

In the previous chapters we said nothing, explicitly, about the relevance of probability in statistics. It is now important to make clear that the use of probability is at the heart of inferential statistics. Inferential statistics, as mentioned in the first chapter, is essential for deciding whether the performances obtained in two experimental conditions are different (e.g., does classical music played in the background during learning improve memory of exam material over a condition where no music is played?). This decision process, which will be described in detail in later chapters, is based on specific assumptions and, in particular, on the probability that a given empirical result can be obtained when these assumptions are true. Thus the decision process performed in statistical inference is based on the probability of obtaining a set of data assuming certain conditions are true.

If we assume that some condition C is true, and if the probability of obtaining an outcome O under condition C is extremely low, then it is inferred that outcome O was due to some condition other than C. In the case of the classical music example described in Chapter 1, the starting assumption could be that the average number of pieces of exam information recalled by the population of students who revised while some classical music was played in the background is identical to the number of pieces of exam information recalled by the population of students who studied with no background music. Let us imagine that students in the classical music sample recall, on average, 20 per cent more items than the students in the no music group. We started with the assumption that the difference between the memory performance between the populations of students revising with or without background music is 0 per cent. Thus we should expect that when we draw pairs of samples from these two populations, the large majority of the differences in memory performances between these pairs of samples should be relatively close to 0 per cent. Now if it turns out that, given this assumption, the probability of getting the difference we observed (i.e., 20 per cent) is extremely low (e.g., less than one in a hundred), it is then inferred that we cannot have much faith in the original assumption. Therefore, it can be concluded that classical music is associated with improved memory for exam material.

The above brief description of the kind of logic used in statistical inference has only been given, at this stage, to show that this process is a probabilistic one. Therefore, before providing a more detailed description of the logic and the processes involved in statistical inference, it is necessary to introduce some concepts of probability.

Some preliminary definitions and the concept of probability

Before defining what probability is, some preliminary definitions are required. The first thing to point out is that an experiment is characterised by the fact that there are different potential outcomes and it is not possible to predict the specific outcome that is going to occur. For example, if a die is rolled, it is not possible to predict which of the six digits will face upward. Similarly, if an experiment involves measuring the intelligence quotient, then it is not possible to predict the actual score that a randomly sampled person will obtain.

The set of *all* possible outcomes of an experiment is called *sample space* and it is denoted by *S* (not to be confused with the symbol used for the standard deviation). Note that the term sample space does not refer to a set of sampled observations. In the case of rolling a die, the sample space is given by the set of all the individual numbers appearing on the six faces of the die, i.e., "1", "2", "3", "4", "5" and "6". Any member of the sample space is called a *simple event*. For example, when a die is rolled, a simple event can be either a "1" or a "2", or a "3", etc. More generally, an *event* is any set of simple events. For example, an event could be "to obtain a number equal or greater than 5" when rolling a die. In this case the event is given by the set of simple events "5" and "6".

Given the above preliminary definitions, let us now try to define what the word probability means. The first thing to note is that there are various definitions of probability. One view (i.e., the *frequentist view*) defines the probability of an event as its *long-term relative frequency of occurrence*. For example, if a fair die is rolled 60 times and the event "1" occurs 9 times, then its relative frequency is $\frac{9}{60} = 0.15$.

If we increase the number of times the die is rolled to a larger number, e.g., to 600, and we observe that the event "1" occurs 95 times, then its relative frequency is $\frac{95}{600} = 0.1583$ (to 4 d.p.). If we further increase the sample to 6000 we may obtain 988 "1"s, thus the relative frequency of the event "1" is $\frac{988}{6000} = 0.1647$ (to 4 d.p.).

We can continue this process by increasing the total number of times a die is rolled, and the larger the number of rolls, the closer the proportion of "1"s is to $\frac{1}{6}$. The number of throws can theoretically be infinite, so the limiting value of the relative frequency of occurrence of "1" is $0.1666\ldots$ or $\frac{1}{6}$. Thus, the probability of the event "1" is said to be $\frac{1}{6}$.

According to the *analytic view* of probability, if a sample space consists of $n(S)$ *equally likely* events, then the probability of occurrence of the event *E* is given by:

$$P(E) = \frac{n(E)}{n(S)}$$

where $n(E)$ is the number of times in which the event *E* occurs, and $n(S)$ is the number of simple events in the sample space *S*.

Thus, for example, the probability of obtaining an even number when rolling a fair die is given by:

$$P(\text{Even number}) = \frac{n(\text{Even number})}{n(S)} = \frac{3}{6} = 0.5$$

where $n(\text{Even number}) = 3$ (i.e., simple events "2", "4" and "6"), and $n(S) = 6$ (i.e., the sample space of all 6 possible numerical outcomes).

Keep in mind that the probability of occurrence of an event is between 0 and 1 (inclusive):

$$0 \leq P(E) \leq 1$$

where 0 indicates that the event is impossible, 1 that it is certain, and intermediate values indicate various degrees of probability of occurrence of an event.

Note also that the probability that an event E does *not* occur is often indicated as $P(\bar{E})$ or as $P(E')$ and is given by:

$$P(\bar{E}) = 1 - P(E)$$

Although there are conceptual differences in the way probability is defined according to the analytic and the frequentist perspectives, the same formulae are used to calculate the probability of the occurrence of various events.

There is also a third way to conceptualise probability. This is the subjective way, and corresponds to the subjective belief that people hold about the likelihood of occurrence of a particular event. Statements like "it is very likely that there will be a lot of traffic this afternoon", capture the subjective appraisal of the probability of occurrence of an event. The subjective view of probability, unlike the analytic and the frequentist views, does not have any mathematical underpinning. It is however important to keep in mind that our behaviour is often dictated by some evaluation of the likelihood of occurrence of some future event. For example, given the above belief about the likelihood of a traffic jam, you may decide to postpone your journey.

As a final point, defining probability is not an easy task. For example, the analytic definition of probability itself contains the term "equally likely", which somehow implies that we have already, before defining it, some kind of definition of probability.

Venn diagrams and probability

As seen above, we have a formula to calculate the probability of occurrence of a particular event. We may also want to calculate the probability of occurrence of more "complex" events which arise from some sort of combination between more than one event (e.g., knowing the probability in the population of being female, and knowing the probability of having blond hair, what is the probability that a person chosen at random has blond hair *and* is female?). In this case we need to use some specific formulae. However, before providing these formulae, it is useful to show how sets of events can be graphically represented using Venn diagrams. In Venn diagrams the sample space is represented by a rectangle, and the events within a sample space are

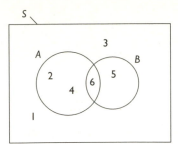

Figure 3.1 Venn diagram of the sets of events *A* (i.e., "obtaining an even number when rolling a die"), *B* (i.e., "obtaining a number equal to or larger than 5 when rolling a die"), and *S* (i.e., the sample space of all possible simple events occurring when rolling a fair die).

represented by circles. This type of representation provides a simple and intuitive way of seeing what are the simple events in the sample space that make up more "complex" events.

Let us take two events *A* and *B*, where *A* is "obtaining an even number when rolling a die", and *B* is "obtaining a number equal to or larger than 5 when rolling a die". If, when rolling a die, we want to know the probability of obtaining an even number *and* that this number is equal to or larger than 5, first we need to know how many simple events are common to *both* events *A* and *B*. These are the simple events that make up the *intersection* between *A* and *B* (i.e., the event comprising only the outcomes that *A* and *B* have in common). On the other hand, if, when rolling a die, we want to know the probability of obtaining an even number *or* a number larger than four, then we need to know how many simple events make up the *union* of *A* with *B* (i.e., the event comprising all the outcomes in *A* and all the outcomes in *B*). In Figure 3.1 a Venn diagram shows the simple events positioned within each of the relevant sets they belong to.

The *intersection* of two sets of events is denoted as *A* ∩ *B*. Using Venn diagrams the intersection of two events *A* and *B* is represented by the grey area displayed in Figure 3.2.

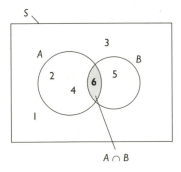

A ∩ *B*

Figure 3.2 Venn diagram representing the intersection between events *A* and *B*. The simple events comprising the event *A* ∩ *B* are in bold within the grey area.

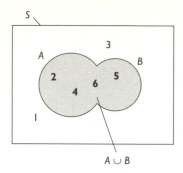

Figure 3.3 Venn diagram representing the union between events A and B. The simple events comprising the event A ∪ B are in bold within the grey area.

The *union* of two sets of events is denoted as $A \cup B$. Using Venn diagrams the union of two events A and B is represented by the grey area displayed in Figure 3.3.

Let us see, in detail, what are the simple events included in the intersection and the union of the events A and B. The first thing to consider is the sample space. This is given by all the possible outcomes obtained when a die is rolled, i.e., $S = \{1, 2, 3, 4, 5, 6\}$. The simple events making up event A are $\{2, 4, 6\}$, while the simple events constituting event B are $\{5, 6\}$. Thus the event $A \cap B$ comprises only the simple events that are common to both A and B, i.e., $A \cap B = \{6\}$. In this case the number of simple events common to both A and B is only one, thus $n(A \cap B) = 1$. Thus, when rolling a die, the probability of obtaining an even number and that this number is equal to or larger than five, is given by:

$$P(A \cap B) = \frac{n(A \cap B)}{n(S)} = \frac{1}{6}.$$

The event $A \cup B$ consists of all the simple events that occur in A and in B. In our rolling die example these are $\{2, 4, 5, 6\}$, thus $A \cup B = \{2, 4, 5, 6\}$ and $n(A \cup B) = 4$. Note that $n(A \cup B)$ is not obtained by simply adding the number of outcomes in A and in B (i.e., $n(A) = 3 + n(B) = 2$, thus $n(A) + n(B) = 5$). If this erroneous procedure had been applied, then the set $A \cup B$ would have contained some duplicates. These duplicates would be all the outcomes making up the intersection of A and B (i.e., those outcomes that are common to both A and B). In this particular case $A \cap B = \{6\}$, thus the outcome "6" would be represented twice. Therefore to obtain the number of simple events comprising the event $A \cup B$ it is necessary to subtract $n(A \cap B)$ from $n(A) + n(B)$, thus:

$$n(A \cup B) = n(A) + n(B) - n(A \cap B),$$

that is

$$4 = 3 + 2 - 1.$$

Then, to calculate the probability of the occurrence of the event $A \cup B$, it is necessary to divide both sides of the above equation by $n(S)$, i.e., the number of all possible outcomes in the sample space. Thus we obtain:

$$\frac{n(A \cup B)}{n(S)} = \frac{n(A)}{n(S)} + \frac{n(B)}{n(S)} - \frac{n(A \cap B)}{n(S)},$$

that is

$$P(A \cup B) = P(A) + P(B) - P(A \cap B).$$

In the case of our example we obtain that:

$$P(A \cup B) = \frac{3}{6} + \frac{2}{6} - \frac{1}{6} = \frac{2}{3}.$$

Thus, when rolling a die, the probability of obtaining either an even number or a number larger than four is $\frac{2}{3}$.

The addition rule and the multiplication rule of probability

The addition rule

Two events A and B are *mutually exclusive* if $n(A \cap B) = 0$, i.e., if the occurrence of one event implies that the other event cannot occur. For example, sexes are mutually exclusive events. If a person is classified as female she cannot be a male, and vice versa. Notice that all simple events in a sample space are mutually exclusive. The above definition can be generalised to any number of mutually exclusive events. Figure 3.4 shows a Venn diagram of three mutually exclusive events. Given that for two mutually exclusive events $n(A \cap B) = 0$, it follows that the probability of the intersection of two mutually exclusive events is 0, therefore, the probability of their union is given by:

$$P(A \cup B) = P(A) + P(B).$$

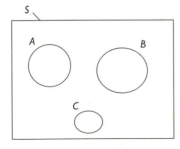

Figure 3.4 Venn diagram representing three mutually exclusive events A, B and C. Notice that there is no overlap between the circles, indicating that no simple event is common to any of the possible pairs of events.

This is known as the *additive rule of probability*, and for N mutually exclusive events it generalises to $P(A \cup B \cup \ldots \cup N) = P(A) + P(B) + \ldots + P(N)$.

From the additive rule it follows that, if two events are *mutually exclusive and exhaustive* (i.e., all the simple events in the sample space have to be included in the union of the two mutually exclusive events), then:

$$P(A \cup B) = 1,$$

which for N mutually exclusive and exhaustive events generalises to:

$$P(A \cup B \cup \ldots \cup N) = 1.$$

Note that the equations

$$P(A \cup B) = P(A) + P(B) - P(A \cap B),$$
$$P(A \cup B \cup \ldots \cup N) = P(A) + P(B) + \ldots + P(N)$$
$$P(A \cup B \cup \ldots \cup N) = 1$$

are valid when events are either equally likely to occur or unequally likely to occur (the last two equations only apply to mutually exclusive events).

The multiplication rule

For mutually exclusive events we know, by definition, that $P(A \cap B) = 0$. Is there a formula to calculate $P(A \cap B)$ for different types of events? Well, it turns out that there is a special formula to calculate the probability of the *joint* occurrence of two or more events provided that these events are *independent*. A set of events are said to be *independent* if the outcome of one event does not influence the outcome of any of the other events. Repeated tosses of a coin constitute independent events. If a coin is tossed and it lands as heads, this outcome does not influence the outcome of the next toss which can be either heads or tails with the same probability as in any of the previous tosses.

The probability of the *joint* occurrence of two independent events is given by:

$$P(A \cap B) = P(A) \times P(B).$$

More generally $P(A \cap B \cap \ldots \cap N) = P(A) \times P(B) \times \ldots \times P(N)$, and this is called the *multiplication rule of probability*, which is valid for equally and unequally likely events. For example what is the probability of obtaining four consecutive "1"s when rolling a die? This is given by:

$$P(\text{four "1"s}) = P("1") \times P("1") \times P("1") \times P("1") = \left(\frac{1}{6}\right)^4 = \frac{1}{1296}.$$

As a further example, assuming that in a given population sex and hair colour (dyed hair is not valid!) are independent events with $P(\text{Female}) = 0.5$ and $P(\text{Blond hair}) = 0.3$, then

$$P(\text{Female and having blond hair}) = P(\text{Female}) \times P(\text{Blond hair}) = 0.5 \times 0.3 = 0.15.$$

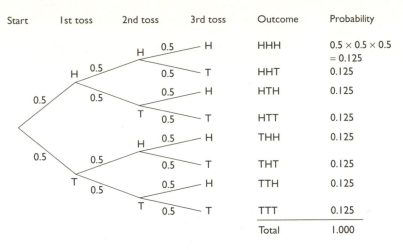

Figure 3.5 Probability tree for a fair coin tossed three times.

Probability trees

Independent events, either with the same or different probability of occurrence, are often combined. It is then useful to see what happens in these cases and what are the probabilities of each of the obtained events. Let us illustrate what we mean using a couple of examples in which independent events are considered. In the first example we want to calculate the probability of each of the possible outcomes obtained when a fair coin is tossed three times. A tree is used to calculate the probability of occurrence of each of these events (see Figure 3.5). Each branch of the tree gives the probability of an outcome. Following each branch tells us the probability of each set of three possible tosses. Since tosses are independent events, it follows that the probability of obtaining a series of three specific tosses is given by applying the multiplication rule of probability, i.e., by the product of the probability of each toss. Furthermore, notice that using the probability tree all possible triplets are obtained, and that these triplets represent mutually exclusive events. Therefore the sum of the probabilities of all possible triplets is 1, i.e., P($HHH \cup HHT \cup \ldots \cup TTT$) = 1.

Consider a second example. Let us assume that a test has been devised to detect children suffering from a specific form of attentional disorder syndrome. Let us also assume that this test is correct 90 per cent of the time (i.e., it classifies sick children as sick 90 per cent of the time, and healthy children as healthy 90 per cent of the time), and that 5 per cent of the child population is affected by the syndrome. We, therefore, want to know what is the probability of occurrence of each of the following outcomes: I) being affected by the syndrome and being diagnosed sick according to the test (i.e., SS); II) being affected by the syndrome and getting a healthy test result (SH); III) being healthy but being diagnosed as sick (HS); IV) being healthy and getting a healthy test result (HH). The probability tree in Figure 3.6 displays these probabilities. From the tree it is expected that 85.5 per cent of the people in the population will be free of the disease and classified as such by the test; 9.5 per cent of the people will be free of the disease, but classified as sick; 0.5 per cent of the people will be sick and classified as healthy; finally, 4.5 per cent of the people will be sick and classified as sick.

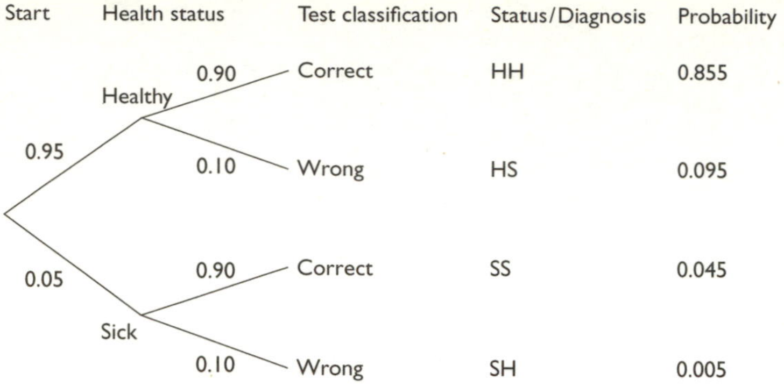

Start	Health status	Test classification	Status/Diagnosis	Probability
		0.90 ⟍ Correct	HH	0.855
	Healthy			
0.95		0.10 ⟍ Wrong	HS	0.095
0.05		0.90 ⟍ Correct	SS	0.045
	Sick			
		0.10 ⟍ Wrong	SH	0.005

Figure 3.6 Probability tree for the attentional disorder example.

Conditional probability

Conditional probability refers to the probability that an event B occurs given that an event A has occurred. This is denoted as:

$$P(B \mid A)$$

i.e., the probability of B given A.

Venn diagrams can be useful in understanding how to calculate conditional probabilities. Let us go back to the die rolling example where we had event A, i.e., "obtaining an even number when rolling a die", and event B, i.e., "obtaining a number *equal to or larger than 5 when rolling a die*". To know the probability of obtaining a number *equal to or* larger than 5, *given that* the obtained number is even, i.e., $P(B \mid A)$, we first need to identify the number of simple events constituting event A, i.e., 3 which are {2, 4, 6}. Then, we need to identify the number of simple events that constitute B and which are also included in A, i.e., 1 which is {6}. To calculate $P(B \mid A)$ we need to take the number of simple events constituting the event B that are also included in the set of simple events making up event A, i.e., 1, and then dividing this value by $n(A) = 3$. It then follows that:

$$P(B \mid A) = \frac{1}{n(A)} = \frac{1}{3}.$$

What are the simple events constituting the event B and that are also included in the set of simple events making up event A? If we inspect the Venn diagram in Figure 3.2 it appears that these simple events are those making up the intersection of events A and B, i.e., $A \cap B$. Thus, we have:

$$P(B \mid A) = \frac{n(A \cap B)}{n(A)}.$$

If we divide both numerator and denominator by $n(S)$, i.e., the total number of simple events in the sample space, we obtain:

$$P(B \mid A) = \frac{\dfrac{n(A \cap B)}{n(S)}}{\dfrac{n(A)}{n(S)}} = \frac{P(A \cap B)}{P(A)}.$$

Thus, for our rolling die example we obtain:

$$P(B \mid A) = \frac{\dfrac{n(A \cap B)}{n(S)}}{\dfrac{n(A)}{n(S)}} = \frac{P(A \cap B)}{P(A)} = \frac{\dfrac{1}{6}}{\dfrac{3}{6}} = \frac{1}{3}.$$

In the special case in which A and B are independent events, then $P(A \cap B) = P(A) \times P(B)$, thus

$$P(B \mid A) = \frac{P(A \cap B)}{P(A)} = \frac{P(A) \times P(B)}{P(A)}.$$

Let us now reconsider the test example from the previous section to further illustrate the concept of conditional probability. An example of conditional probability is the probability of a person being classified as sick, according to the test result, given that he or she is healthy (or equivalently P(Test wrong | Healthy)). To calculate this conditional probability the first thing to do is to obtain the probability of a person being healthy (i.e., $P(H) = 0.95$). This value in this particular case is known already. However, it can be obtained by adding the probability of a person being healthy and correctly declared healthy, i.e., $P(HH) = P(H) \times P(\text{Test correct}) = 0.855$, plus the probability of a person being healthy and wrongly declared sick, i.e., $P(HS) = P(H) \times P(\text{Test wrong}) = 0.095$ (remember that health status and test classification are considered to be independent events). Then,

$$P(B \mid A) = \frac{P(A) \times P(B)}{P(A)}$$

and hence

$$P(\text{Test wrong} \mid \text{Healthy}) = \frac{P(H) \times P(\text{Test wrong})}{P(H)} = \frac{0.095}{0.95} = 0.10.$$

Furthermore, notice that P(Test wrong) × P(Healthy) is rarely identical to P(Test wrong | Healthy). In this case the values are 0.095 and 0.10, respectively.

Summarising, the formulae to calculate conditional probabilities are given by:

$$P(B \mid A) = \frac{P(A \cap B)}{P(A)} \quad \text{and} \quad P(A \mid B) = \frac{P(B \cap A)}{P(B)},$$

and rearranging the formulae we obtain:

$$P(A \cap B) = P(B \mid A) \times P(A) \quad \text{and that} \quad P(B \cap A) = P(A \mid B) \times P(B).$$

Since $(A \cap B) = (B \cap A)$, we obtain:

$$P(A \cap B) = P(B \cap A) = P(B \mid A) \times P(A) = P(A \mid B) \times P(B).$$

As seen earlier, two events are said to be independent if the outcome of one event does not influence the outcome of the other. This is the same as saying $P(B \mid A) = P(B)$ and that $P(A \mid B) = P(A)$. Moreover, as seen earlier, in the case of *independent events*:

$$P(A \cap B) = P(A) \times P(B),$$

but since

$$P(A \cap B) = P(B \mid A) \times P(A) \quad \text{(for *independent events*)},$$

we have that:

$$P(B \mid A) \times P(A) = P(B) \times P(A)$$

and hence

$$P(B \mid A) = \frac{P(A) \times P(B)}{P(A)}.$$

Similarly,

$$P(A \mid B) \times P(B) = P(A) \times P(B), \quad \text{whence} \quad P(A \mid B) = \frac{P(A) \times P(B)}{P(B)}.$$

Therefore, if for events A and B the following are true:

$$P(B \mid A) = P(B)$$
$$P(A \mid B) = P(A)$$
$$P(A \cap B) = P(A) \times P(B)$$

then events A and B are said to be independent.

Table 3.1 Contingency table on opinions about abortion in a sample of 1000 women (either religious or non-religious). The conditional probability of being against abortion while being religious and the unconditional probability of being against abortion are also provided

	Against abortion	Pro abortion	Totals
Religious	280	120	400
Non-religious	190	410	600
Totals	470	530	1000

$$P(\text{Against abortion}) = \frac{470}{1000} = 0.47$$

$$P(\text{Against abortion} \mid \text{Religious}) = \frac{280}{400} = 0.70$$

Independence and conditional probability

Consider a hypothetical study to assess opinions about abortion (pro or against) and religious belief (religious vs non-religious) in young women. A random sample of 1000 women (aged 18 to 30) are selected, and each woman is asked if she is in favour of or against abortion, and if she is religious or not. The summary of the investigation is provided in the contingency table above (see Table 3.1). The researcher wants to know if religious belief and opinions about abortion are independent events. We saw in the previous section that two events are independent if $P(B \mid A) = P(B)$, $P(A \mid B) = P(A)$, and $P(A \cap B) = P(A) \times P(B)$. Thus one way to check if religious belief and opinion about abortion are independent events is to compare the conditional probability of being against abortion given that a woman is religious with the unconditional probability of just being against abortion. If $P(\text{Against abortion} \mid \text{Religious}) = P(\text{Against abortion})$, then the view held on abortion is independent of religious belief (or equivalently, if $P(\text{Religious} \mid \text{Against abortion}) = P(\text{Religious})$).

The *unconditional probability* of being against abortion is found by taking the ratio of the total number of women against abortion divided by the total number of women, that is:

$$P(\text{Against abortion}) = \frac{470}{1000} = 0.47$$

while the *conditional probability* of being against abortion, given that a woman is religious, is calculated by taking the number of religious women who are against abortion divided by the total number of religious women, that is:

$$P(\text{Against abortion} \mid \text{Religious}) = \frac{280}{400} = 0.70.$$

Given that $P(\text{Against abortion} \mid \text{Religious}) \neq P(\text{Against abortion})$, then religious belief and opinion about abortion do not appear to be independent events. Remember, however, that in this example we have been working with sample data. Thus, religious belief and opinion about abortion could be independent in the population of women, and the discrepancy between P(Against abortion) and P(Against abortion | Religious) observed in our sample might simply be due to chance. Therefore, some inferential statistics technique is required to assess if the obtained difference in the conditional and unconditional probabilities can be taken as support for the lack of independence between religious belief and opinion about abortion. The Pearson's χ^2 (where χ is pronounced as either "kye" or "kai") test is used to this aim. This test will be presented in Chapter 6.

Bayes's theorem

When calculating conditional probabilities we are asking what is the probability of an event B occurring given event A has occurred, i.e., $P(B \mid A)$. In some circumstances we may want to ask the reverse question, i.e., what is the probability that event A has previously occurred given that event B has just occurred, i.e., $P(A \mid B)$? How can we answer these types of question?

The starting point to address this question is the equation for calculating the probability of the intersection of two events. As seen earlier this is given by:

$$P(A \cap B) = P(B \cap A) = P(B \mid A) \times P(A) = P(A \mid B) \times P(B),$$

whence

$$P(B \mid A) \times P(A) = P(A \mid B) \times P(B).$$

Therefore, the probability that an event A has previously occurred given that event B has just occurred is given by:

$$P(A \mid B) = \frac{P(B \mid A) \times P(A)}{P(B)},$$

which is a formulation of Bayes's theorem. Note, however, that this theorem is time independent (see the example later in this section). We used a temporal dimension in the description above only to make the exposition clearer.

We can illustrate the application of this theorem with an example. Let us assume that there are two different communities in Atlantis. These are the Blue and the Yellow communities, which make up 80 per cent and 20 per cent of the population, respectively. Hence, P(Blue) = 0.8 and P(Yellow) = 0.2. It is also known that 10 per cent of the members of the Blue community and 20 per cent of the members of the Yellow community are mainly involved in illegal activities. Hence P(Acting illegally | Blue) = 0.1 and P(Acting illegally | Yellow) = 0.2. It turns out that Atlantis police have just arrested a person involved in a robbery. What is the probability that this person acting illegally is a member of the Blue community? Intuitively, we could answer 0.10 to this question, since this is the probability that a person in the Blue community is involved in illegal activities. However this answer would be incorrect since it does not take into account the a priori probability of a person being a member of the Blue community, i.e.,

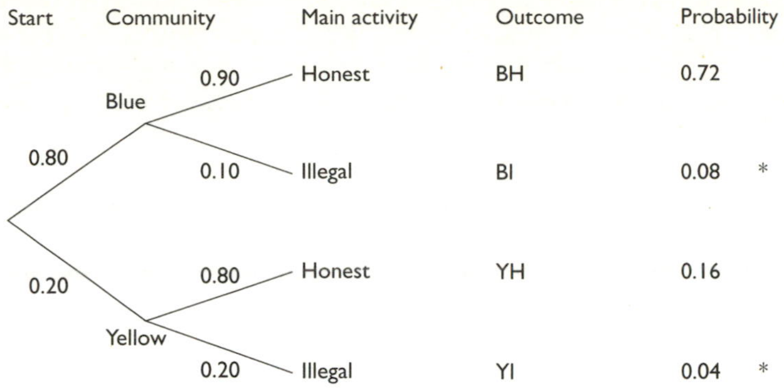

Start   Community   Main activity   Outcome   Probability

                    0.90 ─── Honest   BH   0.72
           Blue

   0.80
                    0.10 ─── Illegal   BI   0.08   *

                    0.80 ─── Honest   YH   0.16
   0.20
           Yellow
                    0.20 ─── Illegal   YI   0.04   *

Figure 3.7 Probability tree representing the activity in the Blue and Yellow communities of Atlantis.

0.8. The correct answer to the question above is $\frac{2}{3}$ or 0.667 (to 3 d.p.). In the following paragraph we will see how this value is calculated.

A probability tree can help to see why the probability that a person being caught acting illegally is a member of the Blue community is $\frac{2}{3}$. From the probability tree displayed in Figure 3.7, it can be calculated that the probability of a person being involved in illegal activities is 0.12. This value is obtained by adding the probability of the outcomes "being involved in illegal activities and being part of the Blue community", i.e., $0.8 \times 0.1 = 0.08$, and "being involved in illegal activities and being part of the Yellow community", i.e., $0.2 \times 0.2 = 0.04$. Thus 12 per cent of the people in Atlantis act illegally (8 per cent of whom are from the Blue community and 4 per cent from the Yellow community). Therefore, the probability that a person committing an illegal activity is from the Blue community is given by $\dfrac{0.08}{0.12} = \dfrac{2}{3}$.

Applying the above formulation of Bayes's theorem

$$P(A \mid B) = \frac{P(B \mid A) \times P(A)}{P(B)}$$

to the Atlantis problem we obtain:

$$P(\text{Blue} \mid \text{Acting illegally}) = \frac{P(\text{Acting illegally} \mid \text{Blue}) \times P(\text{Blue})}{P(\text{Acting illegally})} = \frac{0.1 \times 0.8}{0.12} = \frac{2}{3}.$$

The denominator of the above ratio provides the total probability that a randomly selected person from Atlantis is involved in illegal activities. This is given by:

$$P(\text{Being a criminal}) = [P(\text{Blue}) \times P(\text{Acting illegally} \mid \text{Blue})] + [P(\text{Yellow}) \times P(\text{Acting illegally} \mid \text{Yellow})]$$

$$= 0.8 \times 0.1 + 0.2 \times 0.2$$

$$= 0.12$$

Notice that the percentage of people acting illegally in the Yellow community is higher than the percentage of people acting illegally in the Blue community (i.e., 20 per cent vs 10 per cent). However, the proportion of people in Atlantis who are part of the Blue community is much larger than the Yellow community (i.e., 80 per cent vs 20 per cent). When this difference is taken into account it is evident that more Blue people than Yellow commit illegal activities in Atlantis.

Much research on the psychology of reasoning has demonstrated the difficulty people have in tasks involving probabilities. To properly assess the probability that a person acting illegally is from one of the two communities, the example showed we need to take into account the a priori (or base-rate) probability of being part of each of the two communities, i.e., P(Blue) and P(Yellow). While Bayes's theorem indicates the relevance of these a priori probabilities in correctly answering questions like the one addressed in this section, the majority of people do not seem to take them into account when trying to answer these types of question (for a review on this research see Sutherland, 1994).

Chapter 4

Probability distributions and the binomial distribution

Introduction

The main aim of this chapter is to provide a description of the characteristics of the *binomial distribution and its use in testing hypotheses*. This is a particularly useful distribution. Consider a situation where a series of independent events occurs (e.g., a fair coin is tossed four times), and the outcome of each event can be either a success (e.g., "Head") or a failure (e.g., "Tail"). We can then count the number of successes that are obtained when a coin is tossed four times (i.e., 0, 1, 2, 3, 4), and calculate the probability of obtaining each one of these five outcomes. The binomial distribution describes the probability of each of the outcomes of the above discrete random variable, i.e., "number of successes obtained when a coin is tossed four times". This brief description of the binomial distribution may seem quite obscure at this stage. The introduction of a series of concepts will provide enough background for a more comprehensive presentation of this important probability distribution. We will also describe how the binomial distribution can be used in testing a hypothesis. For example, if you want to test whether a coin is biased you could simply toss the coin 20 times, record the number of "Heads" (e.g., 16), and compare this value with the binomial distribution of the discrete random variable "number of Heads obtained when a fair coin is tossed 20 times". If the observed value is somehow at odds with the values given by the binomial distribution of the above variable, then there is good evidence that the coin is biased. In this chapter we will describe the binomial distribution, and how to apply it in the process of hypothesis testing applied both to relatively abstract situations, like the above example about the coin, and to research in the behavioural sciences.

The first thing to define is the term *discrete random variable*. A variable is considered to be random if each of its values is the result of a random observation. As stated at the beginning of the previous chapter, individual outcomes in an experiment cannot be predicted; thus, the result of an experimental observation can be a legitimate value of a random variable. If it is possible to make a list of all the values that a random variable can take, then this variable is called discrete.

Random variables are often denoted by *capital letters in italics* (usually X, Y, Z) while the observed values of a random variable X are denoted as x_n (i.e., in *lowercase italics*) For example the random variable X is "the face appearing upward when a coin is tossed once". Its values are x_1 (e.g., "Head") and x_2 ("Tail"). Moreover, if we want to indicate that the probability with which the random variable X takes the value x_1 is 0.5, we write:

$$P(X = x_1) = 0.5$$

which is often simplified as $Px_1 = 0.5$. Often, the *values* that a random variable can take are also denoted by capital letters in italics, usually *ex*cluding X, Y, Z since these letters are used to denote random variables. Thus, in the case of the random variable "the face appearing upward when a coin is tossed once", instead of x_1 we could use either A or H or "Head". Hence, the probability associated with a specific value (i.e., H) that a random variable can take can be indicated as $P(H) = 0.5$.

Consider again the case in which the random variable X is "the face appearing upward when a coin is tossed once". This variable can assume either the value $x_1 =$ "Head" or $x_2 =$ "Tail", i.e., the sample space is {H, T}. Thus, if a coin is fair, we have $P(H) = 0.5$ and $P(T) = 0.5$. Similarly, if the random variable X is "the number appearing on the top of a fair die after it has been rolled", then X can take the values 1 to 6, and the probability of each outcome is $Px_i = \frac{1}{6}$. Remember that the total probability of all outcomes in the sample space is 1, thus in the case of the die example we have:

$$P(1) + P(2) + P(3) + P(4) + P(5) + P(6) = 1.$$

Probability distributions

If you go back to Chapter 2, where frequency distributions were described, you will notice that the percentage cumulative frequency distribution reached 100 per cent when all the observations were considered. Similarly, the total probability obtained by adding the probabilities of each simple event in the sample space, as in the rolling die example, is equal to 1. Here each simple event in the sample space has a particular probability associated with it, instead of a particular frequency. If we have a set of mutually exclusive and exhaustive events and we plot the probabilities associated with each event we obtain a *probability distribution*, and the sum of these probabilities is always 1.

What does the probability distribution of, for example, the random variable X named "the number appearing on the top of a fair die after it has been rolled" look like? This can be seen in Figure 4.1. Notice that the sample space is {1, 2, 3, 4, 5, 6} and that each of the values that the random variable X can assume have the same probability, i.e., $P(1) = P(2) = P(3) = P(4) = P(5) = P(6) = \frac{1}{6}$. When the values that a discrete random variable can assume have the same probability of occurrence, and provided that the sum of these probabilities is 1, then the probability distribution is called a *discrete uniform distribution*.

Interestingly, it is not always necessary to list the individual probabilities of each of the simple events in the sample space, as done above, to specify a probability distribution. In some cases it is possible to identify a specific formula, usually called *probability function*, which allows us to generate the probabilities of each event in the sample space. The discrete uniform distribution obtained in the die example is summarised by the following function:

$$Px_i = \frac{1}{6} \quad (i = 1, 2, \ldots, 6),$$

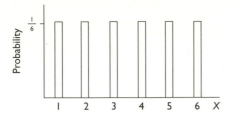

Figure 4.1 Example of discrete uniform distribution: probability distribution of the random variable X, i.e., "the number appearing upwards when rolling a fair die".

or more generally:

$$Px_i = \frac{1}{k} \quad (i = 1, 2, \ldots, k)$$

where k corresponds to the total number of simple events in the sample space, i.e., the total number of values that the random variable X can take (notice that $\Sigma \frac{1}{k} = 1$).

Let us consider another probability distribution called the *Bernoulli distribution*. In this distribution, the random variable X can assume only two values (either success or failure). An example of a random variable that follows the Bernoulli distribution is the variable "number of tails that are obtained when tossing a fair coin". If the coin lands tails up, then the outcome is successful, and its probability of occurrence is $p = 0.5$. If the coin lands heads up, then the outcome is a failure, and its probability of occurrence is $q = 1 - p = 0.5$. If the successful event is denoted as "1", and the failure as "0" (i.e., the absence of a success), then in the case of a fair coin we have:

P(1) = p = 0.5 and P(0) = 1 − p = 0.5.

Similarly, with an unfair coin we may have, for example:

P(1) = p = 0.8 and P(0) = 1 − p = 0.2.

Figure 4.2 displays the Bernoulli distribution with P(1) = 0.8.

The Bernoulli distribution is very simple, and it may appear, prima facie, rather useless since it can only apply to random variables that can take only one of two outcomes. However, consider that many real-life events can only have two possible outcomes, one of which can be labelled as a success and the remaining outcome as a failure. For instance, a student can either pass an exam or fail it; a subject in an experiment, when confronted with a problem-solving task, can either solve the problem or fail to solve it; a new psychotherapy to treat agoraphobia can, for any given patient treated, be either successful or not successful. Furthermore, it often happens that, in an investigation, we need to consider several of these types of events. For example, imagine that 15 patients with a phobic fear of flying undertake a new improved treatment to cure their phobia, and it turns out that 13 of these patients have no more fear of flying at

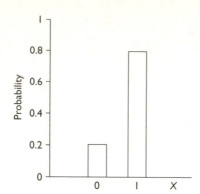

Figure 4.2 Example of Bernoulli distribution with P(1) = 0.8 (thus P(0) = 1 − 0.8).

a follow-up six months after the end of the psychotherapeutic treatment. Let us also assume that it is known that the best available treatment to cure the phobia of flying has a probability of success of 0.6, i.e., 60 per cent of the treated people are free of symptoms at the follow-up. Given this information and the results obtained in the above study, how can we decide if the new treatment is better than the best currently available treatment? The empirical study conforms to a situation where several events, each with a potential outcome that can be either a success or a failure, are combined together. If these events, i.e., the act of treating individual patients, can be considered to be independent, then the sequence of events is called a *Bernoulli trials process.* Given that, as we shall see later in this chapter, the binomial distribution describes the probability of obtaining 0, 1, 2, . . . , up to *n* successes out of *n* Bernoulli trials, this distribution can be used to address the above question. This issue will be discussed later when a full description of the binomial distribution will be provided.

Calculating the mean (μ) of a probability distribution

In Chapter 2, page 33 we showed that the sample mean of a frequency distribution could be obtained by:

$$\bar{x} = \frac{\sum f_i x_i}{n} = \Sigma \left(x_i \times \frac{f_i}{n} \right)$$

where each value of the random variable X (i.e., x_i) is multiplied by its frequency of occurrence divided by n (i.e., the total number of sampled observations). Thus the sample mean is obtained by adding, for each value x_i of the random variable X, the product of x_i and its relative frequency $\left(\dfrac{f_i}{n} \right)$. However, as we said at the beginning of Chapter 3, the long-term relative frequency of occurrence of an event gives its probability. By long-term it is meant that the number of observations increases to the limit of incorporating all possible observations in the population. Hence the long-term relative frequency of an event provides the probability of its occurrence in the population.

Therefore, if instead of $\left(\dfrac{f_i}{n}\right)$ we have the probability of occurrence of an event in the population, then the above formula provides the population mean (i.e., μ) of the random variable X. Thus the long-term average value (or limiting value) of a random variable X provides the population mean value of X. This long-term value, as said in Chapter 2, is called the expected value of X. It is denoted as $E(X)$, and it is equal to μ.

How does the above approach apply to probability distributions? Well in the case of probability distributions we usually know the population probability of an event, thus it is possible to calculate the expected value of a random variable. The formula to calculate the expected value (μ) of any probability distribution is given by:

$$E(X) = \Sigma(x_i \times Px_i)$$

where the x_i are the values that the random variable X can take, and the Px_i are their probabilities.

Let us calculate, for example, the expected value of the Bernoulli distribution with $P(1) = p$ (and more specifically with the population probability of a successful event being 0.80). Applying the above formula the expected value of the Bernoulli distribution is:

$$E(X) = (1 \times p) + [0 \times (1 - p)] = p.$$

Thus if $P(1) = 0.8$, then $E(X) = (1 \times 0.8) + (0 \times 0.2) = 0.8$.

In the case of the discrete uniform distribution we know that $Px_i = \dfrac{1}{k}$, thus

$$E(X) = \Sigma(x_i \times Px_i) = \Sigma\left(x_i \times \frac{1}{k}\right) = \left(1 \times \frac{1}{k}\right) + \left(2 \times \frac{1}{k}\right) + \ldots + \left(k \times \frac{1}{k}\right)$$

$$= (\Sigma x_i) \times \frac{1}{k}.$$

When the random variable X is "the number appearing upwards when rolling a fair die" we obtain that:

$$E(X) = \Sigma(x_i \times Px_i) = \left(1 \times \frac{1}{6}\right) + \left(2 \times \frac{1}{6}\right) + \ldots + \left(6 \times \frac{1}{6}\right) = \frac{21}{6} = 3.5.$$

Remember that, as we saw in the case of the sample mean in Chapter 2, $E(X)$ is not necessarily one of the possible values that a random variable X can take.

Finally, it is useful to know how to calculate the expected value of a function of random variables. For example, you may want to know $E(X^2)$. This is a case where the expected value of a random variable is a function of X, i.e., $f(X)$ where f, in this particular case, is the function that takes the values of the random variable X and returns their squared values. In general, given any function $f(X)$, the expected value of $f(X)$ is given by:

$$E[f(X)] = \Sigma(f(x_i) \times Px_i).$$

In the case of $E(X^2)$ we have:

$$E(X^2) = \Sigma((x_i^2) \times Px_i),$$

(this last formula is equivalent to the more familiar $\frac{\Sigma x^2}{n}$).

For example, if the random variable X has a Bernoulli distribution with $P(1) = p$ then:

$$E(X^2) = (1^2 \times p) + [0^2 \times (1 - p)] = p,$$

and thus, if $P(1) = 0.7$, then $E(X^2) = (1^2 \times 0.7) + (0^2 \times 0.3) = 0.7$.

The formula to calculate $E(X^2)$ will turn out to be very useful when, in the next section, we show how to calculate the variance of a probability distribution, i.e., σ^2 or equivalently $VAR(X)$.

Finally, it can be shown that the expected value of the sum of a finite set of random variables is equal to the sum of the expected value of each random variable, i.e.,

$$E(X + Y + \ldots + Z) = E(X) + E(Y) + \ldots + E(Z).$$

Calculating the variance (σ^2) and the standard deviation (σ) of a probability distribution

In Chapter 2 we defined the population variance as:

$$VAR(X) = \sigma^2 = \frac{\Sigma(x - \mu)^2}{n}$$

where n is the number of observations in the populations and $\mu = E(X)$, or equivalently

$$\sigma^2 = \frac{1}{n}\Sigma(x - \mu)^2.$$

Applying various algebraic operations to this last equation, some shown in Chapter 2, we obtain:

$$\sigma^2 = \frac{1}{n}\left(\Sigma x^2 - \frac{(\Sigma x)^2}{n}\right)$$

$$= \frac{\Sigma x^2}{n} - \frac{(\Sigma x)^2}{n^2} \qquad \text{(multiplying each value within the brackets by } \frac{1}{n}\text{)}$$

$$= \frac{\Sigma x^2}{n} - \left(\frac{(\Sigma x)}{n} \times \frac{(\Sigma x)}{n}\right) \quad \text{(since } \frac{(\Sigma x)^2}{n^2} = \left(\frac{(\Sigma x)}{n} \times \frac{(\Sigma x)}{n}\right)\text{),}$$

but given that $\dfrac{\sum x^2}{n} = \sum((x_i^2) \times \mathrm{P}x_i) = \mathrm{E}(X^2)$, and that $\dfrac{\sum x}{n} = \sum(x_i \times \mathrm{P}x_i) = \mathrm{E}(X)$, we obtain:

$$\mathrm{VAR}(X) = \sigma^2 = \mathrm{E}(X^2) - \mathrm{E}(X)^2.$$

Applying the above formula to calculate $\mathrm{VAR}(X)$ to, for example, a random variable X that follows the Bernoulli distribution with $\mathrm{P}(1) = p$, and knowing that for the Bernoulli distribution, $\mathrm{E}(X^2) = p$ and $\mathrm{E}(X) = p$, we obtain that:

$$\mathrm{VAR}(X) = p - p^2 = p \times (1 - p).$$

Therefore, a random variable X that follows a Bernoulli distribution with $\mathrm{P}(1) = p$ has $\mu = \mathrm{E}(X) = p$ and $\sigma^2 = \mathrm{VAR}(X) = p \times (1 - p)$. If $\mathrm{P}(1) = 0.8$, then $\mu = 0.8$ and $\sigma^2 = 0.8 \times (1 - 0.8) = 0.16$.

Finally, notice that if two random variables X and Y are independent, it can be demonstrated that:

$$\mathrm{VAR}(X + Y) = \mathrm{VAR}(X) + \mathrm{VAR}(Y)$$

which generalises to any finite set of mutually independent random variables as:

$$\mathrm{VAR}(X + Y + \ldots + Z) = \mathrm{VAR}(X) + \mathrm{VAR}(Y) + \ldots + \mathrm{VAR}(Z).$$

The *standard deviation* is, as we know from Chapter 2, the square root of the variance, thus for a random variable X we have:

$$\sigma = \sqrt{\mathrm{VAR}(X)} = \sqrt{\mathrm{E}(X^2) - \mathrm{E}(X)^2}.$$

In the case of a random variable X having a Bernoulli distribution with $\mathrm{P}(1) = p$,

$$\sigma = \sqrt{p \times (1 - p)}.$$

Thus if $\mathrm{P}(1) = 0.8$, then $\sigma = \sqrt{0.16} = 0.4$.

Orderings (or permutations)

The binomial distribution describes the probability of occurrence of a random variable X that is "the number of successes obtained out of n independent *Bernoulli trials*". Since a series of Bernoulli trials can be obtained by combining a series of events in various different ways, it is useful to provide formulae that allow the calculation of the number of all possible combinations of a given number of events. For example, if you want to know in how many ways a fair coin will land as "Heads" once out of two tosses, you can list all combinations of "Heads" and "Tails" that can be obtained, i.e., {HH, HT, TH, TT}, and then count the number of events where there is only one "Head" (i.e., 2). However, even using a tree similar to the one presented in Chapter 3, this procedure is laborious, prone to errors, and very time consuming if the number

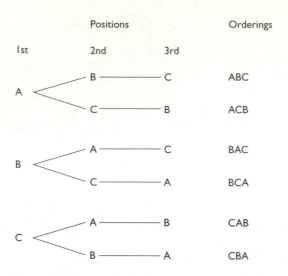

Figure 4.3 Illustration of all the possible orderings (permutations) of three different objects A, B, and C.

of Bernoulli trials is relatively large. Combinatorics is a special branch of mathematics that deals with the way in which various events can be arranged in different ways, thus providing formulae that give quick and efficient solutions to problems like the one just illustrated. What follows is a brief introduction to those aspects of combinatorics that are more relevant to our needs.

If there are, for example, 3 different objects or events (A, B, and C), and we need to find out how many different ways there are for ordering them, what can we do? First, consider that we can chose, as the first object in the sequence, any of the three available objects (i.e., either A, or B, or C). Then, given that the first object is chosen, we only have a choice between the two remaining non-selected objects, for the second position in the sequence. And finally only the last remaining object can be selected as the third choice. Thus we can have $3 \times 2 \times 1 = 6$ different orderings (or permutations) of 3 different objects (see Figure 4.3). The above product is equal to $3 \times (3 - 1) \times (3 - 2)$ which can be written, more conveniently, as 3! (which reads as "3 factorial").

In general, the number of permutations (orderings) of n different objects is given by the factorial of n:

$$n! = n \times (n - 1) \times (n - 2) \times \ldots \times 2 \times 1$$

Thus if there are 10 different objects, the number of all possible different orderings of these objects is equal to $10! = 10 \times 9 \times 8 \times 7 \times 6 \times 5 \times 4 \times 3 \times 2 \times 1 = 3,628,800$. This example should give you an idea of the effort required to provide all possible orderings of a large number of different objects using the procedure illustrated in Figure 4.3.

As an aside, with respect to factorials, the following properties apply:

$$n! = n \times (n - 1)!$$

and it then follows that

$$(n-1)! = \frac{n!}{n}.$$

Thus, if $n = 1$ then $0! = \frac{1!}{1} = 1$.

Now consider that there are 4 different objects (A, B, C and D), where only 2 are selected at a time (i.e., AB, BA, AC, CA, AD, etc.). How many permutations are there for 2 objects chosen from a set of 4 different objects? The number of permutations of r objects from a set of n different objects is denoted by P_r^n and its value is given by:

$$P_r^n = n \times (n-1) \times (n-2) \times \ldots \times (n-r+1)$$

Using the "tree approach" is easy to see how this formula is obtained. If you have, as in the above example, a total of 4 objects from which you select 2 objects at a time, then for the first selection there are 4 objects to chose from. For the second selection there are now only 3 possible objects left since one has already been used during the first selection. Here you stop. No more selections are needed because all possible orderings of 2 objects out of 4 have been identified. Therefore, there are 12 possible different orderings of two objects out of a collection of four different objects, i.e.,

$$n \times (n-r+1) = 4 \times 3 = 12.$$

The above formula to calculate the number of permutations of r objects from a set of n different objects is often presented as

$$P_r^n = \frac{n!}{(n-r)!}$$

which in the case of our example gives: $P_2^4 = \frac{4!}{(4-2)!} = \frac{4!}{2!} = \frac{24}{2} = 12$.

Note that if n out of n objects are selected, then we obtain, as seen previously, that the number of permutations is $n!$. In fact, $P_n^n = \frac{n!}{(n-n)!} = \frac{n!}{0!} = \frac{n!}{1} = n!$. (Recall from the definition of factorials that $0!$ equals 1.)

The above discussion about permutations may appear rather irrelevant to the study of psychology as a scientific subject. This, however, is not the case. Knowing how to order things is useful, for instance, when planning an empirical study. Consider the following example. A group of people are asked to complete 4 different attitude questionnaires (A, B, C and D), and you do not want the order in which the questionnaires are filled in to always be the same. This is because there is a possibility that by the time a subject reaches the last questionnaire (e.g., D), he/she may be tired, thus questionnaire D will always be completed in a less enthusiastic way than the remaining ones. This type of bias can be controlled by presenting each questionnaire in any possible position, so that any bias due to the effect of the order in which the questionnaires are filled is counterbalanced across the sample of subjects. Thus given that there are 4! (i.e., 24) different orderings of the four tests, we know that, with a sample of

24 subjects, each subject will receive the questionnaires in a different order, and any order effect will be controlled for.

Some form of counterbalancing needs to be applied in any empirical study where there is more than one condition administered to a subject (see the section on pages 150–151, "Counterbalancing"). The previous example shows how permutations are relevant to fully counterbalance the order of the conditions in a study. However, counterbalancing does not always need to be full to be effective. For example, in the above case, counterbalancing is considered to be appropriate if it allows each questionnaire to be presented at least once in each of the four positions (i.e., ABCD, BADC, CDAB, DCBA). This type of counterbalancing is called Latin Square (for further details see e.g., Kirk, 1991).

Combinations

Consider the situation where there are four objects (A, B, C and D), and we select two of these at a time. Unlike the cases in the previous section, we now want to identify the number of all different pairs of objects, irrespective of their ordering. So the pairs AB and BA are considered as one exemplar only, since it is of no interest to us that A precedes B or vice versa (in a sense it is as if A and B are considered to be the same object). The *unordered* arrangements of r objects taken from a set of n objects are called *combinations*. The number of combinations of r objects taken from a set of n objects is given by:

$$C_r^n = \frac{n!}{(n-r)! \times r!},$$

or equivalently

$$C_r^n = \frac{n \times (n-1) \times \ldots \times (n-r+1)}{r!}.$$

Thus, the number of combinations of 2 objects taken from a set of 4 objects is:

$$C_2^4 = \frac{4!}{(4-2)! \times 2!} = \frac{4 \times 3 \times 2 \times 1}{(2 \times 1) \times (2 \times 1)} = 6.$$

The binomial distribution

Consider the following example. A fair coin is tossed three times and you place a bet of £10 with a friend that "tails" will be obtained twice. If this outcome occurs, then your friend gives you £10, otherwise you lose £10. Who is most likely to win the money? You or your friend? A way to find out is to use the probability tree presented in Chapter 3 where all possible outcomes (i.e., all possible triplets of heads and tails) are listed with their probability of occurrence (see the probability tree reproduced in Figure 4.4), and then to check the total probability of obtaining "tails" twice out of three tosses, irrespective of the order of heads and tails. From Figure 4.4 it appears that only 3 out of the 8 possible triplets are favourable to you and that the probability

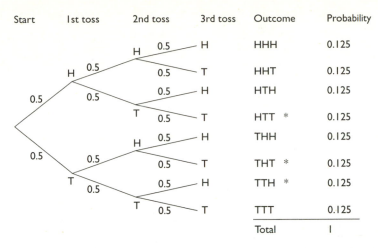

Start	1st toss	2nd toss	3rd toss	Outcome	Probability
			H 0.5 — H	HHH	0.125
	H 0.5	0.5	0.5 — T	HHT	0.125
0.5	0.5	0.5 — H	HTH	0.125
		T 0.5 — T	HTT *	0.125
		H 0.5 — H	THH	0.125
0.5	0.5	0.5 — T	THT *	0.125
	T 0.5	0.5 — H	TTH *	0.125
		T 0.5 — T	TTT	0.125
			Total	1

Figure 4.4 Probability tree illustrating the sequences of heads and tails that can be obtained tossing a fair coin three times. The combination of two tails out of three tosses is obtained three times, thus the probability of occurrence of this event is 0.375.

of winning the bet is only 0.375, while your friend has a much better chance to win (i.e., $1 - 0.375 = 0.625$). Thus you would be better off avoiding the above bet.

The probability tree was useful, in the above example, to calculate the number of sequences where a success, i.e., the event "tails", occurred twice. There is, however, a faster way to calculate the total probability of occurrence of the favourable triplets. In fact, the number of sequences with two successes, i.e., two tails, can be obtained by calculating the number of combinations of two successes out of three trials. Thus for $r = 2$ and $n = 3$ we find that the number of triplets having two tails is:

$C_2^3 = \dfrac{3!}{(3 - 2)! \times 2!} = \dfrac{3 \times 2 \times 1}{1 \times (2 \times 1)} = 3$. Moreover, since we know the probability of a

success and of a failure, i.e., $P(T) = 0.5$ and $P(H) = 0.5$, then the probability of obtaining two successes out of three trials (in this cases tosses) is given by:

$$P(\text{exactly 2 tails}) = C_2^3 \times [P(T)]^2 \times [P(H)]^{(3-2)} = 3 \times (0.5)^2 \times (0.5)^1$$
$$= 3 \times 0.25 \times 0.5 = 0.375.$$

Imagine also that, out of curiosity, we calculate the probabilities of obtaining no successes, only one success, and three successes out of three trials, i.e., P(exactly 0 tails), P(exactly 1 tail), and P(exactly 3 tails), respectively. These probabilities are:

$$P(\text{exactly 0 tails}) = C_0^3 \times [P(T)]^0 \times [P(H)]^{(3-0)} = 1 \times (0.5)^0 \times (0.5)^3$$
$$= 1 \times 1 \times 0.125 = 0.125 \text{ (remember that } x^0 \text{ is always equal to 1).}$$
$$P(\text{exactly 1 tail}) = C_1^3 \times [P(T)]^1 \times [P(H)]^{(3-1)} = 3 \times (0.5)^1 \times (0.5)^2$$
$$= 3 \times 0.5 \times 0.25 = 0.375.$$
$$P(\text{exactly 3 tails}) = C_3^3 \times [P(T)]^3 \times [P(H)]^{(3-3)} = 1 \times (0.5)^3 \times (0.5)^0$$
$$= 1 \times 0.125 \times 1 = 0.125.$$

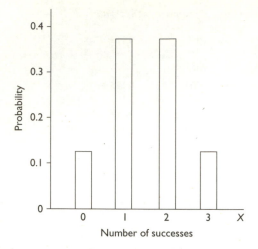

Figure 4.5 Example of a plot of a binomial distribution where the random variable X is the "number of successes out of three independent Bernoulli trials where P(Success) = 0.5"; Success = "Tail".

After this exercise we know the probability of occurrence of 0, 1, 2 and 3 tails (i.e., successes), respectively, out of three independent Bernoulli trials where the probability of obtaining a success in each trial is 0.5. Thus, we could plot the probability distribution of the random variable X named "number of successes out of three independent Bernoulli trials where the probability of a success in each trial is 0.5". This distribution is shown in Figure 4.5 and is an example of the binomial distribution.

In the above exercise, to provide the probability of occurrence of each event of the binomial distribution we made use of a function where the probability of a success was a constant, and the number of successes out of a total of n trials was orderly, changing from 0 to n. In general, the probability of obtaining any of the values of the random variable X in a binomial distribution is given by the equation:

$$P_r = C_r^n \times p^r \times (1-p)^{(n-r)} \quad \text{or equivalently} \quad P_r = \frac{n!}{(n-r)! \times r!} \times p^r \times (1-p)^{(n-r)}$$

where P_r is the probability of obtaining r successes (r varies from 0 to n); n is the total number of Bernoulli trials; p is the probability of occurrence of a success on each trial (the probability of occurrence of a failure is $1-p$), and C_r^n is the number of combinations of r successes out of n independent trials. Thus, any specific binomial distribution is identified by n and p (these are called parameters), with r being the variable that assumes as values any integer between 0 and n, inclusive (thus $n-r$ gives the number of failures). In general the shape of a binomial distribution is symmetrical if $p = 0.5$, positively skewed when $p < 0.50$, and negatively skewed when $p > 0.50$. Figure 4.6 shows three binomial distributions where $n = 12$ and p is either 0.50 (symmetrical), 0.25 (positively skewed), or 0.75 (negatively skewed).

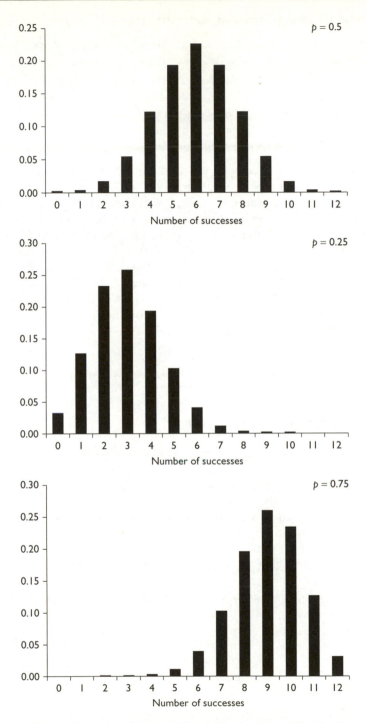

Figure 4.6 Examples of binomial distributions with $n = 12$ and either $p = 0.50$ (symmetrical), or $p = 0.25$ (positively skewed), or $p = 0.75$ (negatively skewed). The scale on the vertical axis reports probabilities.

Mean and variance of the binomial distribution

It is possible to obtain, for any binomial distribution, the mean number of successes, their variance and standard deviation, using the following formulae:

$$\mu = E(X) = n \times p$$

$$\sigma^2 = VAR(X) = n \times p \times (1 - p)$$

$$\sigma = \sqrt{np(1 - p)}$$

where X is a random variable with a binomial distribution, n is the total number of Bernoulli trials, and p is the probability of occurrence of a success on each trial.

If you are curious to know how the above formulae are obtained, then read the following argument. First, let S_n be the number of successes out of n Bernoulli trials with probability p of success on each trial. Remember that the plotting of the probability of occurrence of r successes out of n Bernoulli trials (i.e., 0, 1, 2, ..., n) is a plot of a binomial distribution. Thus, if we call each of the n Bernoulli trials the random variables $X_1, X_2, ..., X_n$, respectively, and, for every jth trial $X_j = 1$ if the trial is a success, and 0 if it is a failure, then $S_n = X_1 + X_2 + ... + X_n$ is the number of successes out of n Bernoulli trials. Since we know, from the section on the Bernoulli distribution, that the expected value of each Bernoulli random variable X_j is:

$$E(X_j) = p$$

and that

$$E(X_1 + X_2 + ... + X_n) = E(X_1) + E(X_2) + ... + E(X_n),$$

it follows that the *expected number of successes* in a binomial distribution is given by:

$$E(S_n) = E(X_1) + E(X_2) + ... + E(X_n) = n \times p.$$

Similarly, the variance of the sum of n independent Bernoulli random variables $X_1, X_2, ..., X_n$ is given by:

$$VAR(X_1 + X_2 + ... + X_n) = VAR(X_1) + VAR(X_2) + ... + VAR(X_n)$$

where $VAR(X_j) = p \times (1 - p)$, and thus the *variance of the number of successes* in a binomial distribution is given by:

$$VAR(S_n) = n \times p \times (1 - p)$$

and its standard deviation is $\sigma = \sqrt{np(1 - p)}$.

How to use the binomial distribution in testing hypotheses

Early in this chapter we referred to the results of an imagined study on the effectiveness of a new improved psychotherapeutic treatment to cure phobics' fear of flying.

We said that 13 out of 15 patients treated were free from phobic symptoms at a follow-up six months after the end of the treatment. Knowing that the best available treatment has a probability of success of 0.6, i.e., 60 per cent of phobic patients recover at follow-up, we want to know if the new therapy is more successful than the best treatment currently available.

In answering the above question we will make use of the binomial distribution, and, in doing so, we will also apply the logic of statistical inference. As mentioned in Chapter 1, inferential statistics techniques allow us to generalise to the entire population the results obtained from sampled observations. Going back to the phobic treatment example, we know that, in the population, the probability of success of the best available treatment is 0.6. We also know that, after having received the new treatment, 13 out of 15 sampled patients are free of symptoms at follow-up. Assuming that the outcome of a patient does not influence the outcome of any other patient, then the above statement is the equivalent of stating that 13 successes were obtained out of 15 independent trials, each of which could either be a success (i.e., recovery), or a failure (i.e., when a patient is still afraid of flying). If trials are not independent, then the binomial distribution will not be suitable for deciding on the improved efficacy of the new treatment. Trials may not be independent if, for example, the therapeutic skill of the clinician administering the treatment improves over trials.

Armed with the above information we want to know how likely it is for 13 patients out of a sample of 15 to be successfully treated, assuming that the population probability of success is 0.6 (i.e., the probability of success of the best available treatment). This assumption is equivalent to saying that the new treatment has the same efficacy as the standard best treatment. In other words we are assuming that in the population P(Success new treatment) = P(Success old treatment) = 0.6. If this hypothesis is true we should find that the probability of having at least 13 recovered patients out of 15 patients treated is relatively large. On the other hand, if under the above hypothesis (usually called the *null hypothesis*), we find that the probability of obtaining at least 13 successes out of 15 treated patients is extremely low, we can then reject the null hypothesis in favour of the *alternative hypothesis* which, in this case, states that in the population P(Success new treatment) > P(Success old treatment). In other words, if the null hypothesis is false, it means that the patients treated with the new approach were not drawn from the population of treated patients with a probability of recovery of 0.6, but that they were sampled from a population where treated patients have more than 0.6 probability of recovery from their phobic fear of flying. Equivalently, and in a less formal way, it would appear that the rate of recovery after the new psychotherapeutic treatment is significantly better than the one provided by the best treatment currently available.

Let us see in detail the application of the above reasoning. The first thing to do is to obtain the binomial distribution where the number of Bernoulli trials is 15 and the probability of success on each trial is $p = 0.6$ (i.e., the probability distribution of the number of patients who recovered out of the 15 patients treated, assuming the null hypothesis is true). This distribution, with the probability of occurrence of each outcome, calculated using the equation defining the binomial distribution, is displayed in Table 4.1. The next step is to decide what outcomes, in terms of the number of patients who recovered, are unlikely to occur under the assumption that the null hypothesis is true. It is a convention to consider extreme outcomes, for which the total probability

Table 4.1
(a) Binomial distribution of *r* successes out of 15 trials, with P(Success) = 0.6
(b) Cumulative version of the binomial distribution shown in Table 4.1(a)

(a)

r	Probability
0	0.000001
1	0.000024
2	0.000254
3	0.001649
4	0.007420
5	0.024486
6	0.061214
7	0.118056
8	0.177084
9	0.206598
10	0.185938
11	0.126776
12	0.063388
13	0.021942
14	0.004702
15	0.000470

(b)

r	Probability
0	0.000001
1	0.000025
2	0.000279
3	0.001928
4	0.009348
5	0.033833
6	0.095047
7	0.213103
8	0.390187
9	0.596784
10	0.782722
11	0.909498
12	0.972886
13	0.994828
14	0.999530
15	1.0

of occurrence is equal to or less than 0.05, as being unlikely to occur. If the observed outcome is among those extreme outcomes for which the total probability of occurrence is equal to or less than 0.05, then it is considered unlikely that the obtained result comes from a sample of observations selected from a population with P(Success) = 0.6. Thus the null hypothesis should be rejected.

The study used in our example intends to assess if the new treatment is better than the old one. To decide on this matter we need to find the probabilities associated with very high numbers of successes using the binomial distribution in Table 4.1a. From this table you can see that the probability of obtaining 15 successes is 0.00047; P(14) = 0.00470 and P(13) = 0.02194. Adding these probabilities we would obtain a total probability of about 0.03. Since this probability is less than 0.05, it is then unlikely, if the null hypothesis stating that $p = 0.6$ is true, that we would have observed 13 or more successes out of a sample of 15 clinical interventions. As a consequence the null hypothesis should be rejected if at least 13 or more patients out of 15 recover from their phobia. This means that, assuming the probability of recovery from a phobic fear of flying after the best available treatment is 0.6 in the population, and if 15 patients are sampled and treated with this treatment, then it is considered *unlikely*, but not impossible, that 13 or more patients will recover. Nevertheless, since we obtained such an unlikely result (i.e., 13 out of 15 patients recovered), then the null hypothesis asserting that P(Success new treatment) = P(success old treatment) = 0.6 is rejected, and it can then be concluded that the new treatment leads to a significantly larger rate of recovery than the old treatment (i.e., the alternative hypothesis stating that, in the population, P(Success new treatment) > P(Success old treatment) is accepted).

Notice that if we had also considered the probability of obtaining 12 successes, i.e., P(12) = 0.06339, and then added this probability to the sum of P(15), P(14) and P(13) we would have obtained a total probability for this new set of extreme events of about 0.1. This is too large a probability to reject the null hypothesis. Thus, 12 successes should not be included in the outcomes that would lead to the rejection of the above null hypothesis. (i.e., if the number of recovered patients in our experiment had been 12 instead of 13, we could have not rejected the null hypothesis.)

Let us now consider a second example of the use of the binomial distribution in hypothesis testing. Imagine that we have been given a coin and we want to know if the coin is fair or not. The first thing to do is to provide the null and the alternative hypothesis for this specific problem. The null hypothesis always expresses, in mathematical terms, the concept that the defendant is assumed innocent unless proven otherwise, i.e., in this case, that the coin to be tested is fair. This is expressed, mathematically as H_0: P(Head) = 0.5, where H_0 denotes the null hypothesis. The alternative hypothesis is usually denoted as H_1. In this case it states that the coin is not fair, which is expressed as H_1: P(Head) $\neq$ 0.5.

Notice the difference between the form of the alternative hypotheses in this and in the previous example. In the coin example we are testing if the coin is unfair; therefore, we want to see if there is enough evidence to suggest that the coin tends to land heads upward with a probability either greater or smaller than 0.5, thus the use of the sign $\neq$. In the phobia example we wanted to see if the new therapy was really an improvement over the best old therapy. In doing this, we assumed that the new therapy was certainly not worse than the old therapy, thus the alternative hypothesis considered only the possibility that the new treatment could lead to a better outcome than the old one, hence H_1: P(success new treatment) > P(success old treatment). More will be said about the implications of choosing this type of directional alternative hypothesis, i.e., in which a specific direction is indicated for the results, when in the next chapter we further elaborate on the issue of hypothesis testing. For the moment it is sufficient to say that when the alternative hypothesis is directional, then the occurrence of the extreme events which lead to the rejection of the null hypothesis is considered only on one side of the binomial distribution, as we did in the phobia case. If however, the alternative hypothesis is non-directional, i.e., it is of the form H_1: P(A) $\neq$ P(B), then the extreme events have to be selected on both sides of the binomial distribution. The region of the binomial distribution that is associated with the rejection of the null hypothesis has to be divided equally between the two sides of the distribution. Thus the critical outcomes that lead to the rejection of the null hypothesis are those extreme outcomes on the right side of the binomial distribution for which the total probability of occurrence is equal to or less than 0.025, and those on the left side for which the total probability of occurrence is equal to or less than 0.025.

Going back to our current problem we want to see if the coin is fair. To assess its fairness we are only allowed to toss the coin 15 times. The first step is to assume that the coin is fair, i.e., that the population probability of a success is 0.5, or equivalently P(Head) = 0.5. If this is true, then the "behaviour" of the coin should follow the binomial distribution with n = 15 and P(Head) = 0.5. This binomial distribution is displayed in Table 4.2. We then know that extreme outcomes, unlikely to occur under the assumption that the null hypothesis is true, are suspicious if they show up in an experiment. As seen earlier, those extreme outcomes whose total probability of

Table 4.2 Binomial distribution of *r* successes out of 15 Bernoulli trials, with P(Success) = 0.5

r	Probability
0	0.00003
1	0.00046
2	0.00032
3	0.01389
4	0.04166
5	0.09164
6	0.15274
7	0.19638
8	0.19638
9	0.15274
10	0.09164
11	0.04166
12	0.01389
13	0.00032
14	0.00046
15	0.00003

occurrence is equal to or less than 0.05 are consider unlikely to occur if the null hypothesis is true. Their occurrence in an experiment indicates that the null hypothesis may be false, and, therefore, that it needs to be rejected in favour of the alternative hypothesis. In the coin case we have stated that H_0: P(Head) = 0.5 and H_1: P(Head) $\neq$ 0.5. As a consequence, outcomes are considered to be extreme when either a very small or a very large number of heads occur out of 15 trials. Inspecting the binomial distribution in Table 4.2, it appears that the total probability of obtaining 0, 1, 2, 3, 12, 13, 14 and 15 heads is about 0.03 which is just less than the critical 0.05 level required to reject the null hypothesis and declare the coin unfair. Hence, if any of the above outcomes occur, then this would suggest that the coin may not be fair. Remember, however, that we can never be certain the coin is unfair because fair coins may, for example, land heads 15 times out of 15 tosses, even if this event is highly unlikely. This issue will be elaborated in the next chapter. For the moment it is important to keep in mind that in rejecting the null hypothesis we run the risk of making a mistake. The probability of making a mistake in rejecting a true null hypothesis is 0.05. This corresponds to the level of risk we are prepared to accept in declaring that a result is not compatible with H_0, despite the fact that, albeit rarely, this result can be observed when H_0 is true.

Finally, you may have noticed that the calculation of the probabilities associated with the binomial distributions is a lengthy process, and because of this, it is not widely used, especially if the maximum number of possible successes is large. We described this process in detail here to emphasise how it is applied to hypothesis testing. In the next chapter we will see how we can make use of the *normal* distribution as an *approximation* of the binomial distribution. This approach simplifies the computation of probabilities. We will also show how to apply the normal distribution in testing hypotheses that would usually require the need of the binomial distribution.

Table 4.3
(a) Individual performances in the recall of lists of categorised and non-categorised words
(b) Binomial distribution of r successes out of 12 trials, with P(Success) = 0.5

(a)

Subject	Categorised	Non-categorised	Successes (+)
1	10	9	+
2	8	7	+
3	7	8	−
4	6	4	+
5	9	5	+
6	7	4	+
7	5	6	−
8	8	7	+
9	9	8	+
10	11	7	+
11	5	4	+
12	7	6	+

(b)

r	Probability
0	0.0002
1	0.0029
2	0.0161
3	0.0537
4	0.1208
5	0.1934
6	0.2256
7	0.1934
8	0.1208
9	0.0537
10	0.0161
11	0.0029
12	0.0002

The sign test

A further application of the binomial distribution in hypothesis testing occurs in the *sign test*, a very simple, but extremely useful inferential test. What follows is an example of how the sign test can be used to test a hypothesis.

A sample of 12 subjects is randomly selected and each subject is asked to commit to memory a series of 24 randomly presented words, where 12 of these words do not have any association between them, while the remaining 12 belong to the same category (e.g., pieces of furniture). At test subjects are asked to recall all the words they remember in any order they want, and the number of categorised and non-categorised words recalled by each subject is recorded. The researcher aims to assess whether or not categorised words are more easily recalled than non-categorised words. A set of fictitious data is presented in Table 4.3. The question to answer is then: Does recall of categorised words differ from recall of non-categorised words?

In applying the sign test, the first thing to do is to obtain the sign of the difference between each pair of performances. In our case we could take the difference between the number of categorised words being recalled minus the number of non-categorised words recalled. A "+" sign next to a subject indicates that the subject recalled more categorised items, while a "−" sign indicates the opposite. If categorisation does not affect recall we would expect the number of "+" signs to be balanced by the number of "−" signs. Thus the null hypothesis capturing the above expectation is the following, H_0: P(Recall categorised word) = P(Recall non-categorised word) = 0.5. On the other hand if categorisation makes a difference, then the number of "+" signs should be either considerably larger or smaller than the number of "−" signs. This alternative hypothesis can be expressed as, H_1: P(Recall categorised word) ≠ P(Recall non-categorised word). Calling the sign "+" a success (we could have equally chosen the sign "−" as a success with no difference in the outcome of the statistical analysis), then, if the null hypothesis is true, the number of successes out of 12 trials is described by the binomial distribution with parameters $n = 12$ and P(Success) = 0.5. This distribution, as well as the empirical data, are provided in Table 4.3. Inspecting the probabilities of each outcome, it can be seen that the extreme number of successes for which the total probability of occurrence is equal to or less than 0.05 are 0, 1, 2, 10, 11 and 12 (i.e., 0.0002 + 0.0029 + 0.0161 + 0.0161 + 0.0029 + 0.0002 = 0.0384). Since we observed 10 successes in the memory experiments, this value is considered unlikely to occur if the null hypothesis is true. Therefore H_0 is rejected in favour of H_1, and it is concluded that categorised items influence (positively) recall performance compared to non-categorised items.

The sign test is applicable to those situations where there are pairs of related observations (this always happens if both observations are obtained from the same subject), and it is possible to determine which is the greatest observation within each pair. On some occasions there may be no difference within a pair of scores (we obtain a "0" sign instead of either "+" or "−"). When this happens, the "0" signs are not included in the analysis and the total number of events is reduced accordingly (i.e., the revised total is given by the total number of pairs of observations minus the number of "0").

Further on the binomial distribution and its use in hypothesis testing

In the section on pages 70–74 we said that it is conventional to reject the null hypothesis in favour of the alternative hypothesis if, assuming that the null hypothesis is true, we obtain one of those extreme outcomes for which the total probability of occurrence is equal to or less than 0.05. However, you may have noticed from the previous examples using the binomial distribution in hypothesis testing, that it is not always possible to select the extreme outcomes so that their total probability of occurrence, under the assumption that the null hypothesis is true, is 0.05. Let us reconsider the phobia of flying example. The null hypothesis was to be rejected if the number of patients who recovered was 13 or more. But for these extreme events we saw that the total probability of occurrence was about 0.027. In a sense we were a bit too stringent in the selection of our extreme events. We could have added another less extreme event to obtain a total probability closer to the 0.05 value used in the decision process about the viability of the null hypothesis. We could have done this by adding to the extreme observations the event "12 patients recovered". However, we saw that this event had a probability of about 0.063 (see Table 4.1a), thus making the total probability of all extreme events about 0.09, a value higher than the standard significance level of 0.05. In allowing an extra critical event we would become somewhat too lenient in rejecting the null hypothesis.

Remember that it is only convention that makes 0.05 the significance level for rejecting the null hypothesis. Moreover, in discrete probability distributions, as in the case of the binomial distribution, probability increases in chunks and not in a continuous smooth manner. Thus, when adding an outcome to the list of extreme outcomes, we add a discrete amount of probability. It is therefore very difficult (very rare) to have a rejection region of the binomial distribution which has an exact probability of 0.05.

An elegant way around this problem has been suggested by Upton and Cook (1997). They suggested using, as the critical "rejection zone", the set of extreme outcomes for which the total probability comes closer to the nominal 0.05 level (thus allowing the actual significance level to be larger than 0.05). In the example on the treatment of the phobic fear of flying, the total probability of obtaining 13, 14 and 15 successes, assuming H_0 is true, was about 0.027. Adding the outcome "12 successes" would have made the total probability about 0.09. Since 0.027 is closer to 0.05 than 0.09, then the critical region for rejection should include only 13, 14 and 15 successes with an actual level of significance of 0.027. In other cases, depending on the values of n and p chosen, the total probability of the extreme outcomes leading to the rejection of the null hypothesis could be larger than the nominal 0.05 significance level. For example, the actual level of significance could be 0.057. In all cases it is recommended that the actual level of significance is reported.

Chapter 5

Continuous random variables and the normal distribution

Introduction

The previous chapter concentrated on some probability distributions, chiefly the binomial distribution and its application in the process of hypothesis testing. The main characteristic of these distributions was that they modelled the "behaviour" of discrete random variables. In this chapter we will focus on the distribution of continuous random variables. These are variables for which the value of each individual outcome is not predictable, and for which it is not possible to make a list of the values these outcomes can take. In particular we will describe the characteristics of the normal distribution and of the standard normal distribution. Furthermore, a more detailed description of the logic of hypothesis testing will be provided using the standard normal distribution. Finally, we will show how the standard normal distribution can be used as an approximation of the binomial distribution.

Continuous random variables and their distribution

In Chapter 1 we said that, in the case of a continuous variable, it is not possible to make a list of all possible values that it can take (i.e., continuous data). Physical quantities like time, weight and speed are examples of continuous random variables. With distributions of continuous random variables, in contrast to discrete random variables, we cannot calculate the probability of any single value that a variable can take. It is only possible to calculate the probability that a continuous random variable X lies between any two values. Why is it not possible to calculate the probability of any single value that a continuous random variable can take?

Well, consider the continuous random variable "the reaction time to press a button in response to a sudden light flashing on a computer screen". For convenience we will only consider a restricted range of possible values that this variable can take. So the upper and lower limits of the distribution are taken as 263 milliseconds and 613 milliseconds (reaction times outside this range are considered to reflect anticipated responses or the effect of irrelevant factors on the task; e.g., getting momentarily distracted, sneezing, etc.). We then know that the total probability for all the values in this range is 1. However, and this is the problem, the probability of any single reaction time within the 263–613 range is zero. This is because if we take any two reaction times, e.g., 321.24 and 321.25 milliseconds, it is always possible to find another reaction time between the two (e.g., 321.245). Moreover, this process goes on forever. For instance, assuming that reaction times are measured extremely accurately, it is possible to find another reaction time between 321.24 and 321.245 (e.g., 321.242), and so on. This means that for any two values of a continuous random variable, even if the difference between these values is infinitesimal, there is always an infinite number of values in the interval between them. It then follows that the probability of any particular value that the continuous random variable can take is infinitely small; it is in fact 0.

Let us try to illustrate the above issue with a graphical example. In Chapter 1 we said that continuous variables, due to limitations in the instruments used to measure them, are often treated as discrete (e.g., reaction times are recorded with millisecond accuracy). Moreover, in Chapter 2 we saw, when describing frequency distributions, that these distributions are often graphically displayed using histograms where the height of each bar represents the frequency of occurrence of an interval of values of the observed variable. Furthermore, the area covered by each bar can be made proportional to the relative frequency of occurrence of the values included within each class (or interval). The histogram in Figure 5.1a displays the distribution of a set of 50 reaction times with the width of each class being 35 milliseconds. In this distribution there are 4 reaction times in the first class. In order to represent the relative density of this class, the area of the first bar is $\frac{4}{50} = 0.08$. Furthermore, adding all the relative densities of the remaining classes, the total area under the histogram should be equal to 1 (in other words it comprises 100 per cent of the values in the distribution).

The histograms in Figure 5.1b and Figure 5.1c display the distributions of 100 and 200 reaction times, respectively (with a class width of 17.5 and 14 milliseconds, respectively). By increasing the number of observations and reducing the class width, the outline of the histogram appears more defined. Now imagine that the number of observations is increased to include the entire population of relevant reaction times (i.e., a potentially infinite number of observations), and that the class interval becomes infinitesimally small (i.e., a dot), so that each bar of the histogram is basically a line (i.e., it has an area of 0). Then, if the top of each line is connected, we will obtain a distribution that appears as a smooth continuous curve. The superimposed smooth continuous curve in Figure 5.1c (see also Figure 5.2) indicates how a histogram would become, applying the procedure just described. A smooth curve like the one in Figure 5.1c and Figure 5.2 displays the distribution of the continuous random variable "the reaction time to press a button in response to a sudden onset of a light flashing on a computer screen". Notice that this distribution has a slightly longer tail on the right side, thus it is moderately positively skewed.

From Chapter 3 we know that, when the number of sampled observations corresponds to the number of observations in the population, then relative frequencies correspond to population probabilities. Thus, the area of each bar in the histogram corresponds to a probability. However, when the number of sampled observations includes the whole, potentially infinite, population, so that it is possible to obtain a continuous smooth curve, each bar is reduced to a line, thus its area is 0 (see Figure 5.2). Therefore it is not possible to calculate the probability of any particular value of a continuous random variable. However, all is not lost. It is in fact possible to calculate the area of the plane delimited by the curve and the x-axis between two values of a continuous random variable (this area can be calculated using the mathematical process of integration). It then follows that it is possible to calculate the probability

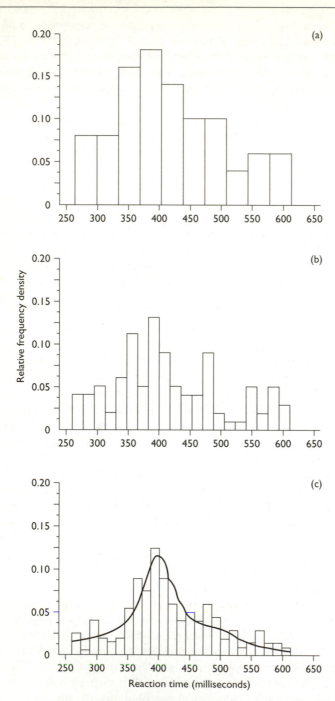

Figure 5.1 Histograms representing the distribution of a set of 50, 100 and 200 reaction times (a), (b) and (c), respectively (with upper and lower limits of the distribution being 263 milliseconds and 613 milliseconds, respectively). The continuous form of the distribution, when the whole population is sampled, is represented by the continuous smooth curve in part (c).

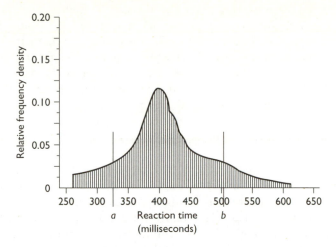

Figure 5.2 Representation of the distribution of a continuous random variable X (i.e., reaction times) obtained by joining the vertices of each histogram bar. After sampling the entire population, each bar has become a line. The probability that X lies between *a* and *b* is given by the area under the curve between the points *a* = 325 milliseconds and *b* = 505 milliseconds.

that a continuous random variable X lies between two values a and b (e.g., the probability of a reaction time between 325 and 505 milliseconds, i.e., $P(325 \leq x \leq 505)$).

In summary, distributions of continuous random variables appear as a smooth curve, with the total area under the curve being equal to 1. Thus the total probability for the range of values of a continuous random variable is 1. The probability that a continuous random variable X takes a value in the interval between a and b is given by the area under the curve delimited by the points a and b and the x-axis (see Figure 5.2 where a = 325 milliseconds and b = 505 milliseconds). Finally, as in the case of discrete random variables, it is possible to have functions (called probability density functions) that specify the distributions of continuous random variables. In the next section we will describe the most important continuous distribution, i.e., the normal distribution.

The normal distribution

The normal distribution is possibly the most important continuous distribution because it describes the "behaviour" of an extremely large number of continuous random variables. For example it describes how the weight of people is distributed in the population, or the distribution of their Intelligence Quotient scores, etc. The distribution of this last continuous random variable is displayed in Figure 5.3. Usually, IQ scores are given in units, but this is because of the limitations of the instruments used to measure IQ. In fact, this variable can, in principle, be treated as continuous. As can be seen from Figure 5.3, the normal distribution is symmetrical, bell shaped and centred around the mean. The median and mode have the same location as the mean. Along the x-axis are the values of the continuous random variable, in this case the IQ scores, while the height of the curve (reported on the y-axis) represents the rate at which the probability increases when moving along the x-axis. The higher the curve, the larger the increments in probability associated with increments in the variable X.

Below the IQ values are indicated, in standard deviation units, i.e., σ, their distances from the population mean. In the case of IQ scores it is known that $\mu = 100$ and $\sigma = 15$. Hence, for example, a score of 95, being 5 IQ units below the mean, is located at $-\frac{1}{3}\sigma$ (or equivalently $-\frac{1}{3}$ SD, i.e., standard deviation units; here each unit corresponds to 15 IQ points) to the left of the population mean, while a score of 145 is located 3 SD to the extreme right of the mean (scores below the mean are expressed as negative, in terms of standard deviation units, while scores above the mean are expressed as positive, in terms of standard deviation units). In Figure 5.3 a line divides the area under the curve into two equal parts. The dotted lines located at -2σ, -1σ, 1σ and 2σ from μ, also slice the area under the normal curve. The percentages within the bell shape indicate that 34.1 per cent of the entire area under the normal distribution is located between μ and either $\mu + 1\sigma$ or $\mu - 1\sigma$ (later in the chapter we will describe how to obtain the size of areas under the normal distribution). Since portions of the area under a continuous distribution curve give the probability of a continuous random variable lying between any two values, it appears that for a randomly sampled person from the population the probability that their IQ score lies between 85 and 100 is 0.341, i.e., $P(85 \leq x \leq 100) = 0.341$ (to 3 d.p.). Similarly, the probability that their IQ score lies between 85 and 115 is 0.682 (to 3 d.p.). Adding all the percentages displayed in Figure 5.3 we obtain the area under the normal curve between $\mu - 2\sigma$ and $\mu + 2\sigma$ (i.e., within the IQ scores of 70 and 130). This portion corresponds to 95.4 per cent of the total area under the normal distribution. Hence, the probability that the IQ of a randomly sampled person lies between 70 and 130 is 0.954 (to 3 d.p.). Given that the total area under the normal curve is 1, it follows that the probability that a randomly sampled person has an IQ either lower than 70, or larger than 130, is fairly small (i.e., $0.046 = 1 - 0.954$).

Generally, the normal distribution captures the fact that, for some continuous random variables, extreme values rarely occur in the population, thus they have a small probability of occurrence, while more common events, i.e., those located around the mean, have a larger probability of occurrence. Finally, at the end of the "measures of dispersion" section (p. 32), we said that, if the distribution of the sampled data is reasonably symmetrical and reasonably bell shaped, then about 95 per cent of the observations lie within ±2 SD from the mean. The argument given in the previous paragraph provides the rationale for that claim.

When describing discrete probability distributions in Chapter 4, we said that in some cases it is possible to provide a function that generates a specific distribution (see for instance the binomial distribution). This is also possible with continuous random variables. In particular, if a continuous random variable X is normally distributed, then its distribution is described by the following function:

$$y = \frac{1}{\sigma\sqrt{2\pi}} \times e^{\left(-\frac{(x-\mu)^2}{2\sigma^2}\right)}$$

where the values of the random variable X range from negative to positive infinite (i.e., $-\infty \leq x \leq \infty$); π and e are constants (i.e., $\pi = 3.1416$ and e = 2.7183, rounded to

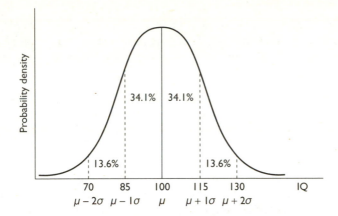

Figure 5.3 Example of a normal distribution where the continuous random variable *X* is the Intelligence Quotient, with $\mu = 100$ and $\sigma = 15$. The percentages indicate the portion of the total area under the normal distribution between two IQ values (e.g., 13.6 per cent of the total area under the normal distribution is between the IQ values of 70 and 85, inclusive).

4 d.p.); μ and σ^2 are the parameters of the distribution (i.e., the values which define the bell shape of the normal distribution). Notice that when *x* takes either extremely large positive values or extremely large negative values, *y* tends to approach zero without ever reaching it. This feature of the normal distribution is captured by the fact that in Figure 5.3 the curve never reaches the *x*-axis. However, for convenience, the range of the normal distribution is limited to ±3 SD around the mean.

While the distribution is always bell shaped and symmetrical around the mean, different values of the parameters affect the appearance of the distribution. Changes in μ produce shifts of the entire distribution along the *x*-axis (i.e., the distribution is centred around different mean values), while changes in σ^2, or equivalently in σ, correspond to changes in the scale of measurement and affect the peak of the distribution and its spread around the mean. With small standard deviations, the peak of the distribution tends to be high and the main body of the bell tends to be narrow, while with large standard deviations, the peak tends to be low and the main body of the bell tends to be wide.

We said earlier that areas under a continuous distribution, between two values of the random variable *X*, correspond to probabilities. We also gave the size of the areas of some portions of the normal curve shown in Figure 5.3. Any area under a curve is obtained by calculating the integral, over a range of values of the random variable *X*, of the function describing the continuous distribution. However, you do not have to worry about the process of integration to calculate probabilities for the most important continuous distributions, because these probabilities are provided in tables. In the case of the normal distribution, a table of probabilities is available for the special case where $\mu = 0$ and $\sigma^2 = 1$ (see Table 5.1 and the more comprehensive *Z* table in the Appendix). A normal distribution with these parameters is called the standard normal distribution. The next section will describe this distribution.

The standard normal distribution

In the last section of Chapter 2 we presented some transformations that can be applied to a set of data. In particular we said that when the mean is subtracted from each score and this difference is divided by the standard deviation of the distribution of the scores, we obtain a new standardised score named z. More formally:

$$z = \frac{x - \mu}{\sigma} \left(\text{or } z = \frac{x - \bar{x}}{s} \text{ when working with sample data} \right).$$

When this standardisation (so called because the units of this new variable are standard deviations) is applied to the values of a normally distributed continuous random variable X, we obtain a new continuous random variable Z which is also normally distributed with $\mu = 0$ and $\sigma = 1$. This distribution is called the *standard normal distribution*. In Figure 5.3, we performed this type of transformation to obtain the distance of IQ scores, in terms of standard deviations, from the mean.

Why is the mean of the standard normal distribution 0 and its standard deviation 1? Let us apply the standardisation procedure to the IQ scores shown in Figure 5.3. We saw that the non-standardised IQ scores have $\mu = 100$ and $\sigma = 15$. Let us calculate the z score corresponding to 100 (i.e., the mean of the IQ scores). Subtracting the mean IQ from the value of 100, and dividing the result by 15 (i.e., the standard deviation of the IQ scores), we obtain: $z = \frac{100 - 100}{15} = 0$. Thus the mean of the standardised scores is 0. Now, let us take an IQ score that is one standard deviation away from the mean (e.g., 115), and calculate its z score. This is $z = \frac{115 - 100}{15} = 1$, thus the standard deviation of the z scores is 1.

The same standardisation process can be applied to all IQ scores to obtain their z scores. With this process we can express each IQ score in standard deviation units. As seen in the previous section, an IQ score of 95 corresponds to a z score of $-\frac{1}{3}$, i.e., $z = \frac{95 - 100}{15} = -\frac{5}{15} = -\frac{1}{3}$. Since every value in any normal distribution can be

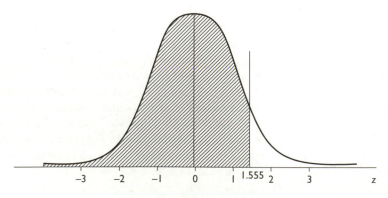

Figure 5.4 Standard normal distribution: The area of the grey portion under the curve can be read in Table 5.1 for $z \leq 1.555$.

Table 5.1 Table of z scores. The cumulative probability from −∞, up to, and including any given z score is also reported. The probability from a given z score to ∞ is 1 minus the cumulative probability for the given z score. A more comprehensive table is provided in the Appendix

z score	Cumulative p value	z score	Cumulative p value	z score	Cumulative p value	z score	Cumulative p value
−4.768	0.000001	−0.915	0.18	0.025	0.51	0.994	0.84
−4.265	0.00001	−0.878	0.19	0.050	0.52	1.036	0.85
−3.719	0.0001	−0.842	0.20	0.075	0.53	1.080	0.86
−3.540	0.0002	−0.806	0.21	0.100	0.54	1.126	0.87
−3.432	0.0003	−0.772	0.22	0.126	0.55	1.175	0.88
−3.290	0.0005	−0.739	0.23	0.151	0.56	1.227	0.89
−3.239	0.0006	−0.706	0.24	0.176	0.57	1.282	0.90
−3.195	0.0007	−0.674	0.25	0.202	0.58	1.341	0.91
−3.156	0.0008	−0.643	0.26	0.228	0.59	1.405	0.92
−3.121	0.0009	−0.613	0.27	0.253	0.60	1.476	0.93
−3.090	0.001	−0.583	0.28	0.279	0.61	1.555	0.94
−2.878	0.002	−0.553	0.29	0.305	0.62	1.645	0.95
−2.748	0.003	−0.524	0.30	0.332	0.63	1.751	0.96
−2.652	0.004	−0.496	0.31	0.358	0.64	1.881	0.97
−2.576	0.005	−0.468	0.32	0.385	0.65	1.96	0.975
−2.326	0.01	−0.444	0.33	0.412	0.66	2.054	0.98
−2.054	0.02	−0.412	0.34	0.444	0.67	2.326	0.99
−1.960	0.025	−0.385	0.35	0.468	0.68	2.576	0.995
−1.881	0.03	−0.358	0.36	0.496	0.69	2.652	0.996
−1.751	0.04	−0.332	0.37	0.524	0.70	2.748	0.997
−1.645	0.05	−0.305	0.38	0.553	0.71	2.878	0.998
−1.555	0.06	−0.279	0.39	0.583	0.72	3.090	0.999
−1.476	0.07	−0.253	0.40	0.613	0.73	3.121	0.9991
−1.405	0.08	−0.228	0.41	0.643	0.74	3.156	0.9992
−1.341	0.09	−0.202	0.42	0.674	0.75	3.195	0.9993
−1.282	0.10	−0.176	0.43	0.706	0.76	3.239	0.9994
−1.227	0.11	−0.151	0.44	0.739	0.77	3.290	0.9995
−1.175	0.12	−0.126	0.45	0.772	0.78	3.353	0.9996
−1.126	0.13	−0.100	0.46	0.806	0.79	3.432	0.9997
−1.080	0.14	−0.075	0.47	0.842	0.80	3.540	0.9998
−1.036	0.15	−0.05	0.48	0.878	0.81	3.719	0.9999
−0.994	0.16	−0.025	0.49	0.915	0.82	4.265	0.99999
−0.954	0.17	0.0	0.50	0.954	0.83	4.768	0.999999

transformed using the process of standardisation, it follows that the standard normal distribution is sufficient to calculate the probability that any normally distributed continuous random variable X lies within any two of its values a and b. The standard normal distribution is shown in Figure 5.4. Table 5.1 allows us to calculate the probabilities of any interval of values of the standard normal distribution.

Let us see how the standard normal distribution table (or Z table) works. The Z table provides the cumulative area (i.e., probability) from −∞ to any z score. Thus, for example, the probability of a z score being included in the interval −∞ and 1.555 (see also Figure 5.4) can be obtained by reading the cumulative p value to the right of $z = 1.555$ in Table 5.1, thus $P(z \leq 1.555) = 0.94$. Conversely, the probability of z being equal to or larger than 1.555 is: $P(1.555 \leq z) = 1 - 0.94 = 0.06$. The Z table also allows us to calculate the probability that a z score can be between any two values a and b. For instance, to calculate $P(-1.96 \leq z \leq 1.96)$, we first read off the cumulative probability associated with -1.96, i.e., 0.025, then the one for 1.96, i.e., 0.975. Finally the smaller probability is subtracted from the larger probability, and we obtain:

$$P(-1.96 \leq z \leq 1.96) = 0.975 - 0.025 = 0.95,$$

and conversely

$$P(z \leq -1.96) + P(z \geq 1.96) = 1 - 0.95 = 0.05.$$

At the beginning of this section we saw how to calculate z scores from non-standardised data. We now give a full example of how, using z scores we can obtain the probability for a range of values of any normally distributed continuous variable. Imagine that we want to know the probability that a randomly sampled person has an IQ between 100 and 121 (given that $\mu = 100$ and $\sigma = 15$). The first thing to do is to obtain the z scores corresponding to the two IQ scores. Then, the cumulative probabilities associated with both these z scores are read off from the Z table (or estimated by linear interpolation). Finally, the difference between the larger and the smaller probabilities gives the answer to our question.

Going step by step, the z score associated with an IQ of 100 is 0, because $\mu = 100$, while for an IQ of 121 we have $z = \dfrac{121 - 100}{15} = 1.4$. The cumulative probabilities associated with $z = 0$ and $z = 1.4$ are 0.5 and 0.919 (to 3 d.p.), respectively. Therefore, $P(100 \leq IQ \leq 121) = 0.919 - 0.5 = 0.419$ (to 3 d.p.).

Let us consider another example. In this case we want to find out what are the two IQ values, symmetrically located around the mean, that would yield a probability of 0.95 for the IQ of a randomly sampled person lying in that interval. We saw above that $P(-1.96 \leq z \leq 1.96) = 0.95$, thus the IQ scores we are looking for are those corresponding to $z = -1.96$ and $z = 1.96$. These values can be obtained in the following way. We know that:

$$z = -1.96 = \frac{x - 100}{15}$$

and thus, we need to find x, i.e., the IQ score corresponding to $z = -1.96$. This is obtained in the following way:

$$100 - (1.96 \times 15) = x, \text{ therefore } x = 70.6.$$

Applying the same procedure to $z = 1.96$ we obtain:

$$100 + (1.96 \times 15) = x, \text{ thus } x = 129.4.$$

Since IQ is measured in increments of 1 unit, rounding the obtained x values we have $P(71 \leq IQ \leq 129) = 0.95$.

In Chapter 4, when the binomial distribution was used in the process of testing hypotheses, we said that those extreme events, whose total probability of occurrence is equal to or less than 0.05, should lead to the rejection of the null hypothesis. Similarly, using the standard normal distribution, we can decide, as seen in the IQ example, which are the values of a variable that could be considered extreme and that, if empirically obtained, would lead to the rejection of the null hypothesis. In the next section we will give an example of the use of the standard normal distribution in the inferential process of testing hypotheses, and in doing this we will also provide a comprehensive presentation of the logic of hypothesis testing. We introduced this topic in Chapter 4. However, since a good understanding of the process of statistical inference is of fundamental importance, this important topic will be presented more than once, and in slightly different ways. Therefore the next section intends to provide both a revision and an in-depth description of the process of hypothesis testing that was presented in Chapter 4.

Hypothesis testing and the normal distribution

Some examples of the application of statistical inference in hypothesis testing were given when discussing the binomial distribution. Our intention is now to provide a thorough presentation of the process of hypothesis testing.

The main aim of statistical inference is to infer some characteristics of the population using sample data. For example, we could be interested in assessing the effectiveness of two different learning strategies, or of two different psychotherapeutic interventions, or maybe we want to know if a group of people differ, with respect to a particular skill, from the normal population, etc. Since the size of the relevant population is usually extremely large, empirical studies tend to be performed on samples. However, the results of these studies would be of little relevance if they could not be generalised to the entire population. As we saw in Chapter 1, a pre-requisite to permit the generalisation of any result obtained from sampled data to the relevant population, is that the selected subjects should be randomly drawn from the population, thus ensuring that the sample provides a fair representation of the characteristics of the entire population (i.e., external validity criterion). Moreover, we said that the manipulation of the variables, and the allocation of the subjects to the various conditions, should occur in such a way that the outcome of the study is not biased (i.e., internal validity criterion). Assuming that a study is both internally and externally valid, then some steps need to be taken to test the hypothesis a researcher intends to investigate.

The *first step* is to clearly formulate the *research hypothesis*. In general, this hypothesis should test some predictions associated with one or more theories in order to provide an empirical test of these theories. The research hypothesis we will work with is that 7-year-old children with no reading disabilities should be faster when reading aloud a test prose passage, than 7-year-old children having reading problems. A study to assess this hypothesis would usually involve at least a sample of children suffering from reading problems and a sample of normal readers. Then, after taking the reading time of each subject, a comparison of the mean reading times of the two samples would be performed. In a study like this, inferential statistics techniques would be applied in order to generalise the results obtained with the two samples to the relevant population. Basically, we would try to assess how likely it is to obtain the observed empirical results assuming that the samples of normal and reading impaired children were drawn from the same population (i.e., that of the normal reader). If this probability is low (usually $p \leq 0.05$), then we would conclude that the two samples were drawn from different populations. In other words, that the mean reading times of normal and impaired children differ significantly. To perform this analysis we need to know the distribution of the sample means. However, the discussion of how the means of samples drawn from a population are distributed will be provided in Chapter 8, when hypothesis testing will be applied to compare means. Because of this, we do not yet have the tools to make a decision about the above problem. Therefore, we will consider a slightly different type of study that will still allow us to make use of the standard normal distribution in hypothesis testing.

Imagine that we have already collected normative data using a reading test on an extremely large number of 7-year-old children with no reading disorders, so we basically know the distribution of reading times for the population of children with no reading problems. We also know that the distribution is normal with $\mu = 50$ seconds (s) and $\sigma = 10$ s. Imagine also that we administer the test to a child with the aim of assessing their reading abilities, and it turn out that the child takes 72.5 s to read the test passage. What can we infer from this performance? Can we suggest that the child's ability to read is normal, or that the child's ability to read is abnormal? This situation is different from the case in which samples are selected and their means are compared, mainly because of the numerosity of the sample. Our sample comprises only one subject! The research hypothesis in this particular case could be something like this: if the assessed child, when compared to normal readers, is exceedingly slow in reading the test material, then he or she suffers from some kind of reading disorder.

The *second step* is to formulate the *null hypothesis* (i.e., H_0). In this case we assume that the sampled child has been taken from the population of children with no reading disorders (i.e., their performance should be equivalent to one of the performances shown by normal readers in the reading test).

The *third step* is to formulate the *alternative hypothesis* (i.e., H_1). Here H_1 states that if the reading time of the assessed child is much too slow, compared to the distribution of the reading times for the normal readers, then the child has not been sampled from the population of normal readers, but from the population of children suffering from some form of reading disorder. Notice that the research (or experimental) hypothesis and the alternative hypothesis may not necessarily be identical. For example the research hypothesis could state that if a child is exceedingly slow in the reading test, then they are considered to suffer from some form of reading disorder. However, the alternative hypothesis states that the rejection of the null hypothesis occurs if the reading time of a child is either exceedingly slow or exceedingly fast. More about this issue will be said in the section on pages 93–95.

The *fourth step* is to identify the distribution of the reading times under the assumption that the null hypothesis is true. We know this distribution. As seen above, it is normal with $\mu = 50$ sec and $\sigma = 10$ sec.

The *fifth step* is to calculate the probability of obtaining, in the population of children with no reading problems (i.e., assuming that H_0 is true), a reading time at least as long as the one obtained by our assessed child (i.e., 72.5 s or more).

Finally, the *sixth step* is as follows. If the probability of obtaining a reading time of 72.5 s is unlikely in the population of children with no reading problems (i.e., it occurs with a probability smaller than 0.05), then the null hypothesis is rejected in favour of the alternative hypothesis. If, on the other hand, the probability of reading the passage in at least 72.5 s is not unlikely in the population of normal readers, we do not have sufficient evidence to reject the null hypothesis. This does not mean that we have proved the null hypothesis to be true. It only means that we are not in a position, given the available evidence, to reject it (this concept will be elaborated later in the chapter).

To decide if the assessed child shows reading difficulties, we need to see if the obtained reading performance allows the rejection of the null hypothesis (H_0) in favour of the alternative hypothesis (H_1). In this process we are going to make use of the standard normal distribution. Therefore the first step is to convert the reading time of 72.5 s into a z score. Applying the required transformation formula we obtain:

$$z = \frac{x - \mu}{\sigma} = \frac{72.5 - 50}{10} = \frac{22.5}{10} = 2.25.$$

The next step is to determine, using the Z table what is the probability of obtaining a z score of at least 2.25. Inspecting the Z table in the Appendix, it appears that the cumulative probability of a z score being in the interval between $-\infty$ and 2.25 is greater than 0.98. Therefore, the probability of obtaining a reading time of at least 72.5 s in the population of normal readers is less than 0.02. Since this probability is less than 0.05, we consider it unlikely that the child has been sampled from the population of normal readers, thus we reject the null hypothesis in favour of the alternative hypothesis, i.e., that the child has been sampled from the population of children with some form of reading disorder. We thus conclude that the child has indeed some form of reading problem and, as a consequence of this diagnosis, we may decide to implement a special intervention aimed to improve the child's reading skills.

Type I and Type II errors

According to the results of the reading test, it was inferred that the assessed child had some form of reading disorder. However, what is the probability that this conclusion could be wrong? This probability is actually known, and it is 0.05. Why 0.05? To decide if the assessed child was reading impaired, their performance was compared against the distribution of the reading times for normal readers. In doing this we decided that, if the child's reading time was among those extreme reading times that have a total probability either equal to or less than 0.05 in the population of normal readers, we would reject the null hypothesis that the assessed child is a normal reader. However, in rejecting the null hypothesis, and thus declaring that the child was sampled from the population of children with some form of reading disorder, we could have made an error. In fact, the child could simply be a member of the population of normal readers, albeit quite a slow reader, but not a child having a reading disorder. Since it was decided, on an a priori basis (i.e., before testing the child), to reject the null hypothesis if an observed reading time corresponded to one of the extreme perform-ances that among normal readers have a probability either equal to or less than 0.05, we could then have mistakenly declared, with a probability of 0.05, that a normal slow reader is in fact a member of the population of reading impaired children. This type of inferential error, i.e., rejecting the null hypothesis when it is true, is called a *Type I error*. Its probability is given by the probability of those extreme outcomes whose occurrence leads to the rejection of the null hypothesis. Usually this "rejection"

Table 5.2 Summary table of the possible outcomes, and probabilities, of the process of statistical inference

Statistical decision	True state of the world	
	H_0 True	H_0 False
Reject H_0	Type I error $p = \alpha$	Correct decision $p = 1 - \beta$ (i.e., Power)
Do not reject H_0	Correct decision $p = 1 - \alpha$	Type II error $p = \beta$

probability is set at 0.05 and it is called α (alpha). The magnitude of α does not need to be 0.05. It can be set either at a more conservative level (e.g., 0.01), or at a more liberal level (e.g., 0.10). In general, however, α levels used in scientific journal articles are rarely larger than 0.05. With an α of 0.01, the probability of wrongly rejecting a true null hypothesis is 0.01.

There is also another type of error in statistical inference. This occurs when the null hypothesis is false and the empirical results do not lead to its rejection. This error is called a *Type II error* and its probability is called β (beta). β is not immediately quantifiable since it depends on various parameters. An example of the occurrence of a Type II error, and a way to calculate the probability of Type II errors follows. Table 5.2 summarises the possible outcomes, and their probabilities, in statistical inference.

We previously said that we knew that the distribution of reading times of children with no reading disorders, in a specific reading test, is normal with $\mu = 50$ s and $\sigma = 10$ s. Imagine that we also know the distribution of the reading times for the population of children with some form of reading disorder. This distribution is normal with $\mu = 65$ s and $\sigma = 10$ s. Figure 5.5 displays the two distributions. The top part of this figure shows the distribution of the reading times of children with no reading disorder. This distribution is divided into two parts. The dark area corresponds to the "rejection" area. Thus if a child obtains a reading time of 66.45 s or slower (i.e., $z \geq 1.645$; $p \leq 0.05$), they are declared to have some kind of reading disorder. As said earlier, reading times equal to or slower than 66.45 s can be found in children with no reading disabilities; thus, the probability of wrongly rejecting a true null hypothesis is $\alpha = 0.05$.

The lower part of Figure 5.5 shows the distribution of the reading time for the population of children having some form of reading impairment. You can notice that this distribution, when compared to the distribution of nonimpaired children, is shifted toward the right. Although the mean reading time of reading impaired children is 1.5 standard deviations slower than the mean reading time of normal children, the two distributions greatly overlap. What is the consequence of this relatively large overlap?

Let us imagine that we administer the reading test to a child whom we know has a reading disorder. The child is a member of the population of impaired readers. Let us assume that the child reads the test passage in 60 s. If we do not know that the child has a reading impairment, and we need to evaluate their reading ability, we would compare the child's performance to the distribution of normal readers. In doing this, the null hypothesis states that the child's performance is one of the performances shown by normal readers in the reading test. Converting the reading time of 60 s into a z score we obtain:

$$z = \frac{60 - 50}{10} = \frac{10}{10} = 1.$$

Inspecting the Z table, it appears that the probability of obtaining a z score of at least 1 is larger than 0.05 (more precisely this probability is 1 minus the cumulative probability from $-\infty$ to $z = 1$; i.e., $1 - 0.841 = 0.159$, to 3 d.p.), thus we would fail to reject the null hypothesis. However, since we know that the child has a reading disorder, and that they have not been sampled from the population of normal readers, we would make a mistake in failing to reject the null hypothesis (i.e., we would commit a Type II error).

How can the probability of committing a Type II error be calculated? In the previous example this is obtained by calculating the area under the curve of the distribution of the impaired children from $-\infty$ to the z score that, in this distribution, corresponds to $z = 1.645$ in the distribution for normal readers. Why? An inspection of Figure 5.5 will help to understand the above argument. We know that we would fail to reject the null hypothesis if, with respect to the distribution for the normal readers, we obtain a z score smaller than 1.645 (or equivalently, for any reading time faster than 66.45 s). Thus every child reading the test passage in less than 66.45 s would not be said to have any form of reading disorder. However, since we know the distribution of the reading times for reading impaired children, we also know that quite a large proportion of these children can read the test passage in a faster time than 66.45 s. Hence, any of these "fast" readers drawn from the population of reading impaired children will be erroneously declared as not having any reading disability on the basis of the test's results. Therefore, in all these cases for which the null hypothesis is false, a mistake will be made because we will fail to reject H_0. The probability of this Type II error is given by the size of the grey area in the lower part of Figure 5.5. Thus we need to calculate this probability.

We know that the distribution of the reading times for the reading impaired children is identical to that of the normal readers with the only difference being that its mean is located at 65 s instead of 50 s. We also know that a reading time of 66.45 s (i.e., corresponding to $z = 1.645$ in the distribution of normal readers), is 1.45 s above the mean of the impaired readers' distribution. The z score corresponding to this reading time in the impaired readers' distribution is given by:

$$z = \frac{66.45 - 65}{10} = \frac{1.45}{10} = 0.145$$

and the cumulative probability from $-\infty$ to $z = 0.145$ is about 0.56, to 2 d.p. (this is β, i.e., the probability of committing a Type II error).

In contrast to the probability of a Type I error, which is known since it corresponds to the "rejection" area decided before conducting the statistical analysis, the probability of a Type II error is not "fixed", but depends on the distance of the mean of the distribution of the impaired population from the mean of the distribution of normal readers,

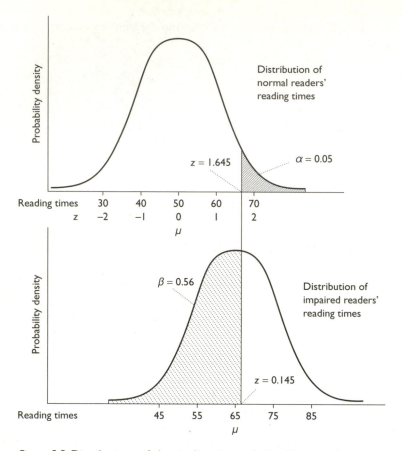

Figure 5.5 Distributions of the reading times obtained in a reading test by the population of normal 7-year-old children (upper part) and of 7-year-old reading impaired children (lower part). Both distributions are normal with $\sigma = 10$.
The dark area within the upper curve corresponds to the probability of committing a Type I error, while the shaded area in the lower curve corresponds to the probability of committing a Type II error, given the data provided in the example described in the main text.

and on the α level selected (in general the size of the sample is also a factor affecting the probability of committing a Type II error; as explained in Chapter 13 larger samples are usually associated with smaller probabilities of committing Type II errors). If α is increased from 0.05 to, for instance, 0.1, then the shaded area in the lower distribution in Figure 5.5 will become smaller, and, as a consequence, β will get smaller. Similarly, if α is kept constant, while the distance of the mean of the impaired population from the mean of the distribution of normal readers is increased, then β will also get smaller. Conversely, if the distance between the means of the two distributions is reduced, then the two distributions tend to overlap to a larger extent; thus, it is more difficult, on the basis of the test results, to discriminate between normal and impaired readers, increasing the probability of a Type II error (i.e., β). *Power* refers to the probability of correctly rejecting a false null hypothesis. This probability is equal to $1 - \beta$.

In the above example we said that we knew the distribution of the reaction times of the children having some form of reading disorder (i.e., we knew the distribution of the data when the alternative hypothesis is true). In general, however, we do not know the distribution of the population data corresponding to the alternative hypothesis (assuming this to be true); as a consequence we often need to do some guesswork to estimate the probability of β (this issue will be recapitulated and expanded upon when the concept of statistical power is discussed in more detail in Chapter 13).

Summarising, in inferential statistics we always assume that the null hypothesis is true. If the evidence against H_0 is strong enough this hypothesis is rejected. This process carries the risk of wrongly rejecting the null hypothesis if this hypothesis is true. This is called a Type I error and its probability is equal to α. The level of α is usually chosen to be 0.05, which means that, on average, out of 100 statistical tests that lead to the rejection of the null hypothesis 5 are wrong. The null hypothesis is assumed to be true and thus, a failure to reject it cannot be taken as evidence that the null hypothesis is true. As we saw in the previous example, it is possible that the null hypothesis is *not* rejected when it *is* actually false. Thus failing to reject the null hypothesis and using this failure as evidence that the null hypothesis is true may lead to incorrect conclusions: Absence of evidence is not evidence for the absence (this issue will be further elaborated in Chapter 13 on statistical power). A second type of error, called Type II, occurs in statistical inference, with probability β, when the null hypothesis is false but it is not rejected. Table 5.2 summarised the possible outcomes of the decision-making process involved in statistical inference with their associated probabilities.

One-tailed and two-tailed statistical tests

The distinction between one- and two-tailed statistical tests was briefly discussed in Chapter 4 when the use of the binomial distribution in hypothesis testing was described. Let us now discuss the issue in more detail.

In the process of statistical inference, the null hypothesis is rejected if the observed empirical results are unlikely to be obtained if the null hypothesis is true. Outcomes can be unlikely because they are either significantly smaller or larger than the mean outcome obtained in the population under the assumption that the null hypothesis is true. Thus, the null hypothesis should be rejected if either of these two classes of outcome occurs. It then follows that equal weight should be given to these two types of extreme outcome. For example, when the standard normal distribution is used in testing a hypothesis, H_0 is rejected if any of the extreme outcomes correspond to either a z score which is equal to or smaller than -1.96 or to a z score which is equal to or larger than 1.96. In this way the total "rejection" area of 0.05 is equally divided between both types of extreme outcome (i.e., very small or very large) that would lead to a rejection of the null hypothesis. When this approach is used in hypothesis testing, the statistical test is said to be *non-directional*, or equivalently, *two-tailed* (because the rejection area is equally divided between the two tails of the distribution used in the statistical test). This is the default approach. Unless there is a strong reason to depart from using a two-tailed test, one should stick to it when performing any statistical analysis.

In the previous example we used the standard normal distribution to determine whether an assessed child suffered from some form of reading disorder. In doing this we considered only very slow reading times as those extreme outcomes leading to the rejection of the null hypothesis, and not the very fast reading times. The 0.05 "rejection" area under the standard normal curve was confined to the right side of the curve. This is an example of a *directional test*, or equivalently, a *one-tailed test* (see also pages 70–73 for another example of the use of a directional test in hypothesis testing). As stated above, one-tailed tests should preferably be avoided. The reason is that, when using a one-tailed test, we do not make provision for rejecting H_0 if an extreme performance unexpectedly occurs on the opposite side to the one where the rejection area has been adopted. Thus, the unexpected occurrence of an extreme result on the opposite side to the predicted one, would not lead to the rejection of the null hypothesis. This situation should always be avoided. A two-tailed test prevents this unwanted situation happening.

In general, one-tailed tests are only used if there is a good enough reason for not considering a particular "side" of the extreme outcomes. In the reading test example we wanted to use the outcome of the test to decide if a child could have some form of reading disorder. Since the presence of a reading disorder, assuming that subjects read the text correctly, does not lead to faster than normal reading times, we had good reason to focus on slow reading times to make a diagnosis about the presence of some form of reading disorder; hence, the use of a one-tailed test. In general, one-tailed tests are legitimate if, for example, a reduction in the magnitude of the dependent variable, when the independent variable increases, is either meaningless or simply due to chance. For instance, when studying the size of the children's vocabularies, it would not be sensible to propose that their vocabulary would shrink as they grew up.

On the other hand, if the occurrence of an unexpected extreme result in the wrong direction is possible, even if it is extremely unlikely, we can use a compromise between a one- and a two-tailed test. This compromise is called a *lopsided test* (Abelson, 1995). When using a lopsided test we set the rejection area in the predicted side as being relatively large (e.g., 4.5 per cent or $p \leq 0.045$), and the rejection area in the supposedly wrong side as being relatively small (e.g., 0.5 per cent or $p \leq 0.005$). In this way α is still set at the standard 0.05 level. A lopsided test combines the virtues of one- and two-tailed tests: it is relatively liberal in rejecting the null hypothesis when extreme results occur in the expected direction, while it still allows the rejection of the null hypothesis, in a more conservative way, if extreme outcomes occur in the non-predicted direction.

On pages 70–73 we described the use of the binomial distribution to assess if a new psychotherapeutic approach to treating the phobic fear of flying was better than the standard treatment available. We used a one-tailed test. At that stage we justified the use of a one-tailed test because it was assumed that the new therapy was certainly not worse than the best available treatment. If, however, for some unknown reason the new treatment is less effective than the old one, then we would not be able to reject the null hypothesis. Unexpected results in the wrong tail should never be ignored. In circumstances like the previous one, the use of a lopsided test would be a safeguard against failing to declare that a new treatment may, in fact, be a fiasco and not an improvement over the old one.

Finally, it is important to keep in mind that the selection of the α level and the decision to use either a one-tailed, a two-tailed or a lopsided test needs to be taken *before* inspecting and analysing the collected data. Imagine you decided to use a *one-tailed* test with $\alpha = 0.05$ to assess the effect of a new Internet-based learning programme compared to a more traditional one, where students attend lectures and tutorials conducted by a teacher. Consider this scenario: you predicted that the new programme would be better, but unexpectedly, the empirical results showed the opposite. You then decide, on the basis of the empirical evidence, to reject the null hypothesis. At this stage your α level is no longer 0.05, but becomes 0.075 (0.05 + 0.025, where 0.05 is the original α level, and 0.025 is the probability corresponding to the size of the rejection region in the opposite direction—half of the 0.05 α level that is usually assigned in a one-tailed test). This was the area used to reject the null hypothesis after noticing that the results were in the opposite direction to those expected. This example shows that the use of a lopsided test on an a priori basis eliminates the risk of changing "direction" on an a posteriori basis (i.e., after having inspected the collected data), thus avoiding an unnecessary increase in the probability of committing a Type I error.

Using the normal distribution as an approximation of the binomial distribution

In all the examples presented in Chapter 4, where we made use of the binomial distribution in hypothesis testing, the total number of observations (i.e., n) in each example was relatively small. If the number of observations is large, e.g., 100, it is unlikely that you will find ready-made tables that give you the probability of each number of successes from 0 to n. In this case you may need to use the formula that defines the binomial distribution to calculate all the relevant probabilities, but this would be a very tedious and long job. (The calculation would be faster using a spreadsheet computer package.) However, it is possible to simplify the entire process by making use of the normal distribution as an approximation of the binomial distribution.

You may be surprised that the normal distribution, which is continuous, can be used to approximate the distribution of discrete random variables. It is, however, possible to prove that if a variable is obtained by adding n independent and identically distributed random variables (either discrete or continuous), the distribution of this new variable approaches normality if n is large. We saw in Chapter 4 that a binomially distributed random variable X is obtained by adding n independent random variables, each having a Bernoulli distribution with an identical probability of success. It then follows that, if n is large, the binomial distribution approximates the normal distribution. As a rule of thumb, when both $n \times p > 5$ and $n \times (1 - p) > 5$ the sample can be considered large. Moreover, the approximation to the normal distribution is better when P(Success) is close to 0.5 (because when $p = 0.5$ the binomial distribution is, like the normal distribution, symmetrical around the mean). If a random variable X is binomially distributed with parameters p and n (where p is the probability of success and n is the total number of observations), then its continuous variable counterpart, that we could call Y, is approximately normally distributed with:

$$\mu = n \times p \quad \text{and} \quad \sigma^2 = n \times p \times (1 - p),$$

i.e., Y has the same mean and variance as the binomially distributed random variable X.

Before giving an example of the use of the normal distribution as an approximation of the binomial distribution, you should keep in mind that the binomial distribution describes discrete events, each having its own associated probability. From the normal distribution we can only calculate the probability of the continuous random variable Y lying within a range of values, e.g., $P(a \leq Y \leq b)$. Thus, in order to use the normal distribution to calculate the probability of a single value of the binomial distribution, we need to identify a range of values of the continuous random variable Y that corresponds to a single value of the binomially distributed random variable X. This so-called *continuity correction* is obtained in the following way. If, for instance, we want to calculate the probability of 10 successes, then we need to calculate the probability of the normally distributed variable being in the interval $(10 - 0.5) \leq Y \leq (10 + 0.5)$. In general:

$$P(X = x) = P(x - 0.5 \leq Y \leq x + 0.5)$$

where x is a value of the binomially distributed random variable X having parameters n and p, and Y is a random variable normally distributed with $\mu = n \times p$ and $\sigma^2 = n \times p \times (1 - p)$. (Incidentally, since the normal distribution provides an approximation to the binomial distribution, we should have used the sign "$\approx$" (i.e., approximately equal to) instead of the sign "$=$" in the above equation. However, for simplicity we will use the sign "$=$" instead of $\approx$.)

To calculate the probability of $X = x$, we need to obtain the z scores corresponding to the limit of the interval of Y, i.e., $x + 0.5$ and $x - 0.5$, using this formula:

$$z = \frac{y - np}{\sqrt{np(1 - p)}}.$$

We then use the Z table to calculate the probability associated with the difference in the relevant z scores difference. The smallest and the largest z scores identifying the relevant portions of the standard normal distribution are:

$$z_{\text{small}} = \frac{(x - 0.5) - np}{\sqrt{np(1 - p)}} \quad \text{and} \quad z_{\text{large}} = \frac{(x + 0.5) - np}{\sqrt{np(1 - p)}}.$$

Thus, $P(X = x)$ is given by the probability associated with the interval between the large and the small z scores.

Let us work through an example. Imagine that a fair coin is tossed 100 times. What is the probability that the coin lands as heads 60 times?

The first thing to do is to identify the values $x - 0.5$ and $x + 0.5$. In this case these are:

60 − 0.5 and 60 + 0.5, i.e., 59.5 and 60.5.

The next step is to calculate the z scores associated with the above values. We know that $n = 100$ and $p = 0.5$ (since the coin is fair), thus we obtain:

$$z_{\text{small}} = \frac{(x - 0.5) - np}{\sqrt{np(1 - p)}} = \frac{59.5 - 50}{\sqrt{25}} = \frac{9.5}{5} = 1.9$$

and

$$z_{\text{large}} = \frac{(x + 0.5) - np}{\sqrt{np(1 - p)}} = \frac{60.5 - 50}{\sqrt{25}} = \frac{10.5}{5} = 2.1.$$

Therefore, the answer to the above question is:

$$P(X = 60) = P(1.9 \leq z \leq 2.1)$$

$$= 0.9821 - 0.9713$$

$$= 0.0108 \text{ (to 4 d.p.)}.$$

In Chapter 4 we mainly used the binomial distribution to calculate, under the assumption that the null hypothesis is true, the probability of obtaining at least a given number of successes. Similarly, we can make use of the approximation to the normal distribution to calculate either

$$P(X \geq x), \quad \text{that is, } P(X = x) + P(X = x + 1) + \ldots + P(X = n)$$

or

$$P(X \leq x), \quad \text{that is, } P(X = 0) + P(X = 1) + \ldots + P(X = x),$$

where $P(X = x)$ indicates the probability of obtaining x successes out of a total of n outcomes; $P(X = x + 1)$ indicates the probability of $x + 1$ successes out of a total of n outcomes and so on.

If n is sufficiently large, then:

$$P(X \geq x) = 1 - P\left(-\infty \leq z \leq \frac{x - 0.5 - np}{\sqrt{np(1 - p)}}\right)$$

and

$$P(X \leq x) = P\left(-\infty \leq z \leq \frac{x + 0.5 - np}{\sqrt{np(1 - p)}}\right).$$

Imagine that 72 patients out of 100 are successfully treated with the new treatment for phobia of flying, and, as in Chapter 4, we compare this performance to P(success) = 0.6 for the best available treatment. To decide if the new treatment is better than the old one we need to calculate $P(X \geq 72)$, where X is the random variable "number of patients recovered", $n = 100$ and $p = 0.6$. Applying the relevant formula we obtain:

$$P(X \geq 72) = 1 - P\left(-\infty \leq z \leq \frac{72 - 0.5 - 100 \times 0.6}{\sqrt{100 \times 0.6 \times 0.4}}\right)$$

$$= 1 - P\left(-\infty \leq z \leq \frac{71.5 - 60}{\sqrt{24}}\right)$$

$$= 1 - P(-\infty \leq z \leq 2.35)$$

$$= 1 - 0.9906 = 0.0094.$$

It therefore appears that the new treatment is more effective than the old one. With the old method, the probability of obtaining at least 72 successes out of 100 is so low that the null hypothesis is rejected in favour of the alternative hypothesis: that the new treatment has a better rate of success than the old one. Notice that, if instead of the one-tailed test just conducted we had applied a lopsided test, we would still have rejected the null hypothesis.

The above approach uses a continuity correction. However, the loss of precision may sometimes be relatively small even if the continuity correction is not used. The relevant formulae without continuity correction are:

$$P(X \geq x) = 1 - P\left(-\infty \leq z \leq \frac{x - np}{\sqrt{np(1 - p)}}\right) \quad \text{and}$$

$$P(X \leq x) = P\left(-\infty \leq z \leq \frac{x - np}{\sqrt{np(1 - p)}}\right).$$

Applying the uncorrected approach to the above example we would have obtained:

$$P(X \geq 72) = 1 - P\left(-\infty \leq z \leq \frac{72 - 60}{\sqrt{24}}\right)$$

$$= 1 - P(-\infty \leq z \leq 2.45) = 1 - 0.9928 = 0.0072.$$

Finally, if we want to make use of the standard normal distribution to find the symmetrical interval (i.e., around np) within which 95 per cent of the values of the binomially distributed discrete random variable X lie, then the procedure used is similar to the one described on pages 86–87.

The first thing to consider is that, as we know already, $P(-1.96 \leq z \leq 1.96) = 0.95$. From here we need to work backwards to find the values of X associated with the above z scores. These values are obtained by solving the following equations:

$$-1.96 = \frac{x - 0.5 - np}{\sqrt{np(1 - p)}} \quad \text{thus} \quad x = np - (1.96 \times \sqrt{np(1 - p)}) + 0.5,$$

and

$$1.96 = \frac{x + 0.5 - np}{\sqrt{np(1 - p)}} \quad \text{thus} \quad x = np + (1.96 \times \sqrt{np(1 - p)}) - 0.5,$$

and hence

$$P\{[np - (1.96 \times \sqrt{np(1 - p)}) + 0.5] \leq x \leq [np + (1.96 \times \sqrt{np(1 - p)}) - 0.5]\} = 0.95.$$

Consider again the example of the fair coin. Given that a fair coin is tossed 100 times, we want to find the interval of values within which the coin would be heads with a probability of 0.95. The limits of this symmetrical confidence interval can be obtained by applying the above formula, where $n = 100$ and $p = 0.5$:

$$P\{[100 \times 0.5 - (1.96 \times \sqrt{100 \times 0.5 \times 0.5}) + 0.5] \leq x$$

$$\leq [100 \times 0.5 + (1.96 \times \sqrt{100 \times 0.5 \times 0.5}) - 0.5]\} = 0.95,$$

$$P\{[50 - (1.96 \times 5) + 0.5] \leq x \leq [50 + (1.96 \times 5) - 0.5]\} = 0.95,$$

$$P(40.7 \leq x \leq 59.3) = 0.95.$$

Thus, a fair coin, if tossed 100 times, should land as heads, with a probability of 0.95, between 41 and 59 times (i.e., the smallest integer larger than 40.7 and the largest integer smaller than 59.3).

If the continuity correction had not been applied the interval would have been calculated as follows:

$$P\{[np - (1.96 \times \sqrt{np(1-p)})] \leq x \leq [np + (1.96 \times \sqrt{np(1-p)})]\} = 0.95$$

and hence,

$$P\{[50 - (1.96 \times 5)] \leq x \leq [50 + (1.96 \times 5)]\} = 0.95$$

and

$$P(40.2 \leq x \leq 59.8) = 0.95.$$

The integer limits of this interval are 41 and 59. Both corrected and non-corrected approaches have provided the same outcome.

Chapter 6

The chi-square distribution and the analysis of categorical data

Introduction

The characteristics of the normal distribution and of the standard normal distribution were described in Chapter 5. These are distributions of continuous random variables which can be used in the process of statistical inference. Similarly, in this chapter, a new continuous distribution is described. This is the chi-square (or alternatively chi-squared) distribution. Furthermore, we show how this continuous distribution can be used in the analysis of discrete categorical (or alternatively frequency) data.

First, the general characteristics of the chi-square distribution are presented. Then the Pearson's chi-square test is described. Examples of its application in the assessment of how well a set of observed frequencies matches a set of expected frequencies (i.e., goodness of fit test), and in the analysis of contingency tables are provided.

The chi-square (χ^2) distribution

"Chi" stands for the Greek letter χ and is pronounced as either "key" or "kai". "Square" or, alternatively, "squared", means raised to the power of two, hence the notation χ^2. The chi-square distribution is obtained from the standardised normal distribution in the following way. Suppose we sample a z score from the z distribution, we square it and its value is recorded. The sampling process is performed an infinite number of times, allowing for the possibility that any z score can be sampled again (i.e., independent sampling). If the z^2 scores obtained are then plotted, the resulting distribution is the χ^2 distribution with one degree of freedom (denoted as χ_1^2). Now suppose we independently sample two χ^2 scores from the χ_1^2 distribution and we add their values, as done above in the case of the z scores. This process is performed an infinite number of times, and all the sums obtained are plotted. The resulting distribution is the χ^2 distribution with two degrees of freedom (denoted as χ_2^2). This process can be generalised to the distribution of any sum of k random variables each having the χ_1^2 distribution. The distribution of a sum of k random variables, each with the χ_1^2 distribution, is itself a χ^2 distribution with k degrees of freedom (denoted as χ_k^2). Furthermore, the distribution of the sum of two random variables distributed as χ_a^2 and χ_b^2, has a $\chi_{(a+b)}^2$ distribution. For example if two independent random variables are distributed as χ_3^2 and χ_2^2, then their sum is distributed as χ_5^2.

The term "degrees of freedom", denoted as df, refers to the positive integer parameter that determines the shape of the chi-square distribution (see Figure 6.1). The mean of a chi-square distribution with k degrees of freedom is equal to k and its variance is $2k$.

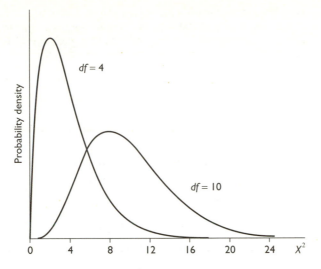

Figure 6.1 Examples of χ^2 distributions.

Table 6.1 The table below gives the critical χ^2 values for each χ^2 distribution, according to the relevant *df*, for significance levels of *p* = 0.05 and *p* = 0.01

df	p = 0.05	p = 0.01
1	3.84	6.63
2	5.99	9.21
3	7.81	11.34
4	9.49	13.28
5	11.07	15.09

Moreover, due to the way in which chi-square distributions are obtained, any χ^2 value cannot be negative (remember that the square of any non-zero number is a positive number, i.e., $- \times - = +$).

As with the normal distribution, the critical values of the chi-square distribution, as a function of the degrees of freedom, are available from tables (see Table 6.1 and the χ^2 table in the Appendix). In contrast to the table of the standardised normal distribution, where most *z* scores and their associated cumulative probabilities are provided, here only the critical χ^2 values that divide the area under each chi-square curve into two parts are reported. In the cases of *p* = 0.05 and *p* = 0.01, 5 per cent and 1 per cent of the total area under the curve is to the right of each of the critical values. The use of this table in statistical inference will be discussed when the Pearson's chi-square test is described in the next section.

The Pearson's chi-square test

Suppose that a coin is tossed 40 times and that 10 heads and 30 tails are observed. We know that if the coin is fair, the probability of obtaining either a head or a tail is identical, i.e., P(Head) = P(Tail) = 0.5. Hence, the expected frequencies of head and

Table 6.2 Observed and expected frequencies for the coin experiment described in pages 101–102. The differences between observed and expected frequencies, their squared values, and the computation of the Pearson's χ^2 test are also reported for each outcome

	Outcomes	
	Head	Tail
Observed frequency (O)	10	30
Expected frequency (E)	20	20
O − E	−10	10
$(O - E)^2$	100	100
$\dfrac{(O - E)^2}{E}$	$\dfrac{100}{20}$	$\dfrac{100}{20}$

$$\chi^2 = \sum_{i=1}^{m} \frac{(O_i - E_i)^2}{E_i} = \frac{100}{20} + \frac{100}{20} = 10 \quad (df = 2 - 1 = 1)$$

tail outcomes are identical (i.e., $40 \times 0.5 = 20$). To decide whether the coin just tossed was fair or not, we need to obtain an index that compares the number of observed and expected frequencies for the two outcomes. The value of this index indicates whether the observed frequencies are too discrepant from those expected. If this is the case, then the coin can be declared biased. In Chapter 4 we saw how to use the binomial distribution to handle this type of problem. Here, however, we provide a more general approach that can also be applied to events which have more than two possible outcomes, or to events that can be sub-classified into two or more categories.

Table 6.2 reproduces the data on the coin experiment. Using the data reproduced in the table it is possible to provide an index of the discrepancy between observed and expected frequencies. This index is called Pearson's χ^2 statistic and it is defined as:

$$\chi^2 = \sum_{i=1}^{m} \frac{(O_i - E_i)^2}{E_i}$$

where O_i is the observed frequency of each outcome, E_i is the expected frequency of each outcome, and m is the total number of the outcomes being compared.

Under the assumption that the null hypothesis is true, then the Pearson's χ^2 statistic is distributed approximately as the χ^2 distribution with $df = m - 1$. The null hypothesis states that the observed frequencies are equal to the expected frequencies, which are themselves given by the product of the sample size and the expected probability of occurrence of each outcome. To decide if there is sufficient evidence to reject H_0, the magnitude of the obtained Pearson's χ^2 statistic needs to be compared with the critical value of the relevant χ^2 distribution. If the obtained Pearson's χ^2 statistic is larger than the critical value of the relevant χ^2 distribution, then H_0 is rejected.

Let us apply the Pearson's χ^2 test to the coin example. The *first* thing to do is to obtain the value of the Pearson's χ^2 statistic. This is given by:

$$\chi^2 = \sum \frac{(O - E)^2}{E} = \frac{(10 - 20)^2}{20} + \frac{(30 - 20)^2}{20} = \frac{100}{20} + \frac{100}{20} = 10.$$

The *second* step requires the comparison of the obtained χ^2 statistic against the critical value of the relevant χ^2 distribution. This is the χ^2 distribution with $df = m - 1 = 2 - 1 = 1$, i.e., χ_1^2, and the critical value, using an α level of 0.05, is 3.84 (see Table 6.1). Since the value of the obtained χ^2 statistic, i.e., 10, is larger than the critical value of the χ_1^2 distribution, i.e., 3.84, the null hypothesis is rejected. This stated that the expected frequencies of the two outcomes were identical, or alternatively that P(Head) = P(Tail) = 0.5. However, on the basis of the observed data, H_0 is rejected in favour of the alternative hypothesis, i.e., that the frequencies of the two outcomes are not identical, or alternatively that P(Head) ≠ P(Tail). Hence, the coin can be considered biased.

Before continuing with the presentation of Pearson's χ^2 test, it is important to make clear that this test is not the same as the χ^2 distribution. Remember that, assuming H_0 is true, the Pearson's χ^2 statistic is approximately distributed as the χ^2 distribution with $df = m - 1$. This is the reason for the use of the χ^2 distribution when the Pearson's χ^2 test is employed in statistical inference. Other statistical tests, for example, the Friedman's test (see Siegel & Castellan, 1988), also make use of the χ^2 distribution in the process of statistical inference.

The Pearson's χ^2 goodness of fit test

In the previous section our example used the Pearson's χ^2 test to assess whether or not there was a good fit between a set of observed and expected frequencies. In this section we generalise the use of this test to situations where the phenomenon studied has more than two outcomes.

Consider a fictitious study where a sample of 120 university lecturers are asked to indicate what they think is the most effective way to assess undergraduate students. Each lecturer has to select only one of these 3 types of assessment:

a) only by end-of-year exams;
b) only by course-work submitted during the year;
c) by a mixture of course-work and end-of-year exams.

The results of this study are shown in Table 6.3. Our aim is to assess whether there is a preferred method of assessment. The null hypothesis states that each of the three methods of assessment has the same probability of being selected, i.e., $\frac{1}{3}$. Thus, the expected frequency of each outcome is given by:

$$120 \times \frac{1}{3} = 40.$$

To calculate the Pearson's χ^2 statistic we need to obtain the differences between observed and expected frequencies and their squared values. These are given in Table 6.3. Applying the appropriate formula we obtain:

$$\chi^2 = \sum \frac{(O - E)^2}{E} = \frac{(35 - 40)^2}{40} + \frac{(23 - 40)^2}{40} + \frac{(62 - 40)^2}{40}$$

$$= \frac{25}{40} + \frac{289}{40} + \frac{484}{40} = 19.95.$$

Table 6.3 Observed and expected frequencies for the study of the most effective way to assess undergraduate students described on pages 103–104. The differences between observed and expected frequencies, their squared values, and their squared values divided by the expected frequency are also reported for each outcome

Outcome	Exams	Course-work	Exams and Course-work	Totals
Observed frequency (O)	35	23	62	120
Expected frequency (E)	40	40	40	120
$O - E$	−5	−17	22	0
$(O - E)^2$	25	289	484	798
$\dfrac{(O - E)^2}{E}$	0.625	7.225	12.100	19.95

(i.e., χ^2 statistic)

We now need to compare the obtained χ^2 statistic against the critical value of the relevant χ^2 distribution with $df = 2$, where $df = m - 1 = 3 - 1 = 2$. From an inspection of the χ^2 table it appears that the critical value, using an α level of 0.05, is 5.99. Since the obtained value of the χ^2 statistic, i.e., 19.95, is larger than the critical value of the χ^2_2 distribution, the null hypothesis is rejected. The null hypothesis stated that the expected frequencies of the three outcomes were identical, or alternatively that P(Exams only) = P(Course-work only) = P(Exams and Course-work). However, on the basis of the observed data, H_0 is rejected in favour of the alternative hypothesis, i.e., that the frequencies of the three outcomes are not identical. Inspecting the observed and expected frequencies of the various outcomes, it then seems that most lecturers are not happy about an assessment that is based only on course-work, and the preferred option seems to be a combination of exams and course-work. This pattern is also evident when inspecting the (O − E) and the $\dfrac{(O - E)^2}{E}$ values. These last values provide an indication of the contribution of the individual outcomes to the size of the obtained χ^2 statistic. For example, the "Exams and Course-work" type of assessment contributed to about 61 per cent of the size of the obtained χ^2 statistic (i.e., $\dfrac{12.1}{19.95}$).

Let us consider another example of the use of Pearson's χ^2 test. In this case the Pearson's χ^2 test is used in assessing how well the distribution of a set of data fits a prescribed distribution. Suppose that a random sample of 318 children performed a test intended to evaluate their reading skills (R) at the end of their first year at school. Assuming that it is known that the distribution of the R scores in the population of children who completed their first year at school is normal with $\mu = 65$ and $\sigma = 15$, we want to know if the distribution of the R scores in the sample of tested children is normal. In other words, we want to assess how close the distribution of the R scores of our sample is to a normal distribution having the mean and the standard deviation of the child population.

The first thing to do is to select the relevant outcomes (or classes). Assuming that the R scores can range from 0 to 125, we need to select a series of classes of R scores and count how many children's scores fall within each class. Knowing that the mean and standard deviation of the R scores in the population are 65 and 15, respectively, we could conveniently select classes with a range of 15 points (i.e., of the size of one standard deviation unit; 1 SD). Moreover, since in a standard normal distribution the cumulative distribution up to −2 SD is less than 2.5 per cent of the total area under the normal curve, then the first class could include all the children who scored less than 2 SD below the population mean; i.e., $65 − (2 \times 15) = 35$. Repeatedly applying this process we select 6 outcomes, and the number of children's scores falling within each class is recorded (see Table 6.4). These data are then the observed frequencies for each outcome.

The next step is to obtain the expected probabilities of each outcome. In the previous example the null hypothesis assumed equal probabilities among the different outcomes, but this is not the case in the current example. In the present case the expected probabilities are calculated in the following way. First, we selected our outcomes so that the scores included in the first outcome were those less than 2 standard deviations below the population mean; the scores included in the second outcome were between −2 SD and −1 SD from the population mean; the scores included in the third outcome were between −1 SD and the population mean, with the remaining 3 outcomes being constructed in the same way but with scores being larger than the population mean. Now, we can make use of the standard normal distribution to calculate the probability associated with each outcome (see Chapter 5). These are reported in Table 6.4 (for example, the cumulative probability of the standard normal distribution from $−\infty$ to $−2z$ is 0.023; the cumulative probability of the standard normal distribution from $−2z$ to $−1z$ is 0.136; remember that one z-score unit corresponds to one standard deviation unit). Having calculated the expected probabilities, the expected frequency for each outcome is then obtained by multiplying the total number of sampled observation, i.e., 318, by the relevant expected probability. For example, the expected number of children scoring less than 35 in the sample is: $318 \times 0.023 = 7.314$ to 3 d.p. (notice that the expected frequencies, unlike the observed frequencies, are not necessarily whole numbers).

The next steps to calculate the Pearson's χ^2 statistic are the same as previously described and they are reported in Table 6.4. The obtained χ^2 statistic, i.e., 8.641, is smaller than the critical χ^2 value, at a 5 per cent significance level, of the χ^2_5 distribution, i.e., 11.07 (df = number of outcomes −1, or $6 − 1 = 5$). Therefore, we do not have sufficient evidence to reject the hypothesis that the reading scores in our sample are normally distributed, hence we retain the hypothesis that our sample data are normally distributed.

Here is a further example of the use of the Pearson's χ^2 test in assessing the goodness of fit to a prescribed distribution. Suppose the number of male children is counted in 200 families each having five children. It is expected that the probability that each child is either male or female is 0.5. Thus the distribution of the number of male children out of 5 children is binomial with $n = 200$ and $p = 0.5$, hence it is possible to calculate the expected probability of each outcome using the binomial distribution. These expected probabilities and the expected frequencies for each outcome are provided in Table 6.5. As can be seen from this table, the obtained Pearson's χ^2 statistic is 4.464. This χ^2 statistic is distributed as χ^2 with $df = 5$ (i.e., number of outcomes minus one). Since the critical value of this distribution, at an α level of 0.05 is 11.07, we cannot reject the null hypothesis stating that our sampled observations are binomially distributed, hence we retain the hypothesis that our data are binomially distributed.

Table 6.4 Observed and expected frequencies of the reading scores (R) in a sample of 318 children at the end of their first year of school. The steps involved in the computation of the Pearson's χ^2 statistic are also provided

Outcomes	$R < 35$ $R < -2\sigma$	$35 \leq R < 50$ $-2\sigma \leq R < -\sigma$	$50 \leq R < 65$ $-\sigma \leq R < \mu$	$65 \leq R < 80$ $\mu \leq R < \sigma$	$80 \leq R < 95$ $\sigma \leq R < 2\sigma$	$95 \leq R$ $2\sigma \leq R$	Totals
Observed frequency (O)	3	40	95	116	54	10	318
Expected probability	0.023	0.136	0.341	0.341	0.136	0.023	1.0
Expected frequency (E)	7.314	43.248	108.438	108.438	43.248	7.314	318
O – E	–4.314	–3.248	–13.438	7.562	10.752	2.686	0.0
$(O - E)^2$	18.611	10.550	180.580	57.184	115.606	7.215	389.744
$\dfrac{(O - E)^2}{E}$	2.545	0.244	1.665	0.527	2.673	0.986	8.641

(i.e., χ^2 statistic $df = 5$)

Table 6.5 Observed and expected frequencies of the number of male children in a sample of 200 families with 5 children each. The expected probability and the expected frequency are reported for each outcome, i.e., the number of male children out of five. Each expected frequency is obtained by multiplying the expected probability of each outcome by the total number of observations (i.e., 200). The remaining steps involved in the computation of the Pearson's χ^2 statistic are also provided

Number of males	0	1	2	3	4	5	Totals
Observed frequency (O)	7	28	63	58	33	11	200
Expected probability	0.0313	0.156	0.313	0.313	0.156	0.0313	1.0
Expected frequency (E)	6.250	31.250	62.500	62.500	31.250	6.250	200
$O - E$	0.750	−3.250	0.500	−4.500	1.750	4.750	0.0
$(O - E)^2$	0.563	10.563	0.250	20.250	3.063	22.563	57.25
$\dfrac{(O - E)^2}{E}$	0.090	0.338	0.004	0.324	0.098	3.610	4.464

(i.e., χ^2 statistic *df* = 5)

Further on the goodness of fit test

In general the Pearson's χ^2 test can be used to assess if the distribution of a set of data has a good fit to any specific distribution (e.g., binomial, normal, uniform). In the coin's fairness and in the students' assessment examples, the observed data were compared to a uniform distribution (i.e., where each outcome has the same probability). In the sex of a child example, the prescribed distribution was binomial with $p = 0.5$ and $n = 200$, while in the reading test example the prescribed distribution was normal with $\mu = 65$ and $\sigma = 15$. However, it is not always possible to know the population parameters of the prescribed distribution. In some cases these may need to be estimated from the sample data. What is the effect of this estimation on the computation of the Pearson's χ^2 test? The answer is none. However some changes need to be made in the selection of the relevant χ^2 distribution to be used in the process of hypothesis testing.

Suppose, for example, that with respect to the reading study described in the previous section, we do not know the population's mean and standard deviation, and that these need to be estimated from the sampled data. Let us assume, for simplicity, that the sample mean is 65 and *s*, the standard deviation of the population estimated using the sample data, is 15. If we want to see if the distribution of the sample data is normal, with these population parameters that have been estimated from the sample, the computation of the Pearson's χ^2 statistic is identical to that described in the previous section; thus, its value is 8.668. However this value needs to be evaluated using the χ^2 distribution with *df* = 3, and not 5 as in the previous example. The reason is that, in this example, the null hypothesis stated that the prescribed distribution is normal, but the characteristics of this distribution, i.e., its parameters—mean and standard deviation —were conveniently selected by the experimenter using the sample data. Therefore, due to this deliberate selection of the parameters of the normal distribution, some constraints are imposed on the expected frequencies. This process leads to a biased χ^2 statistic. Thus, to offset this bias, the number of degrees of freedom is reduced according to the number of the estimated parameters. Since we estimated both the mean and the standard deviation from sample data, then $df = 6 - 1 - 2 = 3$. The critical value of the χ_3^2 distribution at a 0.5 significance level is 7.82. Since the obtained χ^2 statistic is larger than the critical value of the χ^2 distribution, the null hypothesis is rejected. Hence it appears that the sample data are not normally distributed (according to the parameters we imposed). Notice that estimating parameters led to a different statistical conclusion to the one obtained without estimating parameters. In that case the population parameters were known and the obtained χ^2 statistic was not biased.

Assumptions underlying the use of Pearson's χ^2 test

There are some assumptions that need to be fulfilled for the χ^2 distribution to be the appropriate distribution of the Pearson's χ^2 statistic. *First*, observations need to be independent of one another. This means that the outcome of one observation does not affect the outcome of any other observations. It follows from this assumption that each subject can only contribute to one observation. For example, in the coin fairness example, each flip of the coin was independent of any of the other flips. Suppose, however, that 20 ice skaters are observed in three different sessions and in each case their skating performance is rated as either "poor" or "good". When all 60 sessions are rated, it appears that in 45 cases the rating was "good" and in 15 the rating was "poor". This looks like a case where the Pearson's χ^2 test could be applied to assess if there was a difference between the use of the two types of rating. However, its application in this case would be wrong, since each skater contributed to more than one observation. As a rule the number of observations needs to be identical to the number of subjects tested (provided the performances are not somehow related across subjects).

A *second* assumption refers to the size of the expected frequencies. These should not be too small. Unfortunately, there is not a unanimous consensus among statisticians on what size could be considered too small. A useful approach to the minimum size of the expected frequencies has been proposed by Cochran (1952), who suggests that all expected frequencies need to be greater than 1, and no more than 20 per cent of the expected frequencies should be less than 5. In general, with small expected frequencies, the power of Pearson's χ^2 test tends to be low, making it harder to reject a false null hypothesis.

If the expected frequencies of some outcomes do turn out to be too low, it is possible to avoid this problem by combining adjacent outcomes. In order to avoid biasing the results of the χ^2 test, this amalgamation should be performed without considering the observed frequencies of the various outcomes. Suppose we replicate the previous reading test study, and 150 children complete the test at the end of their first year of school. We expect that the distribution of this sample should be normal and we know that the population mean and standard deviation are 65 and 15, respectively. Thus, we could use the chi-square test to assess if the distribution of the R scores in this new sample is normal. Contrary to the earlier example, in this case the expected frequency of some outcomes is below 5 (see Table 6.6). The expected probabilities and the expected frequencies for each outcome are provided in Table 6.6a. It should be noticed that the expected frequencies of the two most extreme outcomes are both less than 5. Since more than 20 per cent of the outcomes have expected frequencies less than 5, some outcomes need to be combined. Thus each of the outcomes with the expected frequency of less than 5 have been combined in Table 6.6b with the adjacent outcome.

Table 6.6 Observed and expected frequencies of the reading scores (R) in a sample of 150 children at the end of their first year of school. In part (a), the expected probability and the expected frequency are reported for each outcome, i.e., number of children performing within each class of R scores. Each expected frequency is obtained by multiplying the expected probability of each outcome by the total number of observations (i.e., 150). In part (b), the two pairs of most extreme outcomes are combined. The steps involved in the computation of the Pearson's χ^2 statistic are also provided

(a)

Outcomes	R < 35 R < -2σ	35 ≤ R < 50 -2σ ≤ R < -σ	50 ≤ R < 65 -σ ≤ R < μ	65 ≤ R < 80 μ ≤ R < σ	80 ≤ R < 95 σ ≤ R < 2σ	95 ≤ R 2σ ≤ R	Totals
Expected probability	0.023	0.136	0.341	0.341	0.136	0.023	1
Expected frequency	3.413	20.386	51.202	51.202	20.386	3.413	150

(b)

Outcomes	R < 50 R < -σ	50 ≤ R < 65 -σ ≤ R < μ	65 ≤ R < 80 μ ≤ R < σ	80 ≤ R σ ≤ R	Totals
Observed frequency (O)	19	53	48	30	150
Expected probability	0.159	0.341	0.341	0.159	1.0
Expected frequency (E)	23.798	51.202	51.202	23.798	150
O − E	−4.798	1.798	−3.202	6.202	0.0
$(O - E)^2$	23.024	3.234	10.251	38.461	74.970
$\dfrac{(O - E)^2}{E}$	0.967	0.063	0.200	1.616	2.847 (i.e., χ^2 statistic)

As can be seen from this last table, the obtained Pearson's χ^2 statistic is 2.847. This χ^2 statistic is distributed as χ^2 with $df = 3$, i.e., 4 outcomes minus 1, since two of the previous outcomes have now been removed. Since, at an α level of 0.05, the critical value of this distribution is 7.81, we cannot reject the null hypothesis that our sampled observations are normally distributed. Notice that no correction in the number of degrees of freedom needs to be applied since we know the population parameters for the distribution of reading scores.

Pearson's χ^2 test and the analysis of 2×2 contingency tables

An example of a contingency table was presented on pages 53–54 when discussing the issue of conditional probabilities. In that context we considered a hypothetical study to assess whether, among women, the two variables "opinion about abortion" (i.e., against vs pro) and "religious belief" (i.e., religious vs non-religious) were independent (i.e., H_0), or associated (i.e., H_1). Table 6.7 provides the observed frequencies for the four cells of the contingency table. As stated on pages 53–54, a way to check if opinion about abortion and religious belief are independent is to compare the unconditional probability of just being against abortion with the conditional probability of being against abortion given that a woman is religious. If P(Against abortion) = P(Against abortion | Religious), then the view held on abortion is independent of religious belief (or equivalently, if P(Religious) = P(Religious | Against abortion)). On the other hand if P(Against abortion) ≠ P(Against abortion | Religious), then opinion about abortion and religious belief are not independent variables.

The simple or unconditional probability of being against abortion is found by taking the ratio of the total number of women against abortion divided by the total number of interviewed women, that is:

$$P(\text{Against abortion}) = \frac{470}{1000} = 0.47.$$

The conditional probability of being against abortion, given that a person is religious, is calculated by taking the number of religious women who are against abortion and dividing by the total number of religious women:

$$P(\text{Against abortion} \mid \text{Religious}) = \frac{280}{400} = 0.70.$$

Table 6.7 Contingency table providing a summary of the opinion about abortion (pro vs against) in a sample of 1000 women (either religious or non-religious)

Religious belief	Opinion about abortion		
	Against abortion	Pro abortion	Totals
Religious	280	120	400
Non-religious	190	410	600
Totals	470	530	1000

Table 6.8 Contingency table providing a summary of the opinion about abortion in a sample of 1000 women (either religious or non-religious). Expected frequencies and the steps involved in the computation of the Pearson's χ^2 statistic are also provided

	Against abortion	Pro abortion
Religious	Observed 280 Expected (188) O − E = 92 $(O − E)^2$ = 8464 $\dfrac{(O − E)^2}{E}$ = 45.021	Observed 120 Expected (212) O − E = −92 $(O − E)^2$ = 8464 $\dfrac{(O − E)^2}{E}$ = 39.925
Non-religious	Observed 190 Expected (282) O − E = −92 $(O − E)^2$ = 8464 $\dfrac{(O − E)^2}{E}$ = 30.014	Observed 410 Expected (318) O − E = 92 $(O − E)^2$ = 8464 $\dfrac{(O − E)^2}{E}$ = 26.616

$$\chi^2 = \sum \frac{(O − E)^2}{E} = 141.576$$

P(Against abortion) = 0.47 and P(Against abortion | Religious) = 0.7 are numerically different. However, to decide whether religious belief and opinion about abortion are independent or not, we need to assess whether the obtained probabilities just differ by chance. It is important to keep in mind that in this example we are working with sample data. So, although religious belief and opinion about abortion could be independent in the female population, it might have happened, by chance, that in our sample there was a discrepancy between P(Against abortion) and P(Against abortion | Religious). Therefore, some inferential statistics technique is required to test if the obtained difference in the simple and conditional probabilities is normally observed in samples that are drawn from a population where P(Against abortion) = P(Against abortion | Religious), i.e., religious belief and opinion about abortion are independent. If the observed difference between simple and conditional probabilities is too large, given the assumption than in the population P(Against abortion) = P(Against abortion | Religious), then this null hypothesis is rejected, and religious belief and opinion about abortion are declared not to be independent. The Pearson's χ^2 test is used for this purpose.

In order to apply Pearson's χ^2 test to the above example we need to calculate the expected frequencies of each of the four cells of the 2×2 contingency table. These are calculated, as seen earlier, by multiplying the total number of observations by the expected probability of each of the 4 cells in the contingency tables. Assuming that the null hypothesis is true, i.e., that religious belief and opinion about abortion are independent, then the expected probability associated with each cell of the contingency table is obtained by applying the multiplication rule of probability, that is:

P(A and B) = P($A \cap B$) = P(A) × P(B).

Therefore we obtain:

P(Religious and Against abortion) = P(Religious) × P(Against abortion)

$$= \frac{400}{1000} \times \frac{470}{1000} = 0.4 \times 0.47 = 0.188,$$

where 0.4 is obtained by dividing the marginal total number of religious women (400) by the total number of women sampled (1000); and where 0.47 is obtained by dividing the marginal total number of women against abortion (470) by the total number of women sampled (1000).

Using the same approach we obtain:

P(Religious and Pro abortion) = P(Religious) × P(Pro abortion)

$$= \frac{400}{1000} \times \frac{530}{1000} = 0.4 \times 0.53 = 0.212$$

P(Non-religious and Against abortion) = P(Non-religious) × P(Against abortion)

$$= \frac{600}{1000} \times \frac{470}{1000} = 0.6 \times 0.47 = 0.282$$

P(Non-religious and Pro abortion) = P(Non-religious) × P(Pro abortion)

$$= \frac{600}{1000} \times \frac{530}{1000} = 0.6 \times 0.53 = 0.318.$$

Having calculated the expected probability of each of the cells in the contingency table, the expected frequencies are easily obtained by multiplying each probability by the total number of sampled observations, i.e., 1000. Table 6.8 provides the observed and expected frequency of each cell in the contingency table. In addition, the relevant quantities involved in the computation of the Pearson's χ^2 statistic are also provided. Thus the Pearson's chi-square for the data in Table 6.7 is:

$$\chi^2 = \sum \frac{(O - E)^2}{E} = \frac{(280 - 188)^2}{188} + \frac{(120 - 212)^2}{212} + \frac{(190 - 282)^2}{282} + \frac{(410 - 318)^2}{318}$$

$$= 45.021 + 39.925 + 30.014 + 26.616 = 141.576.$$

The Pearson's χ^2 statistic obtained is compared with the critical value of the appropriate χ^2 distribution, i.e., $df = 1$ (the way to calculate the appropriate number of degrees of freedom for contingency tables will be given in the next section). Since the critical value for this distribution at a significance level of $p = 0.05$ is 3.84, the null hypothesis is rejected, and it is concluded that religious belief and opinion about abortion are associated. Inspecting the observed and expected frequencies it appears that religious women tend to be mostly against abortion while most of the non-religious women are not.

Finally, we would like to draw attention to the fact that while the chi-square distribution is continuous, categorical variables are discrete. Therefore, various corrections for continuity have been suggested to improve the approximation of the Pearson's χ^2 statistic to the relevant χ^2 distribution. The most well known is that suggested by Yates (1934) for 2×2 contingency tables. This consists of subtracting 0.5 from each difference between observed and expected frequencies before calculating the Pearson's χ^2 statistic. While Yates' correction is often used, it is overly conservative (i.e., it does reduce the probability of rejecting a false null hypothesis), when either the column marginal totals or the row marginal totals or both are random (i.e., non-fixed). Since constant marginal totals across repeated studies rarely exist in the behavioural sciences, several statisticians have argued against the use of Yates' correction. To appreciate what it is meant by random marginal totals, imagine that the religious belief and opinion about abortion study is repeated with another sample of 1000 women. It will be unlikely that the new marginal totals will be the same as those in Table 6.7. This basically means that marginal totals are not fixed across replications of a study (for further details see Howell, 1997).

Further on the degrees of freedom and the calculation of the expected frequencies for any contingency table

In describing the application of the Pearson's χ^2 test to the 2×2 contingency table in the previous section, we said that the obtained χ^2 statistic had to be evaluated using the χ^2 distribution with $df = 1$, but no explanation was provided as to why there was only one degree of freedom, given that in the example there were four different cells. As a rule, for any contingency table having r rows and c columns, the number of degrees of freedom is:

$$df = (r - 1) \times (c - 1).$$

In the case of a 2×2 contingency table $df = (2 - 1) \times (2 - 1) = 1$. While, for a 3 rows by 4 columns contingency table we have $df = (3 - 1) \times (4 - 1) = 6$.

Why then does the above formula give us the correct number of degrees of freedom? Consider the calculation of the expected frequencies in the case of the 2×2 contingency table presented in Tables 6.7 and 6.8. For any type of contingency table, the sum of the expected frequencies in each row and in each column is always equal to the observed marginal totals (for example the sum of the expected frequencies of the cells in the first row of Table 6.8 is $188 + 212 = 400$). Because of this, when the estimated frequency has been obtained for the first cell of the 2×2 contingency table, the remaining expected frequencies are fixed because we have to reproduce the marginal observed frequencies. Thus, when one frequency is estimated, we are not free to choose the remaining expected frequencies, hence we have only one degree of freedom. A similar situation applies to larger contingency tables. In these cases, however, due to the sizes of the tables, the degrees of freedom are more. The application of the above formula will give the correct number of degrees of freedom for any type of bi-dimensional contingency table.

In the computation of the expected frequencies given in the previous section we first calculated the expected probability under the assumption that the factors under study (i.e., religious belief and opinion about abortion) were independent, and then we multiplied each expected probability by the total number of observations to obtain the relevant expected frequencies. There is, however, a short cut to obtain the expected frequencies. This is given by multiplying, for each cell, the relevant row and column marginal totals, and then dividing this product by the total number of observations, that is:

$$\frac{\text{"Row marginal total"} \times \text{"Column marginal total"}}{\text{"Total number of observations"}}$$

Take for example the cell of religious women against abortion. The expected frequency for this cell is given by multiplying the number of religious women by the number of women against abortion and then dividing this product by 1000 (i.e., the total number of observations); thus, the expected number of religious women against abortion is:

$$\frac{400 \times 470}{1000} = 188.$$

Notice that the relevant expected probability of the same cell was: $\frac{400 \times 470}{1000 \times 1000}$, thus the short cut method to obtain the expected frequency corresponds to the method used to calculate the expected probabilities (the only difference being that, for the denominator, we do not take the squared value of the total number of observations). This method to calculate cells' expected frequencies applies to contingency tables of any size.

The analysis of R × C contingency tables

The procedure used to analyse 2 × 2 contingency tables can easily be generalised to larger contingency tables having any R number of rows and any C number of columns. Consider a study to assess the effect of the perceived age of children on bullying. A sample of 131 12-year-old male children were interviewed and asked if they had been bullied in the past month, either more than once a week, once a week, or less once a week, by older children attending their same school. The sample of children was divided into three groups according to their perceived age: those who looked older than their age, those who looked their age, and those who looked younger than their age. The result of the study is summarised in a 3 × 3 contingency table (see Table 6.9a). The null hypothesis of this study states that there is no association between physical appearance and bullying attacks. The calculation of the Pearson's χ^2 statistic is performed as usual:

$$\chi^2 = \frac{(3 - 9.04)^2}{9.04} + \frac{(4 - 7.34)^2}{7.34} + \ldots + \frac{(3 - 16.72)^2}{16.72} = 46.93.$$

The relevant χ^2 distribution to be used is χ^2_4 (i.e., $df = (r - 1) \times (c - 1) = (3 - 1) \times (3 - 1) = 4$). Since the critical value for this distribution at a significance level of $p = 0.05$ is 9.49, the null hypothesis is rejected, and it is concluded that there is a relationship between physical appearance and bullying attacks. By inspecting the value

Table 6.9 Contingency table providing a summary of the episodes of bullying suffered by 12-year-old children who either look older than their age, same as, or younger than their age. Observed frequencies are in italic, expected frequencies (to 2 d.p.) in roman. Section (b) of the table provides the $\frac{(O - E)^2}{E}$ quantities for each cell, and the obtained Pearson's χ^2 test

(a)

	More than once a week	Once a week	Less than once a week	Totals
Look older than their age	3 9.04	4 7.34	30 20.62	37
Look as old as their age	9 15.63	15 12.7	40 35.66	64
Look younger than their age	20 7.33	7 5.95	3 16.72	30
Totals	32	26	73	131

(b)

	More than once a week	Once a week	Less than once a week
Look older than their age	4.0	1.5	4.3
Look as old as their age	2.8	0.4	0.5
Look younger than their age	21.9	0.2	11.3

$$\chi^2 = \sum \frac{(O - E)^2}{E} = 46.93 \quad df = (3 - 1) \times (3 - 1) = 4$$

of the $\frac{(O - E)^2}{E}$ quantities for each cell of the contingency table (see Table 6.9b), i.e., those cells that mostly contribute to the size of the obtained χ^2 statistic, it appears that the children who look younger than their age are usually bullied more than once a week, and rarely less than once a week. Moreover it appears that children who look older than their age are those who are the least bullied in the sample. Summarising the results of the study, it appears that children who look younger than their age are those who tend to be the most likely victims of bullying perpetrated by older school colleagues.

One- and two-tailed tests

On pages 93–95 we wrote that when either the normal or the binomial distributions are used in the process of hypothesis testing, it is possible to conduct either a one-tailed or a two-tailed test (remember however that the default approach employs a two-tailed test, alternatively called a non-directional test). However, in the case of the Pearson's χ^2 test, this test is always non-directional.

Consider for example the use made of the Pearson's χ^2 test in deciding if a coin was fair or not (pages 101–102 above). In that case, the null hypothesis about the fairness of the coin could have been rejected either if too many tails or too few tails had occurred, since both types of outcome would have produced a large χ^2 statistic. Thus large values of the χ^2 statistic could have been obtained either because one outcome rarely occurred or because it was very frequent. Thus the application of the χ_1^2 distribution in the decision process about the fairness of the coin was compatible with a non-directional (or two-tailed) inferential approach. More so, the use of the χ^2 distribution provides a non-directional approach in the process of statistical inference associated with the use of Pearson's χ^2 test.

How to measure the strength of the association between variables in a contingency table

As we saw in the previous sections, when data are in the form of a contingency table, the null hypothesis at the basis of the process of statistical inference states that the two investigated variables are independent. Hence, if the Pearson's χ^2 statistic is large enough, the null hypothesis is rejected and the variables are considered to be associated. However, the χ^2 statistic does not tell us how strong the association is between the variables, but only indicates that they may not be independent. Therefore it would be useful to have a measure of the strength of the association between two variables.

Before describing how to measure the strength of the association between variables in a contingency table, we will use an example to illustrate why the magnitude of the χ^2 statistic does not inform us about the strength of the association between two variables. Consider the following fictitious experiments conducted by a health psychology researcher on the relationship between exercise and weight loss. In this research every participant has the same dietary regime, but the participants in the experimental conditions are also asked to perform a series of prescribed aerobic activities. In the first experiment 100 men were randomly allocated to each of the two groups (i.e., Exercise + Diet vs Diet only). Participants in the Exercise + Diet condition performed 30 minutes of aerobic exercise every day. Participants' weight was taken at the beginning of the training regime and a week after the 6-week treatment period ended. The number of people who lost weight in each group was recorded and the data entered in the 2×2 contingency table shown in Table 6.10a. The Pearson's χ^2 statistic for these data is 20.11. Since the critical value for the χ^2 distribution with $df = 1$ at a significance level of $p = 0.05$ is 3.84, the null hypothesis is rejected, and it is concluded that there is a positive relationship between exercising and weight reduction (i.e., increasing the amount of exercise from none to some is associated with more weight loss).

In a second experiment the same variables were studied. However, participants in the Exercise + Diet group were only asked to perform 15 minutes of aerobic exercise 3 days a week. Moreover, 1000 men were randomly allocated to each group, instead of 100 men as in the previous study. The results of this second study are shown in Table 6.10b. The Pearson's χ^2 statistic for these data is 20. Since the critical value for the χ^2 distribution with $df = 1$, at a significance level of $p = 0.05$, is 3.84, the null

Table 6.10 Contingency tables providing a summary of the relationship between exercising and weight loss in a sample of 200 men exercising 30 minutes a day (a), and in a sample of 2000 men exercising 15 minutes 3 times per week (b)

(a)

	Weight reduced	No weight loss	Totals
Exercise + Diet	76	24	100
Diet only	45	55	100
Totals	121	79	200

$$\chi^2 = \sum \frac{(O - E)^2}{E} = 20.11 \quad \phi = \sqrt{\frac{\chi^2}{N}} = \sqrt{\frac{20.11}{200}} = 0.317$$

(b)

	Weight reduced	No weight loss	Totals
Exercise + Diet	550	450	1000
Diet only	450	550	1000
Totals	1000	1000	2000

$$\chi^2 = \sum \frac{(O - E)^2}{E} = 20 \quad \phi = \sqrt{\frac{\chi^2}{N}} = \sqrt{\frac{20}{2000}} = 0.1$$

hypothesis is rejected, and, as in the previous study, it is concluded that there is a positive relationship between exercising and weight reduction.

The χ^2 statistics obtained in the two studies are almost identical. Although the null hypothesis was rejected in both cases, it seems that the relationship between exercising and weight loss was stronger in the first rather than the second study. In the first study 76 of the 100 men (i.e., 76 per cent) who exercised and dieted reduced their weight, while only 45 per cent of the men who dieted only lost weight. Thus men in the Exercise + Diet condition were 1.69 times more likely to lose weight than those in the Diet only condition (1.69 is obtained as 0.76/0.45). In the second study only 55 per cent of the 1000 men who exercised and dieted reduced their weight, while 45 per cent of the men who dieted only lost weight. Thus men in the Exercise + Diet condition were 1.22 times more likely to lose weight than those in the Diet only condition (1.22 is obtained as 0.55/0.45). Thus, despite the fact that the Pearson's χ^2 statistics obtained in the two studies are almost identical, the exercise regime in the first study seemed more effective in leading to a weight reduction than the exercise regime in the second study (i.e., in the first study men who exercised were 1.69 times more likely to lose weight than those in the Diet only condition, while men who exercised in the second experiment were only 1.22 times more likely to lose weight than those in the Diet only condition).

The above example demonstrates that in the analysis of contingency tables, while the magnitude of the χ^2 statistic informs us about the presence of a relationship between two variables, this statistic does not provide an index of the strength of the association between variables. In the case of *2 × 2 contingency tables* the most common index of the strength of the association between two variables is called phi (ϕ). This is calculated as:

$$\phi = \sqrt{\frac{\chi^2}{N}}$$

where χ^2 is the value of the χ^2 statistic calculated using the data in the 2 × 2 contingency table, and N is the total number of observations.

Applying this formula to the two experiments on the effect that exercise has on weight loss, it appears that in the study where participants exercised 30 minutes a day,

$\phi = \sqrt{\dfrac{20.11}{200}} = 0.317$, while in the study where men exercised 15 minutes three days per

week $\phi = \sqrt{\dfrac{20}{2000}} = 0.1$. Thus, the association between exercise and weight loss was

stronger in the first rather than the second experiment.

Phi (ϕ) can vary between 0 and 1, where 0 indicates that there is no relationship between two dichotomous variables (i.e., variables that can take only one of two discrete values) and 1 indicates a perfect relationship between two dichotomous variables (see Table 6.11). As a rule of thumb, $\phi = 0.1$ indicates that the association between two dichotomous variables is weak (or alternatively that the effect size is small); $\phi = 0.3$ indicates that the effect size is medium; and $\phi = 0.5$ indicates that the association between two dichotomous variables is quite strong (or alternatively that the effect size is large). If the null hypothesis is true, then in the population $\phi = 0$.

Table 6.11 Examples of contingency tables where there is no relationship between two dichotomous variables Q and P (i.e. $\phi = 0$; (a)), and where there is a perfect relationship between two dichotomous variables (i.e. $\phi = 1$; (b))

(a)

$\phi = 0$ $\chi^2 = 0$	Q_1	Q_2	Totals
P_1	55	55	110
P_2	30	30	60
Totals	85	85	170

(b)

$\phi = 1$ $\chi^2 = 170$	Q_1	Q_2	Totals
P_1	110	0	110
P_2	0	60	60
Totals	110	60	170

For larger contingency tables the effect size index is called Cramer's phi (usually symbolised as ϕ_c), and its value is calculated as follows:

$$\phi_c = \sqrt{\frac{\chi^2}{N(k-1)}}$$

where χ^2 is the value of the χ^2 statistic calculated using the data in any $c \times r$ contingency table (recall that c = number of columns; r = number of rows), N is the total number of observations, and k is the smaller of the values r and c.

Applying this formula to the study on bullying we obtain that:

$$\phi_c = \sqrt{\frac{46.93}{131(3-1)}} = \sqrt{\frac{46.93}{262}} = 0.423,$$

thus indicating a medium effect size. Notice that when $k = 2$, the formula to obtain ϕ_c is identical to that for ϕ.

Observe also that the interpretation of the effect size, in the case of large contingency tables, is not as immediate as for 2×2 contingency tables, where the direction of the effect is immediately evident. For example, in the first study, performing exercise appeared associated with greater weight loss (i.e., it led to more people losing weight). In the case of larger contingency tables, it is more difficult to specify the type of association between two variables. As seen in the study on bullying it may be useful to inspect the pattern of the $\frac{(O-E)^2}{E}$ quantities to provide a plausible interpretation of the type of association occurring between the variables.

A fundamental conceptual equation in data analysis: Magnitude of a significance test = Size of the effect × Size of the study

If both sides of the formula for ϕ are squared we obtain $\phi^2 = \frac{\chi^2}{N}$, and after some rearrangement this becomes:

$$\chi^2 = \phi^2 \times N.$$

This is a very important equation showing that, when the Pearson's χ^2 test statistic is distributed as the χ^2 distribution with $df = 1$, the magnitude of the Pearson's χ^2 test is a function of the effect size (ϕ^2, i.e., the squared size of the relationship between two dichotomous variables) and of the size of the study (i.e., N). This equation represents an application of a fundamental conceptual equation of data analysis which states that:

Magnitude of a significance test = Size of the effect × Size of the study.

The above relationship between the magnitude of a significance test, the effect size, and the size of the study has a very important consequence on the way data analysis should be conducted. To fully answer our research questions, we should not only provide the size of a statistical test, but also a measure of the size of the effect of the variables studied. The exercise and weight loss study provided an example of the importance of the above relationship between effect size, size of the study, and magnitude of the significance test. In both experiments the χ^2 test statistics were almost identical. However, the effect size obtained in the first experiment showed that more regular exercise had a greater effect on weight loss than shorter bouts of exercise fewer times per week, as in the second experiment (i.e., the values of ϕ were 0.317 and 0.1, respectively).

Given that the effect sizes between the two studies differed, why then were the Pearson's χ^2 test statistics almost identical? The answer lies in the fact that 200 men took part in the 30-minutes-a-day exercise experiment, while 2000 men were recruited in the second experiment. Applying the above formula to these data you can see that the greater number of subjects compensated for the small effect size, producing a significant χ^2 test statistic of the same magnitude as that detected in the experiment with a smaller sample size, but larger effect size.

The χ^2 test statistic in the study where men exercised 30 minutes a day is:

$$\chi^2 = \phi^2 \times N = (0.317)^2 \times 200 = 20.11$$

while the χ^2 test statistic in the study where men exercised for 15 minutes 3 times a day in the experimental condition is:

$$\chi^2 = \phi^2 \times N = (0.1)^2 \times 2000 = 20.$$

Assuming that only 200 men had been tested in this second experiment, and that the same effect size had been obtained, i.e., $\phi = 0.1$, then the χ^2 test statistic would have been equal to $2 = (0.1)^2 \times 200$. This would have not been significant since the critical value of the χ^2 distribution with $df = 1$ (at an α level of 0.05) is 3.84. Therefore the important message is that the magnitude of a statistical test only provides a partial picture (i.e., it tells us if we can reject the null hypothesis stating that the effect size in the population is zero). To provide a more comprehensive analysis of the data, a measure of the effect size should also be included.

The same conceptual relationship holds for Pearson's χ^2 test statistics for contingency tables bigger than 2×2 (i.e., $df > 1$). In this case we have:

$$\chi^2 = \phi_c^2 \times N(k - 1).$$

where χ^2 is the value of the Pearson's χ^2 statistic calculated using the data in any $r \times c$ contingency table, N is the total number of observations, and k is the smaller of the values R and C.

An important note on the inclusion of nonoccurrences in contingency tables

The issue of nonoccurrences was not explicitly dealt with when describing the use of the Pearson's χ^2 test in the analysis of contingency tables. It is, however, useful to spend some time on this issue in order to understand the risk of committing serious

Table 6.12 Contingency table summarising the opinion of pub landlords and pub customers on keeping pubs open between 6pm and 2am. Yes = in favour; No = against. Part (a) includes nonoccurrences (i.e., no answers), while in part (b) nonoccurrences are omitted. The value of the Pearson's χ^2 statistic for both tables is provided. For explanation of part (c), see text

(a)

$\chi^2 = 9.83$	Landlords	Customers	Totals
YES			
Observed	52	68	120
Expected	63.36	56.64	
NO			94
Observed	61	33	
Expected	49.64	44.36	
Totals	113	101	214

(b)

$\chi^2 = 2.13$	Landlords	Customers	Totals
YES Observed	52	68	120
YES Expected	60	60	120

(c)

$\chi^2 = 214.74$	Landlords	Customers	Totals
YES			
Observed	52	68	120
Expected	103.3	16.97	
NO			
Observed	561	33	594
Expected	509.97	84.03	
Totals	613	101	714

errors, in the analysis of frequency data, when frequencies of nonoccurrences are not considered. Imagine a study where a sample of pub landlords and a sample of pub customers are asked if they are in favour of extending evening opening hours every day of the week until 2am. The results are displayed in Table 6.12. From the data in Table 6.12a, it appears, not surprisingly, that customers are keener than landlords to see pubs opened for longer hours at night, $\chi^2(df = 1) = 9.83$, $p < 0.05$, $\phi = 0.214$.

Imagine, however, that you fail to consider the negative responses or nonoccurrences, and that a chi-square test is performed only on "YES" responses. An analysis of these data (see Table 6.12b) would suggest that the empirical evidence is not strong enough to lead to the rejection of the null hypothesis that landlord and customers have the same view about pubs closure times, $\chi^2(df = 1) = 2.13$, $p > 0.10$. However, this analysis is wrong since it only took into account when participants were in favour of having extended hours, but it failed to take into account how many participants in each category (i.e., Landlords and Customers) were opposed to the late night closure. In fact, the percentage of customers against extended opening hours at night was much smaller than the percentage of landlords opposing extended hours.

To further clarify the reason why it is incorrect not to consider nonoccurrences, imagine that the sample of landlords is increased to 613 (i.e., 500 more landlords), but none of the new landlords is in favour of keeping their pub open for longer hours. This inclusion of new subjects should have an effect on the size of the cells of the previous contingency table. This new set of opinions would leave the number of "YES" responses the same as in Table 6.12a, while the number of "NO" responses would now be 561 among landlords, and 33 among customers. From the analysis of this revised 2×2 contingency table (see Table 6.12c) we would obtain, $\chi^2(df = 1) = 214.17$, $p < 0.05$, $\phi = 0.548$ (notice the increased size of both the χ^2 statistics and the effect size). On the other hand, the analysis failing to include nonoccurrences would have remained unchanged, i.e., $\chi^2(df = 1) = 2.33$, $p > 0.10$. Thus, remember that to correctly analyse contingency tables, nonoccurrences, if present, have always to be included.

Chapter 7

Statistical tests on proportions

Introduction

In Chapters 4 and 6 we saw how to use the binomial and the Pearson's χ^2 tests to test hypotheses about the number of successes out of n independent trials. Quite often, however, researchers are interested in the proportion of successes (i.e., the number of successes divided by the number of trials). In this section, we will describe how to perform statistical tests on proportions of successes, and how to calculate, using sample data, confidence intervals that have a given probability of including the true population proportion.

Statistical tests on the proportion of successes in a sample

Let us assume that the proportion of successes in a population is $p = 0.4$, then the proportion of failures $q = 1 - p$ (hence $q = 1 - 0.4 = 0.6$). Let us take all possible independent samples of n observations from the above population and calculate the proportion of successes in each sample. Provided that $n \times p > 5$, the distribution of the sample proportions will then be approximately normal with $\mu = p$ and with a standard error $\sigma_p = \sqrt{\dfrac{pq}{n}}$ (important note: the standard deviation of any distribution of sample statistics, like proportions or means, is usually called *standard error*). Therefore, we can obtain the following standardised normal variable:

$$z = \frac{p_{obs} - p}{\sqrt{\dfrac{pq}{n}}}$$

where p_{obs} is the proportion of successes observed in a sample of n independent observations, in which each observation can either be a success or a failure; p is the proportion of successes in the population from which the sample has been drawn; $q\ (= 1 - p)$ is the proportion of failures in the population; and n is the size of the sample. If the sampled observations were not drawn from a population where the proportion of successes is p, then we should obtain a z score which is relatively large in absolute terms. For an α level of 0.05, the null hypothesis, stating that our sample was drawn from a population where the proportion of successes is p, is rejected if the calculated z score lies outside the ± 1.96 critical region (or if $z = \pm 1.96$). For simplicity this last statement will be omitted later in the text. However, remember that the limits of the critical region allow the rejection of the null hypothesis.

Let us use an example to illustrate the application of the above procedure. Imagine that a new type of hair conditioner is advertised, and that the manufacturer claims that 30 per cent of the people who regularly use any type of hair conditioner will move to their new product after trying it. A group of sceptical consumers decides to assess this claim asking an independent organisation to test it. This organisation randomly samples 400 regular users of hair conditioner who then try the new product for a month. After this trial period it appears that 92 out of the 400 participants (i.e., 23 per cent of the sample) are prepared to move to the new product. Can these data support the claim of the manufacturers?

The null hypothesis states that the sample has been drawn from a population where the proportion of people moving to the new conditioner is 0.30, while the alternative hypothesis states that the sample has not been drawn from a population where the proportion of people moving to the new conditioner is 0.30. The null hypothesis is tested using the above formula for z, where $p_{obs} = 0.23$, $p = 0.30$, $q = 0.7$ ($= 1 - p = 1 - 0.3$) and $n = 400$. Thus we obtain:

$$z = \frac{p_{obs} - p}{\sqrt{\dfrac{pq}{n}}} = \frac{0.23 - 0.3}{\sqrt{\dfrac{0.3 \times 0.7}{400}}} = \frac{-0.07}{\sqrt{\dfrac{0.21}{400}}} = -3.055.$$

Since -3.055 lies outside the ± 1.96 critical region, for an α level of 0.05, the null hypothesis is rejected and it is concluded that fewer than 30 per cent of the users who try the new conditioner will move to this new product.

Confidence intervals for population proportions

In some circumstances researchers may want to use sample proportions to estimate the proportion in the population. Although the sample proportion is an unbiased estimate of the population proportion, (i.e., the long-term average or expected value of the sample proportion corresponds to the population proportion), we do not know how close the sample proportion is to the population proportion. Therefore, we may want to use sample data to find a range of values which should contain the population proportion with a given probability (i.e., we construct confidence intervals for the population proportion). Confidence intervals are regions in which a population parameter is likely to be found. Let us illustrate how to calculate confidence intervals for the population proportion (this procedure has also been described within different contexts in the sections on pages 86–87 and pages 98–99).

As shown above, we know that the proportions of successes in samples of size n, drawn from a population with p proportion of successes, are normally distributed with $\mu = p$ and $\sigma_p = \sqrt{\dfrac{pq}{n}}$. Inspecting the standardised normal distribution tables we know that the probability that z is equal to or larger than 1.96 is 0.025. More formally:

$$P(z \geq 1.96) = 0.025,$$

and for the opposite tail of the distribution:

$$P(z \le -1.96) = 0.025$$

and hence the probability that z lies within ± 1.96 is 0.95, i.e., $P(-1.96 \le z \le 1.96) = 0.95$ or equivalently

$$P(1.96 \ge z \ge -1.96) = 0.95.$$

Since $z = \dfrac{p_{obs} - p}{\sqrt{\dfrac{pq}{n}}}$ we can substitute $\dfrac{p_{obs} - p}{\sqrt{\dfrac{pq}{n}}}$ for z in the previous formula, thus:

$$P\left(1.96 \ge \dfrac{p_{obs} - p}{\sqrt{\dfrac{pq}{n}}} \ge -1.96\right) = 0.95.$$

Since $\sqrt{\dfrac{pq}{n}} = \sigma_p$ we obtain:

$$P\left(1.96 \ge \dfrac{p_{obs} - p}{\sigma_p} \ge -1.96\right) = 0.95.$$

Rearranging the terms within the brackets:

$$P(1.96 \times \sigma_p - p_{obs} \ge -p \ge -1.96 \times \sigma_p - p_{obs}) = 0.95.$$

Since we want to find the interval containing p and not $-p$, we multiply the components of the inequality by -1 (this implies that the "greater than" symbols become "less than" symbols) and we obtain:

$$P(-1.96 \times \sigma_p + p_{obs} \le p \le 1.96 \times \sigma_p + p_{obs}) = 0.95$$

or equivalently,

$$P(p_{obs} - 1.96 \times \sigma_p \le p \le p_{obs} + 1.96 \times \sigma_p) = 0.95.$$

The above statement indicates that the interval $p_{obs} \pm 1.96 \times \sigma_p$ has 0.95 probability of including the true population proportion. This interval is called the *95% symmetric confidence interval* for p (i.e., the population proportion).

One problem with the above procedure for calculating the confidence interval is that we do not know the population proportion p, so we cannot calculate the standard error, since $\sigma_p = \sqrt{\dfrac{pq}{n}}$. We can, however, use the proportion of successes obtained in the sample to estimate the standard error. This estimate is denoted as s_p and it is calculated as

$$s_p = \sqrt{\frac{p_{obs} \times q_{obs}}{n}}.$$

Hence, the formula to obtain the *95% symmetric confidence interval* ($CI_{95\%}$) for the proportion of success in the population, i.e., p, using sample data is the following:

$$CI_{95\%} = p_{obs} \pm 1.96 \times s_p$$

where p_{obs} is the proportion of successes in the sample; $q_{obs} = 1 - p_{obs}$; $s_p = \sqrt{\frac{p_{obs} \times q_{obs}}{n}}$; and n is the sample size.

Imagine that a random sample of 900 people are interviewed about which party they intend to support in the next UK general election. From the interview it appears that 42 per cent of the people in the sample intend to vote Labour. Given these data what is the 95% symmetric confidence interval for the proportion of people voting Labour in the whole population?

The first thing to do is to calculate s_p:

$$s_p = \sqrt{\frac{p_{obs} \times q_{obs}}{n}} = \sqrt{\frac{0.42 \times (1 - 0.42)}{900}} = \frac{0.2436}{30} = 0.00812.$$

Thus, the 95% confidence interval for the proportion of the population intending to vote Labour is:

$$p_{obs} \pm 1.96 \times s_p = 0.42 \pm 1.96 \times 0.00812 = 0.42 \pm 0.0159,$$

that is, the $CI_{95\%} = 0.4041 \le p \le 0.4359$, and the limits of the 95% confidence interval for p are 0.4041 and 0.4359.

The probability that a confidence interval will include the true population mean can be changed by simply selecting a different critical value of z depending on the desired probability to be associated with the confidence interval. For example, in the case of a 99% confidence interval, denoted as $CI_{99\%}$, the critical z value to be inserted in the above formula is 2.576. In the case of the voting study, the 99% confidence interval for the proportion of the population intending to vote Labour is:

$$p_{obs} \pm 2.576 \times s_p = 0.42 \pm 2.576 \times 0.00812 = 0.42 \pm 0.0209$$

and thus, the $CI_{99\%} = 0.3991 \le p \le 0.4409$, and the limits of the 99% confidence interval for p are 0.3991 and 0.4409.

The more general formula for confidence intervals is:

$$CI = \bar{x} \pm c \times s_p$$

where c is the two-tailed critical value of z for any desired α level (i.e., $z_{\frac{\alpha}{2}}$).

Notice that when confidence intervals are calculated using test statistics other than z (e.g., t), then c will refer to the specific test statistic used.

Statistical tests on the difference between the proportions of successes from two independent samples

Consider again the study described in the section on pages 110–113 about religious belief and opinion about abortion. In that section we saw that 120 out of the 400 sampled religious women (i.e., 30 per cent) were, in principle, pro abortion, while 410 out of the 600 non-religious women (i.e., 68.33 per cent) were in favour of abortion. In that section we used Pearson's χ^2 to test the null hypotheses that there was no relationship between religious belief and view about abortion. In this section we are going to do the same thing using a different approach. We are going to assess if the proportions of non-religious and religious women in favour of abortion differ significantly. If being religious is associated with being against abortion, then we should find that the proportion of religious women who are pro abortion is significantly smaller than the proportion of non-religious women who are pro abortion. From a slightly different angle, if the null hypothesis (H_0) is true, then the proportion of pro-abortion women in the population of religious women is the same as the proportion of pro-abortion women in the population of non-religious women. The alternative hypothesis (H_1) states that the population proportion of religious pro-abortion women differs from the proportion of non-religious pro-abortion women.

If (H_0) is true then $p_1 = p_2 = p$ (i.e., the probability of success in the first population is identical to the probability of success in the second population; thus, these probabilities are equal to the common population probability p). An alternative formulation of the null hypothesis is $H_0: p_1 - p_2 = 0$. Under this condition it can be shown that the distribution of the differences between pairs of sample proportions is approximately normal with $\mu = 0$ and with standard error $\sigma_{p_1-p_2} = \sqrt{\dfrac{pq}{n_1} + \dfrac{pq}{n_2}}$, where p is the proportion of successes in the common population; $q = 1 - p$; and n_1 and n_2 are the sizes of the two samples. Therefore, we can obtain the following standardised normal variable:

$$z = \frac{(p_{obs1} - p_{obs2}) - 0}{\sigma_{p_1-p_2}},$$

where p_{obs1} and p_{obs2} are the proportions of successes obtained in the two samples, and $\sigma_{p_1-p_2}$ is the standard error of the distribution of differences between two sample proportions.

Here, however, we face the problem of not knowing the value of p in the common population, nor the values of p_1 and p_2, hence we cannot calculate $\sigma_{p_1-p_2}$. However, there is a way around this problem. In H_0 we assumed that $p_1 = p_2 = p$; hence, we can make use of sample data to estimate p_1 and p_2 (i.e., p_{obs1} is taken as an estimate of p_1 and p_{obs2} is taken as an estimate of p_2). Therefore we can pool p_1 and p_2 (or better still, their available estimates p_{obs1} and p_{obs2}) to obtain a *pooled estimate of the common population proportion p*. This is denoted as $\hat{p}$ and is calculated as:

$$\hat{p} = \frac{n_1 \times p_{obs1} + n_2 \times p_{obs2}}{n_1 + n_2}$$

and instead of $\sigma_{p_1-p_2}$ we can calculate its estimate $s_{p_1-p_2}$:

$$s_{p_1-p_2} = \sqrt{\frac{\hat{p}\hat{q}}{n_1} + \frac{\hat{p}\hat{q}}{n_2}}$$

where $\hat{q} = 1 - \hat{p}$ and n_1 and n_2 are the sizes of the two samples. Hence, we can obtain the following standardised normal variable:

$$z = \frac{p_{obs1} - p_{obs2}}{s_{p_1-p_2}} = \frac{p_{obs1} - p_{obs2}}{\sqrt{\dfrac{\hat{p}\hat{q}}{n_1} + \dfrac{\hat{p}\hat{q}}{n_2}}}$$

and we can make use of the z score to decide if the null hypothesis can be rejected. This procedure is appropriate provided that, as a rule of thumb, $\hat{p}$ or $\hat{q}$ (whichever is smaller) times n_1 or n_2 (whichever is smaller) is larger than 5.

Let us apply this procedure to the data on religious belief and view about abortion. The proportion of successes (i.e., the proportion of women in favour of abortion) is 0.30 and 0.6833 in the samples of religious ($n = 400$) and non-religious women ($n = 600$), respectively. Therefore,

$$\hat{p} = \frac{n_1 \times p_{obs1} + n_2 \times p_{obs2}}{n_1 + n_2} = \frac{400 \times 0.3 + 600 \times 0.6833}{400 + 600} = 0.53,$$

thus $\hat{q} = 1 - 0.53 = 0.47$ and hence,

$$s_{p_1-p_2} = \sqrt{\frac{\hat{p}\hat{q}}{n_1} + \frac{\hat{p}\hat{q}}{n_2}} = \sqrt{\frac{0.53 \times 0.47}{400} + \frac{0.53 \times 0.47}{600}} = 0.0322 \text{ (to 4 d.p.).}$$

The relevant z is then calculated as follows:

$$z = \frac{p_{obs1} - p_{obs2}}{s_{p_1-p_2}} = \frac{0.3 - 0.6833}{0.0322} = -11.8986.$$

Since this value lies outside the critical range of z scores for an α level of 0.05, i.e., ± 1.96, the null hypothesis is rejected and it is concluded that there is a significant difference between the proportion of religious pro-abortion women and non-religious pro-abortion women.

As an addendum, if the value of the z score (i.e., -11.8986) is squared, then we obtain the value of the Pearson's χ^2 (i.e., 141.576) calculated on the same data expressed as frequencies instead of proportions of successes. This happens because, as stated in Chapter 6, the χ^2 distribution with one degree of freedom, and the distribution of z^2 scores, are identical.

Confidence intervals for the difference between two independent population proportions

Researchers may be interested in identifying a range of values within which the difference between two independent population proportions lies with a given probability. The procedure to be used is comparable to the one described earlier, where we illustrated how to calculate confidence intervals for the population proportion.

The formula for the *95% symmetric confidence interval* for the difference between two independent population proportions is the following:

$$\text{CI}_{95\%} = (p_{obs1} - p_{obs2}) \pm 1.96 \times s_{p_1-p_2}$$

where p_{obs1} and p_{obs2} are the proportions of successes obtained in the two samples, and $s_{p_1-p_2}$ is the estimated standard error of the distribution of differences between two sample proportions. Unlike the case of the z test on the difference between two independent proportions, this estimate should be calculated without using a pooled estimate of the common population proportion p. (The reason is that here we do not assume any null hypothesis stating that the proportions of successes in the two populations from which the samples are drawn are identical. So there is no reason to obtain a pooled estimate of the common population proportion of successes p.) The estimated standard error of the difference between two independent proportions is therefore:

$$s_{p_1-p_2} = \sqrt{\frac{p_{obs1} \times (1 - p_{obs1})}{n_1} + \frac{p_{obs2} \times (1 - p_{obs2})}{n_2}}$$

where n_1 and n_2 are the sizes of the two samples.

Imagine the case in which we obtain the percentage, from two independent samples of female and male drivers, of those people who have not had an accident in the last 5 years (i.e., success). The proportion of successes is 0.67 among women ($n = 200$) and 0.55 among men ($n = 220$). What is the 95 per cent confidence interval for the difference between the male and female populations' proportion of successes? To obtain this we first calculate the estimated standard error of the differences between the two proportions:

$$s_{p_1-p_2} = \sqrt{\frac{p_{obs1} \times (1 - p_{obs1})}{n_1} + \frac{p_{obs2} \times (1 - p_{obs2})}{n_2}}$$

$$= \sqrt{\frac{0.67 \times (1 - 0.67)}{200} + \frac{0.55 \times (1 - 0.55)}{220}} = 0.0472 \text{ (to 4 d.p.)}.$$

Thus the 95% confidence interval for the difference between the male and female populations' proportion of successes is:

$$(p_{obs1} - p_{obs2}) \pm 1.96 \times s_{p_1-p_2} = (0.67 - 0.55) \pm 1.96 \times 0.0472$$

$$= 0.12 \pm 0.0926 \text{ (to 4 d.p.)},$$

that is, the $\text{CI}_{95\%} = 0.0274 \leq p \leq 0.2126$, and the limits of the 95% confidence for the difference between the male and female populations' proportion of successes are 0.0274 and 0.2126, respectively. Since zero is not within the limits of the interval, this indicates that there is a significant difference between the proportions of safe female drivers and safe male drivers. Different levels of confidence other than 0.95 can be selected by simply inserting the z score for the desired level of probability in the above formula. Hence the general formula for confidence intervals for the difference between proportions of successes is:

$$CI = (p_{obs1} - p_{obs2}) \pm c \times s_{p_1 - p_2},$$

where c is the two-tailed critical value of z for any desired α level (i.e., $z_{\frac{\alpha}{2}}$).

Statistical tests on the difference between nonindependent proportions of successes (McNemar test)

In some cases researchers may be interested in assessing if there is a significant difference between two nonindependent proportions of successes. This situation is most likely to arise when the same subjects are asked to provide responses under two different conditions. Imagine, for instance, that a sample of 144 subjects are asked to indicate if they are in favour of liberalising cannabis (i.e., yes = success), and that 45 people respond affirmatively (hence the proportion of successes is $\frac{45}{144} = 0.3125$). After collecting these data, the same sample watch a documentary where a panel of experts discuss the pros and cons of liberalising this drug. Then the subjects are asked again to indicate if they are in favour of liberalising cannabis, and it appears that 72 subjects are now in favour (i.e., the proportion of successes is $\frac{72}{144} = 0.5$). Thus the proportion of successes in the sample has increased from 0.3125 to 0.5 (i.e., by 0.1875) following the documentary. Do these proportions differ significantly? Or in other words, is 0.1875 significantly different from zero (i.e., this is the null hypothesis)?

To test the above null hypothesis we need to display the data obtained in the cannabis study in a specific 2×2 contingency table. The cells of this table need to provide the number of subjects in favour of liberalising cannabis in both conditions (i.e., yes–yes); the number against in both conditions (no–no); the number in favour in the first but not in the second condition (yes–no); and the number against in the first but in favour in the second condition (no–yes). The sum of the frequencies of the four cells gives the total number of observations in the sample (i.e., n). Proportions are obtained by dividing cell and marginal frequencies by n.

Table 7.1a shows which frequencies should be entered in the 2×2 contingency table to perform the McNemar test. The letters A, B, C, D represent the frequencies for yes–no, yes–yes, no–no, and no–yes responses, respectively; (A + B) represents the frequency of successes in the first condition; (B + D) represents the frequency of successes in the second condition. Table 7.1b shows the proportions of successes and failures associated with each cell and the marginal frequency (e.g., the proportion of successes in the first condition is given by $p_{obs1} = \frac{A + B}{n}$; the proportion of successes in the second condition is given by $p_{obs2} = \frac{B + D}{n}$).

Table 7.1 Contingency tables for handling proportions obtained from the same sample of subjects

(a) Frequencies

		Second condition		
		No (failures)	Yes (successes)	Totals
First condition	Yes (successes)	A	B	A + B
	No (failures)	C	D	C + D
	Totals	A + C	B + D	n

(b) Proportions

		Second condition		
		No (failures)	Yes (successes)	Proportions
First condition	Yes (successes)	$a \left(= \dfrac{A}{n} \right)$	$b \left(= \dfrac{B}{n} \right)$	$p_{obs1} \left(= \dfrac{A + B}{n} \right)$
	No (failures)	$c \left(= \dfrac{C}{n} \right)$	$d \left(= \dfrac{D}{n} \right)$	$q_{obs1} \left(= \dfrac{C + D}{n} \right)$
	Proportions	$q_{obs2} \left(= \dfrac{A + C}{n} \right)$	$p_{obs2} \left(= \dfrac{B + D}{n} \right)$	1

The null hypothesis underlying the McNemar test states that the proportion of successes in the two conditions studied is the same. This does not imply that nobody should change their opinion. Some people are likely to change their point of view. However, if the null hypothesis is true, it is expected that the number of changes from "yes to no" will balance the number of changes from "no to yes". To assess if the proportion of successes in the first condition differs from the proportion of successes in the second condition, the McNemar test is based on a comparison between the number of subjects changing their type of response (i.e., from yes-to-no vs from no-to-yes). If this number is too high then the null hypothesis is likely to be false; thus, the alternative hypothesis stating that two nonindependent proportions differ is accepted. Notice that the number of successes in the first condition is obtained by adding A and B frequencies, and that the number of successes in the second condition is given by adding B and D frequencies (see Table 7.1a). Hence, the difference in the number of successes between the second and the first condition is given by: $(B + D) - (A + B) = D - A$.

How can we decide if the quantity $D - A$ is big enough to warrant the rejection of the null hypothesis? Well, it can be shown that if $(A + D) > 10$, then the quantity $\dfrac{D - A}{\sqrt{A + D}}$ is a standard normal deviate (i.e., z). Hence we can make use of the Z table to decide if the null hypothesis about the difference between two nonindependent

Table 7.2 Contingency tables for handling the nonindependent proportions obtained in the cannabis study

(a) Frequencies

		Opinion after documentary		
		Against	In favour	Totals
Opinion before documentary	In favour	A 5	B 40	45
	Against	C 67	D 32	99
	Totals	72	72	n = 144

$$z = \frac{D - A}{\sqrt{A + D}} = \frac{32 - 5}{\sqrt{5 + 32}} = \frac{27}{\sqrt{37}} = 4.44$$

(b) Proportions

		Opinion after documentary		
		Against	In favour	Totals
Opinion before documentary	In favour	a 0.0347	b 0.2778	0.3125
	Against	c 0.4653	d 0.2222	0.6875
	Totals	0.5	0.5	1

$$z = \frac{\dfrac{D - A}{n}}{\sqrt{\dfrac{A + D}{n^2}}} = \frac{d - a}{\sqrt{\dfrac{a + d}{n}}} = \frac{0.2222 - 0.0347}{\sqrt{\dfrac{0.0347 + 0.2222}{144}}} = \frac{0.1875}{0.0422} = 4.44$$

proportions can be rejected. When this procedure is applied to the cannabis example we obtain (see Table 7.2(a)):

$$z = \frac{D - A}{\sqrt{A + D}} = \frac{32 - 5}{\sqrt{5 + 32}} = \frac{27}{\sqrt{37}} = 4.44.$$

Since 4.44 lies outside the ±1.96 critical region, for an α level of 0.05, the null hypothesis is rejected and it is concluded that watching the documentary led to a significant increase in the proportion of people in favour of liberalising cannabis. Although all calculations were performed on frequencies, we reached a decision on proportions. This choice was made simply for convenience. The same conclusion would be reached if the frequencies were transformed into proportions by dividing each frequency by *n*.

Table 7.2(b) provides the relevant proportions. If we had calculated the required standard normal deviate, to test the difference between the proportions of people in favour of liberalising cannabis before and after the documentary, we would have obtained the same result as when using frequencies:

$$z = \frac{\dfrac{D - A}{n}}{\sqrt{\dfrac{A + D}{n^2}}} = \frac{d - a}{\sqrt{\dfrac{a + d}{n}}} = \frac{0.2222 - 0.0347}{\sqrt{\dfrac{0.0347 + 0.2222}{144}}} = \frac{0.1875}{0.0422} = 4.44$$

where the numerator (i.e., $d - a$) is the difference between two nonindependent proportions; and the denominator (i.e., $\sqrt{\dfrac{a + d}{n}}$) is the estimated standard error of the difference between two nonindependent proportions.

Knowing the standard error of the difference between two nonindependent proportions, estimated using sampled observations, we can then calculate the confidence interval within which the difference between two nonindependent proportions of successes in the population should lie. This is given by:

$$CI = (p_{obs1} - p_{obs2}) \pm c \times s_{p_1 - p_2}$$

where $(p_{obs1} - p_{obs2})$ is the difference between the two nonindependent proportions obtained from the sampled data; c is the two-tailed critical value of z for any desired α level (e.g., $z_{\frac{\alpha}{2}}$ for 95% confidence intervals); and $s_{p_1 - p_2}$ (i.e., $\sqrt{\dfrac{a + d}{n}}$) is the estimated standard error of the difference between nonindependent proportions.

When the above formula is applied to the cannabis study we obtain that:

$$(p_{obs1} - p_{obs2}) \pm 1.96 \times s_{p_1 - p_2} = 0.1875 \pm 1.96 \times 0.0422,$$

thus the $CI_{95\%} = 0.1047 \leq p \leq 0.2703$, and the limits of the 95% confidence for the difference between proportions of successes are 0.1047 and 0.2703. Since zero is not contained within the limits of the interval, it indicates, as seen previously, that there is a significant difference between the proportions of people in favour of liberalising cannabis before and after viewing the documentary. As usual, different levels of confidence can be selected by simply inserting the z score for the desired level of probability in the above formula.

Chapter 8

Sampling distribution of the mean and its use in hypothesis testing

Introduction

In Chapter 5 we described how the standardised normal distribution is used when deciding if an observation could have been drawn from a given population with a known mean and standard deviation. In this chapter we will do something similar, but, instead of applying the process of hypothesis testing to individual observations, the process will be applied to sample means. For example, imagine we know that the population distribution of scores in a standardised test measuring reading speed is normal with $\mu = 200$ words per minute and $\sigma = 30$. Moreover, imagine that a random sample of 36 people are given a crash course on how to read fast and that at the end of the course they read, on average 218 words per minute in the reading speed test. If we want to know whether the course was effective or not, we need to know how likely it is that our sample, with a mean of 218, is drawn from a population whose scores in the reading speed test are distributed as indicated above. If this probability is very low, then it is concluded that the sample was *not* drawn from a population with $\mu = 200$ (i.e., that the reading course was effective). In this chapter we will give a detailed explanation of how to use the standardised normal distribution to answer questions of this type.

Before explaining how to apply the standardised normal distribution in testing hypotheses about means, we will first describe what the sampling distribution of the mean is, and give a brief outline of the Central Limit Theorem. The Student's t-distribution, and the application of the t-test to the above type of problem will also be considered. The t-test, and its associated t-distribution, are used to examine hypotheses about means when the standard deviation of the population of the individual observations is not known. In the majority of cases where means are compared, we do not know the population standard deviation, so it is estimated using the sampled data, and the t-test is an appropriate way to test hypotheses about the mean. Finally, we will show how to use sample data to construct intervals that have a given probability of containing the true population mean.

The sampling distribution of the mean and the Central Limit Theorem

Imagine we know that the distribution of the population of individual scores in a manual dexterity test is normal with $\mu = 50$ and $\sigma = 8$. Now imagine that we draw an infinite number of independent samples, each of 16 observations, from this population. We then record these means and plot their values. What would the distribution of these sample means look like? It turns out that the distribution of these sample means (also called the *sampling distribution of the mean*) is normal with a mean of 50 (i.e., equal to the mean of the distribution of the population of the individual scores; the mean of the sampling distribution of the mean is usually denoted as $\mu_{\bar{x}}$) and a standard deviation of 2 (note that the standard deviation of the sampling distribution of the mean is usually called the *standard error of the mean* and is denoted as $\sigma_{\bar{x}}$). The value of the standard error is obtained by taking the value of the standard deviation of the population of the individual scores (i.e., 8), and dividing this value by the square root of the number of observations in each sample (i.e., $\sqrt{16}$).

This is formalised in the *Central Limit Theorem*, which states that: for a population of values with mean μ and variance σ^2, the sampling distribution of the mean will have a mean equal to μ (i.e., $\mu_{\bar{x}} = \mu$), variance denoted as $\sigma_{\bar{x}}^2 = \dfrac{\sigma^2}{n}$, and standard error $\sigma_{\bar{x}} = \dfrac{\sigma}{\sqrt{n}}$, where n is the sample size. Moreover, the shape of the sampling distribution of the mean will be approximately normal if the distribution of the parent population from which the samples are drawn is normal (see Figure 8.1). On the other hand, if

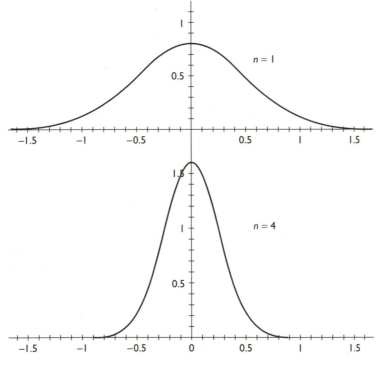

Figure 8.1 Examples of sampling distributions of the mean. The upper part provides the distribution of the population of single observations (i.e., sample size $n = 1$) with $\mu = 0$ and $\sigma^2 = 0.25$. The lower part provides the sampling distribution of the mean for samples of 4 observations taken from the population of single observations shown in the upper part of the figure. Notice that the sampling distribution of the mean is normal, centred at zero, but now the variance is 0.0625 (i.e., $\dfrac{\sigma^2}{n} = \dfrac{0.25}{4}$).

the distribution of the parent population from which the samples are drawn is not normal, then the sampling distribution of the mean will be approximately normal when n (i.e., the size of samples) increases. In general, with a sample size of 30 observations or more, irrespective of the shape of the distribution of the population of individual observations, the sampling distribution of the mean becomes approximately normal.

In summary, if we want to test hypotheses about means we need to know the characteristics of the distribution of the sample means. As seen above, the Central Limit Theorem tells us that the sampling distribution of the mean is usually normal with $\mu_{\bar{x}} = \mu$ and $\sigma_{\bar{x}} = \dfrac{\sigma}{\sqrt{n}}$, where μ and σ are the mean and the standard deviation of the parent population of individual observations from which the samples are drawn, and n is the sample size.

Testing hypotheses about means when σ is known

It is usually uncommon to know the standard deviation of a population of scores, so the technique described in this section is of limited application, but it is still worth knowing since there are circumstances in which it can be successfully applied. For example, when a standardised test is applied to a sample of subjects, we then know the population standard deviation and the mean of the individual scores. Let us consider the example described in the Introduction. As stated earlier, we know that the distribution of the population of individual scores in a standardised test measuring reading speed is normal with $\mu = 200$ words per minute and $\sigma = 30$. We also know that a random sample of 36 people achieved a mean performance of 218 words per minute in this test after having attended a crash course on how to read fast. The question we want to answer, on the basis of these data, is the following: has the course been effective in improving reading speed?

To answer this question we need to know the characteristics of the sampling distribution of the mean of samples of 36 observations drawn from the parent population. According to the Central Limit Theorem this distribution is approximately normal with the mean being $\mu_{\bar{x}} = \mu = 200$ and the standard error being $\sigma_{\bar{x}} = \dfrac{\sigma}{\sqrt{n}} = \dfrac{30}{\sqrt{36}} = 5$. Hence, using these pieces of information, we can calculate the value of the standardised z score corresponding to the obtained sample mean. If the z score is either equal to or larger or smaller than the critical values ± 1.96 (i.e., $\alpha = 0.05$), then the null hypothesis is false. In this case H_0 states that the sample of 36 people is drawn from the normal population, i.e., H_0: $\mu = 200$. The alternative hypothesis states that the sample of 36 people has *not* been drawn from the population of normal readers (with respect to reading speed), i.e., H_1: $\mu \neq 200$.

The way in which the z score corresponding to the obtained sample mean is calculated is equivalent to that described in the section on pages 84–89. Here however we are working with sample means and not individual scores, thus

$$z = \frac{x - \mu}{\sigma} \text{ becomes } z = \frac{\bar{x} - \mu}{\sigma_{\bar{x}}} \text{ (or equivalently } z = \frac{\bar{x} - \mu}{\frac{\sigma}{\sqrt{n}}}\text{)}$$

where $\bar{x}$ is the sample mean, μ is the population mean under the null hypothesis, and $\sigma_{\bar{x}}$ is the standard error of the mean.

Applying the relevant formula to the sample of 36 people who took the crash course in speed reading:

$$z = \frac{\bar{x} - \mu}{\dfrac{\sigma}{\sqrt{n}}} = \frac{218 - 200}{\dfrac{30}{\sqrt{36}}} = \frac{18}{5} = 3.6.$$

Since this value lies outside the ± 1.96 range, we reject the null hypothesis and conclude that the reading speed of the subjects who attended the reading course is significantly different (faster) than the average performance expected from samples of normal readers. Note that we used a two-tailed test since we allowed the null hypothesis to be rejected if the sample mean was either larger or smaller than the population mean.

Testing hypotheses about means when σ is unknown: the Student's *t*-distribution and the one-sample *t*-test

In the majority of cases it is unlikely that we know the mean and the standard deviation of the population of individual observations. Nevertheless, as we saw in the section on pages 31–32, we can estimate the standard deviation of the population using sample data, i.e., s. As a reminder, s is given by:

$$s = \sqrt{\frac{\sum (x - \bar{x})^2}{n - 1}}.$$

Hence, knowing s we can also obtain an estimate of the standard error of the sample distribution of the means (denoted as $SE_{\bar{x}}$):

$$SE_{\bar{x}} = \frac{s}{\sqrt{n}}.$$

In principle, if we need to test some hypotheses about the mean, and we do not know σ, we could calculate its estimate s, then $SE_{\bar{x}}$ and substitute this estimate of the population standard error for $\sigma_{\bar{x}}$ in $z = \dfrac{\bar{x} - \mu}{\sigma_{\bar{x}}}$ to calculate z. Then, as in the previous section, we could use the z value to decide whether or not to reject the null hypothesis.

However, the above procedure is inappropriate because its application would, more often than it should, wrongly reject the null hypothesis when it is true. This means that although the alpha level may be set at 0.05, the probability of wrongly rejecting a true null hypothesis, and thus the probability of committing a Type I error, is larger than 0.05. The reason is that the values of the variable $\dfrac{\bar{x} - \mu}{SE_{\bar{x}}}$ obtained by inserting $SE_{\bar{x}}$ instead of $\sigma_{\bar{x}}$ in the z formula, are not normally distributed; so the z distribution cannot be used in the process of statistical inference. The solution to this problem

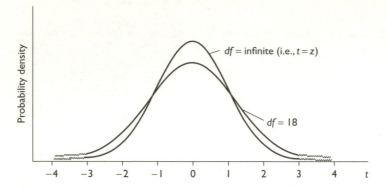

Figure 8.2 Examples of *t*-distributions with *df* = 18, and when the *t*-distribution corresponds to the z-distribution.

resides in the fact that the variable $\dfrac{\bar{x} - \mu}{SE_{\bar{x}}}$, or equivalently $\dfrac{\bar{x} - \mu}{\dfrac{s}{\sqrt{n}}}$, which is called *t*, is known to be distributed in a similar, but slightly different way to the standardised normal distribution. In particular the variable $t = \dfrac{\bar{x} - \mu}{SE_{\bar{x}}} = \dfrac{\bar{x} - \mu}{\dfrac{s}{\sqrt{n}}}$ is distributed as the Student's *t*-distribution with degrees of freedom *n* − 1. There is a loss of one degree of freedom because the sample mean is used to calculate *s*. As seen in Chapter 2, *s* is based on *n* − 1 *df*, hence we have *n* − 1 *df* for the one-sample *t*-test. Like the standard normal distribution, the Student's *t*-distribution is bell shaped, symmetrical around its mean, with $\mu = 0$ and $\sigma = 1$. However, unlike the z-distribution, there is not only one *t*-distribution, but an infinite number. As in the case of the χ^2 distribution, the number of degrees of freedom is the parameter that characterises each *t*-distribution. The *t*-distribution is very like the z-distribution, but just higher above the *x*-axis towards the end of the two tails (see Figure 8.2). The lower the number of degrees of freedom, the higher the tails (thus the critical values, within which 95 per cent of the area under the curve lies, are bigger, in absolute values). As the degrees of freedom increase (i.e., the sample size increases), the *t*-distribution approaches the z-distribution, and when the degrees of freedom are infinite, the *t*-distribution is identical to the z-distribution. In this last case it is as if we sampled the whole population, thus $SE_{\bar{x}} = \sigma_{\bar{x}}$, hence the *t*- and z-distributions are identical.

Let us now describe an example showing how the Student's *t*-distribution, and its associated *t*-test, are used in testing hypotheses about the mean when σ is unknown and needs to be estimated using sample data. Consider a study assessing recognition memory for unfamiliar faces. During learning, a sample of 32 subjects are asked to study a series of 100 previously unseen faces for a memory test to be carried out later. A day later, during the test phase, each subject is given a booklet where on each page there are the pictures of two faces, one on the left and another on the right. Each page always contains one of the 100 faces studied the previous day, as well as a new previously

Table 8.1 Percentage of correctly recognised faces, ordered from the lowest to the highest performance, of the 32 subjects who undertook the forced choice recognition memory test for unfamiliar faces. The sample mean, the population standard deviation estimated using sample data, the population mean assumed by the null hypothesis, and the computation of the *t*-test are also provided

44	48	54	58
44	49	55	58
45	51	55	60
45	52	56	62
46	52	56	62
46	53	57	63
47	53	57	65
48	54	58	65

$n = 32 \quad \bar{x} = 53.69 \quad s = 6.26 \quad \mu = 50$

$$SE_{\bar{x}} = \frac{s}{\sqrt{n}} = \frac{6.26}{\sqrt{32}} = 1.107$$

$$t = \frac{\bar{x} - \mu}{SE_{\bar{x}}} = \frac{53.69 - 50}{1.107} = 3.33 \quad df = n - 1 = 31$$

unseen face (new and old faces are randomly positioned in each of the 100 test pairs). The subjects' task is to say, for each pair of faces, which is the face that was studied during the learning phase (a two-alternative forced choice recognition memory test). The data from this fictitious experiment are shown in Table 8.1, and it appears that, on average, about 53.7 per cent of the studied faces are correctly recognised.

Given these results we are interested to know if the performance was, on average, better than chance. If people were asked to guess which were the old faces without having seen them during the study phase, they would have no knowledge of the right answer, so they would be expected to perform at a chance level. Since only one of the two faces in each pair is the correct one (i.e., the old one), chance is then 50 per cent. Therefore if the null hypothesis, stating that the forced choice recognition memory performance in the population is at chance, is true (and the scores obtained are normally distributed), the population mean is then 50 per cent. Note that although the expected mean is 50 per cent, not every subject will necessarily obtain a performance of 50 per cent; some random variation in the performances is expected. If we do not know what the population standard deviation (σ) is, we then need to make use of the sample data to obtain an estimate of it, i.e., *s*. As displayed in Table 8.1 it appears that $s = 6.26$. Thus the standard error of the distribution of the means from samples of 32 subjects drawn from the population of subjects performing at chance is:

$$SE_{\bar{x}} = \frac{s}{\sqrt{n}} = \frac{6.26}{\sqrt{32}} = 1.107.$$

According to the above information we know that the sampling distribution of the mean of samples of 32 observations drawn from this population has $\mu_{\bar{x}} = \mu = 50$, expressed in percentages, and an estimated standard error $SE_{\bar{x}} = 1.107$. This information can be used to assess the probability that the mean performance of our sample (i.e., 53.69) could be obtained by drawing a sample from the population of people

Table 8.2 Table of the critical values of the Student's *t*-distribution as a function of the degrees of freedom. Critical values are given in absolute terms (e.g., 2.015 corresponds to −2.015 and 2.015). For two-tailed tests the critical portions of the area under the curve are located on both tails. For one-tailed tests the critical portion of the area under the curve is located only on the relevant tail of the curve (either positive or negative, as specified by the alternative hypothesis)

df	alpha = 0.10 two tails	alpha = 0.05 two tails	alpha = 0.01 two tails
5	2.015	2.571	4.032
10	1.812	2.228	3.169
12	1.782	2.179	3.055
16	1.746	2.120	2.921
18	1.734	2.101	2.878
20	1.725	2.086	2.845
22	1.717	2.074	2.819
24	1.711	2.064	2.797
30	1.697	2.042	2.750
31	1.696	2.040	2.744
35	1.690	2.030	2.724
44	1.680	2.015	2.692
50	1.676	2.009	2.678
100	1.660	1.984	2.626
1000	1.646	1.962	2.581
∞	1.645	1.960	2.576
	alpha = 0.05 one tail	alpha = 0.025 one tail	alpha = 0.005 one tail

performing at chance in the forced choice recognition memory test. If this probability is equal to or less than 0.05, the null hypothesis is rejected and the alternative hypothesis, stating that the sample was drawn from a population whose average performance is different from 50 per cent (i.e., different from chance), is then accepted. In order to test if we can reject the null hypothesis we need to calculate the value of *t* corresponding to a mean of 53.69 per cent and then decide if this value lies outside the critical range of values for the relevant Student *t*-distribution (i.e., with $df = n - 1 = 32 - 1 = 31$).

From the formula for *t* applied to our data we obtain that:

$$t = \frac{\bar{x} - \mu}{SE_{\bar{x}}} = \frac{\bar{x} - \mu}{\frac{s}{\sqrt{n}}} = \frac{53.69 - 50}{\frac{6.26}{\sqrt{32}}} = \frac{3.69}{1.107} = 3.33.$$

The next step is to calculate the values of the *t*-distribution for $df = 32 - 1 = 31$, between which 95 per cent of the area under the *t*-curve lies. The critical values of *t* for a large number of degrees of freedom are provided in the *t* table in the Appendix. A smaller version of the *t* table is presented in Table 8.2. If the *t*-test performed is two-tailed, then the critical values for the above example are ±2.04. Since 3.33 lies outside this range, the null hypothesis is rejected and it is concluded that the performance in the forced choice recognition memory test is different from chance (i.e., better than chance). If the nature of the investigation had allowed us to conduct a one-tailed test (e.g., if it was unreasonable that subjects, on average, could perform at a less than chance level), then the critical value, at alpha = 0.05, would have been 1.696.

Two-sided confidence intervals for a population mean

In the previous example we applied the one-sample *t*-test to assess if the performance in the forced choice recognition memory test was different from chance. Since the obtained *t*-value was sufficiently large we rejected the null hypothesis, and concluded that our sample was most likely drawn from a population whose mean performance differs from 50 per cent. However, our test did not tell us what was the mean of this population. As we saw in the section on pages 36–38, the best point estimate of the unknown population mean is the sample mean (i.e., $\bar{x} = 53.69$). Although $\bar{x}$ is an unbiased estimator of μ (i.e., the long-term average or expected value of $\bar{x}$ corresponds to μ), we do not know how close this point estimate is to the true population mean. Hence it would be useful to identify intervals of values with a relatively high probability to include the true population mean. In the remaining part of this section we use sampled data to obtain (infer) ranges of values within which the true population mean lies with a given probability (i.e., we construct confidence intervals for the population mean). The width of a confidence interval offers a basis to decide if the sampled data provide a precise estimate for the location of the population mean (i.e., when the limits of the interval are close, then the location of the population mean is more precise).

Let us describe the method used to calculate two-sided confidence intervals for a population mean. The term two-sided (which is usually omitted) indicates that the same attention is given to both tails of the distribution. First we show how to calculate confidence intervals for situations in which σ is known. Then this method is modified so that it can be applied to situations where σ is not known (i.e., s is used as an estimate of σ). This last method will then be applied to the study described in the previous section about recognition memory.

Confidence intervals for a population mean when σ is known

According to the Central Limit Theorem we know that $\bar{x}$ is normally distributed with mean = μ and standard error = $\dfrac{\sigma}{\sqrt{n}}$, where n = sample size. Inspecting the standardised normal distribution tables we know that the probability that z is equal to or larger than 1.96 is 0.025. More formally:

$$P(z \geq 1.96) = 0.025$$

and for the opposite tail of the distribution:

$$P(z \leq -1.96) = 0.025$$

hence,

$$P(-1.96 \leq z \leq 1.96) = 0.95 \quad \text{or equivalently,} \quad P(1.96 \geq z \geq -1.96) = 0.95.$$

Since $z = \dfrac{\bar{x} - \mu}{\dfrac{\sigma}{\sqrt{n}}}$ we can substitute $\dfrac{\bar{x} - \mu}{\dfrac{\sigma}{\sqrt{n}}}$ for z in the previous formula, thus:

$$P\left(1.96 \geq \dfrac{\bar{x} - \mu}{\dfrac{\sigma}{\sqrt{n}}} \geq -1.96\right) = 0.95.$$

Since $\dfrac{\sigma}{\sqrt{n}} = \sigma_{\bar{x}}$:

$$P\left(1.96 \geq \dfrac{\bar{x} - \mu}{\sigma_{\bar{x}}} \geq -1.96\right) = 0.95.$$

Rearranging within the brackets:

$$P(1.96 \times \sigma_{\bar{x}} - \bar{x} \geq -\mu \geq -1.96 \times \sigma_{\bar{x}} - \bar{x}) = 0.95.$$

Since we want to find the interval containing μ and not $-\mu$, we multiply the components of the inequality by -1 (this implies that the "greater than" symbols become "less than" symbols) and we obtain:

$$P(-1.96 \times \sigma_{\bar{x}} + \bar{x} \leq \mu \leq 1.96 \times \sigma_{\bar{x}} + \bar{x}) = 0.95$$

or equivalently

$$P(\bar{x} - 1.96 \times \sigma_{\bar{x}} \leq \mu \leq \bar{x} + 1.96 \times \sigma_{\bar{x}}) = 0.95.$$

The above statement indicates that the interval $\bar{x} \pm 1.96 \times \sigma_{\bar{x}}$ has a probability of 0.95 of including the true population mean. This interval is called the *95% confidence interval* for μ. When the above formula is applied, the value of a specific sample mean is entered for $\bar{x}$ (remember that $\bar{x}$ depends on the sample being drawn). However, since different values of the sample mean can be entered to calculate this interval, intervals obtained using different samples will have different limits. In any case, out of one hundred 95% confidence intervals obtained from one hundred random samples of n observations drawn from a given population with variance $= \sigma^2$, on average, 95 of these intervals will include the true population mean. The probability that a confidence interval will include the true population mean can be changed by simply selecting a different critical value of z, depending on the desired probability to be associated with the confidence interval. For example, in the case of a 99% confidence interval, denoted as $CI_{99\%}$, the critical z value to be inserted in the above formula is 2.576. Therefore:

$$P(\bar{x} - 2.576 \times \sigma_{\bar{x}} \leq \mu \leq \bar{x} + 2.576 \times \sigma_{\bar{x}}) = 0.99$$

(or equivalently, the interval $\bar{x} \pm 2.576 \times \sigma_{\bar{x}}$ has a probability of 0.99 of including the true population mean).

Hence, the general formula for confidence intervals for μ is:

$$\mathrm{CI} = \bar{x} \pm c \times \sigma_{\bar{x}}$$

where c is the two-tailed critical value of z for any desired α level (i.e., $z_{\frac{\alpha}{2}}$).

As an example, imagine that a random sample of 25 8-year-old children have been given a new treatment to improve IQ, and that the mean IQ at the end of the treatment in this sample is 108. We also know that the distribution of the IQ scores in the 8-year-old children is normal with $\mu = 100$, and $\sigma = 15$. Given these data, we want to find the 95% confidence interval for the population mean from which our sample was drawn. The first thing to do is to calculate the standard error of the mean:

$$\sigma_{\bar{x}} = \frac{\sigma}{\sqrt{n}} = \frac{15}{\sqrt{25}} = 3.$$

Then, applying the formula for confidence intervals to our data, we find that μ lies within the following values:

$$\bar{x} \pm 1.96 \times 3 = 108 \pm 1.96 \times 3.$$

Thus, the $\mathrm{CI}_{95\%} = 102.12 \leq \mu \leq 113.88$ i.e., the 95% confidence limits for μ are 102.12 and 113.88, indicating that it is unlikely that our sample was drawn from a population with $\mu = 100$. If this had been the case, the value of 100 would have fallen within the limits of the 95% confidence interval for the population mean. In other words, the outcome of this fictitious study could be summarised by saying that the treatment used to improve children's IQ was successful.

Confidence intervals for a population mean when σ is unknown

If the population standard deviation needs to be estimated using sample data (i.e., σ is unknown), then we know that $\bar{x}$ is distributed as t, with $df = n - 1$ (where n is the sample size), with mean $= \mu$, and $SE_{\bar{x}} = \frac{s}{\sqrt{n}}$. If we want to construct a confidence interval for the population mean, we need to modify the previous formula for confidence intervals by substituting $SE_{\bar{x}}$ for $\sigma_{\bar{x}}$, and by using the critical value of the relevant t-distribution instead of the z-distribution. Remember that the critical value of t depends on the degrees of freedom of the relevant t-distribution. For example, if we want to calculate the 99% confidence interval using the data from a sample of 45 subjects (i.e., $df = 44$), then the two-sided critical value of the t-distribution is 2.692 (see Table 8.2). Denoting this critical value as c, the limits of any confidence interval are:

$$\bar{x} \pm c \times SE_{\bar{x}}.$$

Let us apply the above procedure to construct a 95% confidence interval for the forced choice recognition memory example previously described. In this case we know that $\bar{x} = 53.69$, and that $s = 6.26$. Therefore the standard error is $SE_{\bar{x}} = \frac{s}{\sqrt{n}} = \frac{6.26}{\sqrt{32}} = 1.107.$

The relevant t-distribution has 31 degrees of freedom (i.e., $df = n - 1 = 32 - 1 = 31$), thus c is 2.04 (see Table 8.2). Hence:

$$\bar{x} \pm c \times SE_{\bar{x}} = 53.69 \pm 2.04 \times 1.107 = 53.69 \pm 2.258 \text{ (to 3 d.p.)}.$$

We can conclude that the 95% confidence limits for μ are 51.432 and 55.948, and that the 95% confidence interval is:

$$CI_{0.95} = 51.432 \leq \mu \leq 55.948.$$

Note that this interval does *not* include the value $\mu = 50$. This was expected since the one-sample t-test carried out on these data in the previous section was significant. This meant that we accepted the alternative hypothesis stating that our sample was drawn from a population with $\mu \neq 50$. Accordingly, the 95% confidence interval does not include $\mu = 50$ within its limits. If this value had been included within the 95% confidence interval, then the corresponding one-sample t-test, for an alpha level of 0.05, would not have been significant (i.e., the null hypothesis stating that our sample was drawn from a population with $\mu = 50$ could not have been rejected).

Now consider the case in which we want to construct a 99.9% confidence interval for the forced choice recognition memory study. Now c would be 3.633 (this is the critical value of the t-distribution, $df = 31$, for an alpha of 0.001, two tails). Therefore:

$$\bar{x} \pm c \times SE_{\bar{x}} = 53.69 \pm 3.633 \times 1.107 = 53.69 \pm 4.022 \text{ (to 3 d.p.)}.$$

Thus, the 99.9% confidence limits for μ are 49.668 and 57.712, with the 99.9% confidence interval being:

$$CI_{0.999} = 49.668 \leq \mu \leq 57.712.$$

Note that the interval now includes 50. This reflects the fact that we have constructed the interval with a more stringent procedure that allows, on average, 999 out of 1000 intervals, instead of 950 out of 1000 as before, to include the true population mean. Similarly, if we had performed a one-sample t-test with an α level of 0.001, this would not have been significant. The critical value of the t-distribution ($df = 31$, for an α level of 0.001, two tails) is 3.633, and our calculated t value was 3.33. With such a low probability of committing a Type I error we cannot reject the null hypothesis stating that our sample was drawn from a population with $\mu = 50$.

As an addendum it should be noted that a statement of the type:

$$P(\bar{x} - c \times SE_{\bar{x}} \leq \mu \leq \bar{x} + c \times SE_{\bar{x}}) = 0.95$$

indicates that this type of confidence interval has a 0.95 probability of containing μ. However, when we sample n observations, we obtain a specific value of the variable $\bar{x}$ and of the standard error $SE_{\bar{x}}$ and when these values are entered into the above equation, with the appropriate value of c (according to the relevant df and the selected probability), the specific confidence interval we obtain ($51.432 \leq \mu \leq 55.94$) either includes or excludes μ. Unlike $\bar{x}$ which is a variable, μ, although unknown, is fixed, so any specific confidence interval either includes μ or it does not. Hence, any specific confidence interval has a probability of either 1 or 0 of containing μ. We cannot say that a specific confidence interval contains μ or not, but we can say, for example, that intervals of the type $\bar{x} \pm c \times SE_{\bar{x}}$ will include the true population mean with the probability associated with the selected value of c.

Finally, we reiterate that it is important to use several decimal places during the intermediate stages of any computation. Rounding at an early stage of the computational process may lead to low accuracy. To simplify the presentation of the computations we only showed either 2 or 3 decimal places here. You need to employ more places during computation and to leave any rounding to the end.

Chapter 9

Comparing a pair of means

The matched- and the independent-samples t-test

Introduction

In Chapter 8 we mainly described how to decide if a set of observations was drawn from a given population. We showed how to apply the t-test in assessing the probability that a set of observations, with their observed mean, was drawn from a population with a given mean. In that chapter we also showed how to use sample data to construct confidence intervals that have a given probability of containing the true population mean. In this chapter we will extend the application of the t-test to situations in which we intend to compare the means obtained from two sets of observations. The aim of this comparison is to decide if the two sets are sampled from the same population or not.

If the outcome of the t-test gives a sufficiently small probability of the two sets of observations being drawn from the same population, then we declare that the two sets of observations are drawn from different populations (i.e., there is a significant difference between the means). Two different conditions in which the t-test is applied to compare a pair of means will be described:

a) when the means are obtained from two sets of related observations; and
b) when the two sets of observations are independent.

We also explain how to construct confidence intervals for the difference of a pair of population means, and we describe the conditions where the t-test may not be appropriate for comparing pairs of means. This occurs when some of the assumptions underlying the use of the t-test are violated. For these cases we indicate alternative ways to analyse the data. Given the strong similarity to the one-sample t-test, we first describe the application of the t-test to sets of related observations.

The matched-samples t-test

The matched-samples t-test (also called related- or paired- or nonindependent-samples t-test) is used to compare means obtained from two sets of related scores (these two sets are assumed to have been drawn from normally distributed populations with equal variances). The most common way to obtain related sets of scores occurs when the same subjects are measured twice in some task. For example, when a sample of people have their pulse rates measured, at rest, and after 5 minutes of aerobic exercise. We would expect each subject's pulse rate to increase after exercising, compared to the resting baseline. We would also expect people with a relatively high resting pulse rate to have a relatively high post-exercise pulse rate and, conversely, people with a relatively low resting pulse rate to have a relatively low pulse rate after aerobic exercise. Overall, we would expect the measurements of pulse rate before and after exercising to be related.

We will now describe a fictitious memory experiment to provide an example of the application of the *t*-test in the analysis of matched samples. Consider the following study designed to assess if pictures are easier to remember than words. In this experiment 21 people are asked to commit to memory a series of 40 stimuli individually displayed on a computer screen for 4 seconds each. The study list includes 20 words, referring to objects, randomly intermixed with 20 pictures depicting objects. At the end of the learning phase subjects are required to recall, in any order they want, all the items they can remember from the list of pictures and words just presented. The number of pictures and words recalled by each subject is recorded, and we want to make use of these data to test if pictures are easier or more difficult to recall than words. When all the data are collected we will have a set of paired scores, i.e., the number of pictures and number of words recalled by each subject (see Table 9.1); thus, the matched-samples *t*-test seems suitable to analyse these data.

To decide if pictures are easier or more difficult to recall than words, we need to state the null hypothesis. This states that the mean number of words and pictures recalled should be identical, thus H_0: $\mu_{pictures} = \mu_{words}$, or equivalently, H_0: $\mu_{pictures} - \mu_{words} = 0$, hence H_0: $\mu_D = 0$, where D is the difference between the mean number of pictures and words recalled. The alternative hypothesis states that the mean number of pictures and words recalled differs, thus H_1: $\mu_{pictures} \neq \mu_{words}$, or equivalently H_1: $\mu_{pictures} - \mu_{words} \neq 0$, hence H_1: $\mu_D \neq 0$. So to decide if we can reject the null hypothesis, we need to establish whether the mean of the sampled difference scores, i.e., $\bar{D}$, shown in Table 9.1, is significantly different from 0 (zero being the population mean of the difference scores under the assumption that the null hypothesis is true). If the value of $\bar{D}$ is large, it is unlikely that the sampled difference scores are drawn from a population where $\mu_D = 0$, then we can conclude that there is a significant difference between the number of pictures and words recalled.

As you may have noticed the steps involved in assessing the null hypothesis are the same as those used when we described the one-sample *t*-test in the previous chapter. We are going to test the null hypothesis using only one set of data, obtained by subtracting pairs of related observations. To test the null hypothesis assumes that the population mean of the difference scores is zero. Therefore, in order to test the null hypothesis in our memory experiment we need to calculate the appropriate value of *t*, with the mean of the sampled difference scores $\bar{D} = 2.048$ (Table 9.1), and the population mean assumed by H_0, i.e., $\mu_D = 0$. In fact:

$$t = \frac{\bar{D} - 0}{\dfrac{s_D}{\sqrt{n}}} = \frac{\bar{D} - 0}{SE_{\bar{D}}}$$

Table 9.1 The number of pictures and words recalled by each subject is displayed in the second and third columns. The column headed "Difference scores" gives the difference between the number of pictures recalled and the number of words recalled by each subject. The computation of the matched-paired *t*-test on the difference scores (degrees of freedom in brackets) and of the 95% confidence interval are also provided

Subjects	Pictures	Words	Difference scores (D)
1	12	10	2
2	14	10	4
3	11	11	0
4	10	7	3
5	9	6	3
6	12	8	4
7	11	10	1
8	10	10	0
9	8	7	1
10	15	11	4
11	11	8	3
12	7	4	3
13	8	7	1
14	10	9	1
15	13	11	2
16	12	10	2
17	9	10	−1
18	11	9	2
19	12	8	4
20	12	9	3
21	11	10	1
Mean	10.857	8.810	2.048
Standard Deviation	1.982	1.834	1.465

Standard error:
$$SE_{\bar{D}} = \frac{s_D}{\sqrt{n}} = \frac{1.465}{\sqrt{21}} = 0.320$$

Matched-samples *t*-test (*df = n* − 1)

$$t(20) = \frac{\bar{D} - 0}{SE_{\bar{D}}}$$

$$t = \frac{2.048 - 0}{\frac{1.465}{\sqrt{21}}} = \frac{2.048 - 0}{0.32} = \frac{2.048}{0.32} = 6.4$$

Critical values of *t*(20) = ±2.086 (*α* = 0.05)

95% Confidence interval:

$$\bar{D} \pm c \times SE_{\bar{D}} = 2.048 \pm 2.086 \times 0.32$$

$$CI_{0.95} = 1.381 \leq \mu_D \leq 2.715$$

where $\bar{D}$ and s_D are the mean and the standard deviation of the difference scores, respectively, *n* is the number of difference scores, and $SE_{\bar{D}}$ is the standard error of the mean of the difference scores. Applying this formula to our data:

$$t = \frac{2.048 - 0}{\frac{1.465}{\sqrt{21}}} = \frac{2.048 - 0}{0.32} = \frac{2.048}{0.32} = 6.4.$$

The calculated t value is distributed as the t-distribution with $n - 1$ degrees of freedom, hence $df = 20$. For a two-tailed test at the 0.05 level of significance the critical values are ±2.086. Since the calculated t lies outside this range, it appears that significantly more pictures than words are recalled, possibly due to the fact that pictures can be named and therefore, unlike words, both visual and verbal representations may support free recall. There is a loss of one degree of freedom, hence $df = n - 1$, because the sample mean, i.e., $\bar{D}$, has been used to calculate s_D as an estimate of the unknown population parameter σ_D.

Although we wanted to see if pictures are more easily recalled than words we did not use a one-tailed test. This protected us from the possibility that words could have been more easily recalled than pictures. Therefore, despite predicting that $\mu_{\text{pictures}} > \mu_{\text{words}}$, the alternative hypothesis was of the form $\mu_{\text{pictures}} \neq \mu_{\text{words}}$.

It is important to know that the matched-samples t-test is not only used when we obtain pairs of measurements from each subject. While this is the most obvious way to obtain paired samples, there are other ways to obtain such samples. In general this occurs when for each pair of observations, even if obtained from different individuals, knowing something about one observation in a pair tells us something about the other observation in the pair, i.e., the observations within each pair are related. When this happens, we have matched samples.

For example, imagine a study carried out on several pairs of newly born identical twins to assess if first born twins tend to be more physically active than second born twins. Due to the fact that identical twins have an identical genetic make-up, we expect that the measurements of physical activity will be related within each pair of twins, i.e., if one twin is very active we expect the other twin to be very active too. Despite having pairs of scores from different individuals, these scores are nevertheless related, and we should use a matched-samples t-test to analyse the data. Whenever we have sets of pairs of related observations, then the matched-samples t-test is the appropriate statistical technique to test if there is a significant difference between the means of the two sets of observations.

Finally, in order to apply the matched-samples t-test, it is assumed that the variances of the populations from which the two sets of scores have been drawn are normally distributed with roughly equal variances (see the section on pages 158–159 for further details on the assumptions underlying the use of the t-test).

Confidence intervals for a population mean

Although $\bar{D}$ is an unbiased estimator of μ_D, we do not know how close this point estimate is to the true population mean of the difference scores. As shown in Chapter 7, confidence intervals specify a range of values within which the true population mean of the difference scores lies, with a given probability. In the remaining part of this section we will show how these confidence intervals are calculated. The approach used in the section on pages 143–145 can be applied to cases where we have a mean of a set of difference scores obtained from matched samples. To show how to calculate two-sided confidence intervals from matched samples we will make use of the data from Table 9.1.

In general, for difference scores, the limits of any two-sided confidence interval are:

$$\bar{D} \pm c \times SE_{\bar{D}},$$

where $\bar{D}$ and $SE_{\bar{D}}$ are the mean and the standard error of the mean of the difference scores, respectively, and c is the two-tailed critical value for the desired level of significance of the t-distribution with $df = n - 1$.

Let us apply the above procedure to construct a 95% confidence interval for the free recall data. In this case we know that $\bar{D} = 2.048$, and that $SE_{\bar{D}} = 0.32$. The relevant t-distribution has 20 degrees of freedom (i.e., $df = 21 - 1$), thus c is 2.086 (see the t table in the Appendix). Hence:

$$\bar{D} \pm c \times SE_{\bar{D}} = 2.048 \pm 2.086 \times 0.32 = 2.048 \pm 0.688 \text{ (to 3 d.p.)}.$$

Thus, we can conclude that the 95% confidence limits for μ_D are 1.381 and 2.716, and that the 95% confidence interval is:

$$CI_{0.95} = 1.381 \leq \mu_D \leq 2.716.$$

Note that this interval does not include the value of $\mu_D = 0$. Hence, the difference between the mean of the population of the number of pictures recalled and the mean of the population of the number of words recalled should be different from zero. This was expected since the matched-samples t-test carried out on the data in Table 9.1 was significant at an α level of 0.05. This meant that we accepted the alternative hypothesis, which stated that our sample of difference scores was drawn from a population with $\mu_D \neq 0$. Accordingly, the 95% confidence interval does not include zero within its limits. If this value had been included within the 95% confidence interval, then the corresponding matched-samples t-test, for an α level of 0.05, would not have been significant (i.e., the null hypothesis stating that our sample of difference scores was drawn from a population with $\mu_D = 0$ could not have been rejected).

Counterbalancing

Counterbalancing the conditions in which a subject gives repeated measurements is fundamentally important to obtaining an accurate interpretation of the results of an experiment. However, not all studies using matched samples may require counterbalancing. For example, if we want to study the effect of training on performing a task, it would be normal for the first measurement to occur at baseline, and the second to follow some training (cf. the example on the effect of aerobic exercise on pulse rate described earlier on pages 146–147). Similarly, in the memory experiment described in the same section on pages 147–149 the two conditions manipulated by the experimenter, i.e., pictures vs words, were randomly intermixed during learning, to prevent any spurious order effect potentially affecting the results. However, in some experiments there is the risk of, so-called, carry-over effects, when, for example, the order in which tasks are administered to the subjects is not counterbalanced. In these cases the outcome of an experiment would be difficult to evaluate, because it is not possible to distinguish the effect of the experimental manipulation from the effect of the order in which the conditions are administered. For example, consider a study intended to investigate the effect of study time on memory for lists of words. In this study there are two conditions:

Table 9.2 Example of a possible counterbalancing of the lists and the order of the administration of the study conditions to be used in the experiment assessing the effect of study time on memory. A minimum of 4 subjects is required for a full counterbalancing of the list and order variables

I condition	II condition
2 sec / List-a	4 sec / List-b
2 sec / List-b	4 sec / List-a
4 sec / List-b	2 sec / List-a
4 sec / List-a	2 sec / List-b

a) subjects see each word of List-a displayed for 4 seconds on a computer screen; and
b) subjects see each word of List-b displayed for 2 seconds on a computer screen.

If the two learning conditions are always administered in the same order, e.g., first subjects study the 4 seconds list followed by its recall, then the 2 seconds list followed by its recall. If significantly more words are recalled with the 4 s, it is not clear if this effect is due to differences in study time or to some noninteresting factors. For example, subjects may be more tired while trying to commit to memory the second list, and this may then lead to a disadvantage for the second list which is also the one for which subjects have less time at their disposal to commit the words to memory. To avoid this type of confounding effect it is important to counterbalance the order in which the conditions are administered. A random half of the subjects tested should perform the 2 s condition first, while the remaining half should perform the 4 s condition first. This would control for any unwanted effect from spurious non-relevant variables.

Note also that in this fictitious experiment, subjects study two different lists of words. You should avoid always using one list in conjunction with a specific study condition. If for some unexpected reason List-a, i.e., the one associated with the longer study condition, is easier to remember than List-b, i.e., the one associated with the shorter study condition, then any apparently significant effect of study time may well be due to the spurious effect of list difficulty. Therefore, in this case the type of list used should also be counterbalanced across subjects. Table 9.2 provides an example of a possible counterbalancing of lists and study conditions for this last experiment.

In summary, counterbalancing is usually required to obtain a correct experimental design where subjects are repeatedly tested under different conditions. More complex experimental designs, which are not covered in this introductory book, make use of more complex forms of counterbalancing. The reader interested in this topic can consult Roberts and Russo (1999) or a more advanced book such as Kirk (1991).

The sampling distribution of the difference between pairs of means and the independent-samples *t*-test

The sampling distribution of the difference between pairs of means

The independent-samples *t*-test is used to decide if there is a significant difference between the means of two *independent* sets of data. Independent sets of data are usually obtained when two different groups of people are tested under different conditions. In particular, for any pair of scores, where the first score is taken from the first sample and the second score from the second sample, knowing something about one of the two scores in one pair will *tell us nothing* about the other score in the pair, i.e., the two sets of scores are not related. In this section we will describe how to calculate the independent-samples t-test.

For the independent-samples t-test the null hypothesis always states that the population mean for Condition-1 is identical to the population mean for Condition-2, thus H_0: $\mu_1 = \mu_2$, or equivalently, H_0: $\mu_1 - \mu_2 = 0$. The alternative two-tailed hypothesis states that μ_1 and μ_2 differ, thus H_1: $\mu_1 \neq \mu_2$, or equivalently H_1: $\mu_1 - \mu_2 \neq 0$. Therefore, to decide if the difference between the means of two sets of sampled observations, $(\bar{x}_1 - \bar{x}_2)$, is significantly different from zero, we need to know the characteristics, under the assumption that the null hypothesis is true, of the *sampling distribution of the difference between pairs of means*. This distribution is obtained by taking, for the first member of each pair, the mean of a sample of size n_1, drawn from the population with mean = μ_1, and, for the second member of each pair, the mean of a sample of size n_2, drawn from the population with mean = μ_2. (Note the important caveat that, in order to apply the independent-samples t-test, it is assumed that these two populations are normally distributed and have identical variances, i.e., $\sigma_1^2 = \sigma_2^2$. Assuming that the null hypothesis is true, these two populations are, de facto, the same population.) For each of the possible pairs of independent samples drawn from these two populations, the difference between the observed means is recorded and then plotted. If the observed difference between the means of our two samples, i.e., $(\bar{x}_1 - \bar{x}_2)$, is located at the extreme of the sampling distribution of the difference between pairs of means, then it is concluded that it is unlikely that our samples were drawn from the same population; hence, the difference is declared significant.

To construct the sampling distribution of differences between pairs of means we need to repeatedly take random samples from two independent populations with the same mean. Thus the mean of the sampling distribution of the difference between pairs of means is zero. It can be demonstrated that the shape of this distribution is normal with its variance, $\sigma_{\bar{x}_1 - \bar{x}_2}^2$, being:

$$\sigma_{\bar{x}_1 - \bar{x}_2}^2 = \sigma_{\bar{x}_1}^2 + \sigma_{\bar{x}_2}^2$$

where $\sigma_{\bar{x}_1}^2$ is the variance of the distribution of the means of all possible samples of a given size drawn from the population with mean = μ_1, and $\sigma_{\bar{x}_2}^2$ is the variance of the distribution of the means of all possible samples of a given size drawn from the population with mean = μ_2.

As seen in the section on pages 134–136, we know, according to the Central Limit Theorem, that $\sigma_{\bar{x}}^2 = \dfrac{\sigma^2}{n}$ where n is the sample size, thus

$$\sigma_{\bar{x}_1 - \bar{x}_2}^2 = \sigma_{\bar{x}_1}^2 + \sigma_{\bar{x}_2}^2 = \frac{\sigma_1^2}{n_1} + \frac{\sigma_2^2}{n_2},$$

where σ_1^2 and σ_2^2 are the variances of the normally distributed observations in the populations with means equal to μ_1 and μ_2, respectively; n_1 and n_2 are the sizes of the samples of people drawn from populations 1 and 2, respectively.

Summarising, the distribution of the differences between pairs of means obtained from samples independently drawn from normal populations having identical means, i.e., $\mu_1 = \mu_2$, and identical variances, i.e., $\sigma_1^2 = \sigma_2^2$, is:

normal

with Mean = 0

with Variance $\sigma_{\bar{x}_1 - \bar{x}_2}^2 = \dfrac{\sigma_1^2}{n_1} + \dfrac{\sigma_2^2}{n_2}$,

and Standard error $\sigma_{\bar{x}_1 - \bar{x}_2} = \sqrt{\dfrac{\sigma_1^2}{n_1} + \dfrac{\sigma_2^2}{n_2}}$.

(Remember that the standard deviation of the sampling distribution of means is called standard error.)

Since we know the characteristics of the sampling distribution of the difference between pairs of means, we can then calculate, under the assumption that the null hypothesis is true, if the probability of obtaining the observed difference between our sampled means, $(\bar{x}_1 - \bar{x}_2)$, is too low. If this probability is equal or less than 0.05, then the null hypothesis is rejected, the alternative hypothesis is accepted, and the two samples are declared to be drawn from populations with different means, i.e., there is a significant difference between the means of the two sets of sampled observations. The independent-samples *t*-test is used in reaching this decision.

The independent-samples t-test

We have just seen that the shape of the standard distribution of the differences between pairs of means is normal, with mean = 0 and standard error = $\sqrt{\dfrac{\sigma_1^2}{n_1} + \dfrac{\sigma_2^2}{n_2}}$. We could use the *z*-test to assess if the observed difference between the sampled means is significantly different from zero. This *z* value would then be:

$$z = \frac{(\bar{x}_1 - \bar{x}_2) - (\mu_1 - \mu_2)}{\sqrt{\dfrac{\sigma_1^2}{n_1} + \dfrac{\sigma_2^2}{n_2}}} = \frac{(\bar{x}_1 - \bar{x}_2)}{\sqrt{\dfrac{\sigma_1^2}{n_1} + \dfrac{\sigma_2^2}{n_2}}}$$

where $(\bar{x}_1 - \bar{x}_2)$ is the difference between the sample means; n_1 and n_2 are the number of observations in each of the two samples; $(\mu_1 - \mu_2)$ is the difference between the population means from which the two samples should be drawn assuming that the null hypothesis is true, thus $\mu_1 - \mu_2 = 0$; and $\sqrt{\dfrac{\sigma_1^2}{n_1} + \dfrac{\sigma_2^2}{n_2}}$ is the standard error of the difference between pairs of means.

Unfortunately, to calculate the standard error we need to know the variances of the populations of individual observations having means equal to μ_1 and μ_2. As we saw in the previous chapter, it is rarely the case that we know these population variances, i.e., σ_1^2 and σ_2^2. In Chapter 8 we saw that to circumvent this problem we could estimate the population variance using sample data, i.e., s^2, and consequently, use the t-test instead of the z-test. The same approach will be used in testing the difference between means obtained from independent samples. In this case we will obtain an estimate of the standard error of the difference between means by substituting s_1^2 and s_2^2 for σ_1^2 and σ_2^2, respectively, in the above formula to calculate the standard error. Therefore the estimated standard error of the difference between pairs of means, denoted as $SE_{\bar{x}_1-\bar{x}_2}$, is as follows:

$$SE_{\bar{x}_1-\bar{x}_2} = \sqrt{\frac{s_1^2}{n_1} + \frac{s_2^2}{n_2}}$$

and the formula for the t-test is then:

$$t = \frac{(\bar{x}_1 - \bar{x}_2) - (\mu_1 - \mu_2)}{\sqrt{\dfrac{s_1^2}{n_1} + \dfrac{s_2^2}{n_2}}} = \frac{(\bar{x}_1 - \bar{x}_2)}{\sqrt{\dfrac{s_1^2}{n_1} + \dfrac{s_2^2}{n_2}}}.$$

Since the two estimated variances s_1^2 and s_2^2 are obtained using the sample means $\bar{x}_1$ and $\bar{x}_2$, respectively, then *two degrees of freedom are lost*. The number of degrees of freedom for the independent-samples t-test is:

$$df = (n_1 - 1) + (n_2 - 1) = n_1 + n_2 - 2.$$

Before showing an application of the independent-samples t-test, it is important to notice that the above formula to calculate t is only appropriate when the two independent samples have the same number of observations. The reason for this is that, to apply the independent-samples t-test, it is assumed, irrespective of the null hypothesis being true or false, that the two samples are drawn from populations with identical variances, i.e., $\sigma_1^2 = \sigma_2^2 = \sigma^2$. In the formula for the t-test we used estimates of these variances based on sample data, i.e., s_1^2 and s_2^2. These estimates are likely to differ due to variability in the samples (i.e., not all samples drawn from the same population have the same variance as the population). However, since s_1^2 and s_2^2 are estimates of the same population variance, they can be averaged to obtain a more accurate estimate of the population variance. Their average should take into consideration the sample size to give more weight to the estimate of the population variance obtained from the larger sample (i.e., the larger the sample the more accurate the estimate of σ^2). Therefore, a weighted average of the estimated variances, weighted by their degrees of freedom, should be calculated and used in the formula to obtain t.

This new estimate of the common population variance σ^2 is called a *pooled variance estimate*, and it is denoted as s_P^2:

$$s_P^2 = \frac{s_1^2 \times (n_1 - 1) + s_2^2 \times (n_2 - 1)}{(n_1 - 1) + (n_2 - 1)} = \frac{s_1^2 \times (n_1 - 1) + s_2^2 \times (n_2 - 1)}{n_1 + n_2 - 2}$$

where $(n_1 - 1)$ and $(n_2 - 1)$ are the degrees of freedom used to calculate s_1^2 and s_2^2, respectively.

The pooled variance estimate is used to calculate the standard error of the sample mean which is:

$$SE_{\bar{x}_1 - \bar{x}_2} = \sqrt{\frac{s_P^2}{n_1} + \frac{s_P^2}{n_2}} = \sqrt{s_P^2 \times \left(\frac{1}{n_1} + \frac{1}{n_2}\right)}$$

and thus, the independent-samples *t*-test is calculated as:

$$t = \frac{(\bar{x}_1 - \bar{x}_2)}{SE_{\bar{x}_1 - \bar{x}_2}} = \frac{(\bar{x}_1 - \bar{x}_2)}{\sqrt{s_P^2 \times \left(\frac{1}{n_1} + \frac{1}{n_2}\right)}}.$$

Note that this and the previous formula for the independent-samples *t*-test give identical values of *t*, provided that the number of observations in the two samples is identical, i.e., $n_1 = n_2$. If the number of observations in the two samples is different, then this last formula should be used since it provides a more accurate estimate of the population variance and of the standard error. In general, to avoid making mistakes, the formula with the pooled variance estimate should be used to calculate the independent-samples *t*-test whether the sample sizes are different or not. The next section provides an example of the application of the independent-samples *t*-test.

An application of the independent-samples t-test

In the section on pages 17–20 we described two hypothetical sets of marks obtained at the end-of-year exam in an introductory course in biology from two independent samples of 60 university students. One sample included students who regularly attended the course (at least 80 per cent of the lectures), while the remaining sample included those students who did not regularly attend the course (less than 50 per cent of the lectures). On that occasion we said that a visual comparison of the two distributions of marks, shown in Table 2.5, seemed to suggest that students who regularly attended received higher marks than poor attenders. We also said that inferential statistics techniques were necessary to substantiate that type of claim. We now know that the independent-samples *t*-test is the appropriate inferential statistics technique to assess if there is a significant difference between the mean obtained from the good and the poor attenders in the biology exam.

Table 9.3 provides the data required to calculate the independent-samples *t*-test to assess whether or not "good attenders" received, on average, higher exam marks than "poor attenders". Since $t = \dfrac{(\bar{x}_1 - \bar{x}_2)}{SE_{\bar{x}_1 - \bar{x}_2}} = \dfrac{(\bar{x}_1 - \bar{x}_2)}{\sqrt{s_P^2 \times \left(\frac{1}{n_1} + \frac{1}{n_2}\right)}}$, we need to calculate

the various individual quantities before determining *t*.

The first quantity is the difference between the two sample means:

$$(\bar{x}_1 - \bar{x}_2) = 59.3 - 54.7 = 4.6.$$

Table 9.3 This table provides means, standard deviations, and estimated population variances, using sample data, of the exam marks of two group of students, i.e., "good attenders" vs "poor attenders", in an end-of-year-exam in biology. The pooled variance estimate and the computation of the independent-samples *t*-test are provided. The degrees of freedom of the *t*-distribution used to assess the significance of the results are also reported, as well as the computation of the 95% confidence interval

	Good attenders ($n_1 = 60$)	Poor attenders ($n_2 = 60$)
Mean	59.3	54.7
Standard Deviation	11.032	11.6
Variance (s^2)	121.705	134.553

Pooled variance estimate

$$s_P^2 = \frac{s_1^2 \times (n_1 - 1) + s_2^2 \times (n_2 - 1)}{n_1 + n_2 - 2} \qquad s_P^2 = \frac{121.705 \times (60 - 1) + 134.553 \times (60 - 1)}{60 + 60 - 2} = 128.129$$

$$t = \frac{(\bar{x}_1 - \bar{x}_2)}{\sqrt{s_P^2 \times \left(\frac{1}{n_1} + \frac{1}{n_2}\right)}} = \frac{59.3 - 54.7}{\sqrt{128.129 \times \left(\frac{1}{60} + \frac{1}{60}\right)}} = \frac{4.6}{2.0667} = 2.226$$

$df = n_1 + n_2 - 2 = 60 + 60 - 2 = 118$

Critical values of $t(118) = \pm 1.98$ ($\alpha = 0.05$, two tails)

95% Confidence interval: $(\bar{x}_1 - \bar{x}_2) \pm c \times SE_{(\bar{x}_1 - \bar{x}_2)} = 4.6 \pm 1.98 \times 2.0667$

$CI_{0.95} = 0.508 \le (\mu_1 - \mu_2) \le 8.692$

Then to calculate the standard error of the difference between means, we need to calculate the pooled variance estimate. This is the weighted average of the estimated population variances, weighted by their degrees of freedom. Hence:

$$s_P^2 = \frac{s_1^2 \times (n_1 - 1) + s_2^2 \times (n_2 - 1)}{n_1 + n_2 - 2},$$

$$s_P^2 = \frac{121.705 \times (60 - 1) + 134.553 \times (60 - 1)}{60 + 60 - 2} = 128.129.$$

So the standard error of the difference between pairs of means is:

$$SE_{\bar{x}_1 - \bar{x}_2} = \sqrt{s_P^2 \times \left(\frac{1}{n_1} + \frac{1}{n_2}\right)} = \sqrt{128.129 \times \left(\frac{1}{60} + \frac{1}{60}\right)} = 2.0667$$

and hence,

$$t = \frac{59.3 - 54.7}{2.0667} = 2.226 \text{ (3 d.p.).}$$

To assess whether or not there is a significant difference between the mean exam marks obtained by the two groups of students we need to compare the calculated value of t against the Student's t-distribution with $df = n_1 + n_2 - 2 = 60 + 60 - 2 = 118$. Inspecting the t table in the Appendix, it appears that, for a two-tailed test at the 0.05 level of significance, the critical values for this t-distribution are ± 1.98. Since the calculated t lies outside this range of values, it appears that the mean exam mark of the students who regularly attended the biology course was significantly higher than the mean exam mark obtained by the poor attenders.

Confidence intervals for the difference between two population means

As in the matched-samples case, it is possible to calculate two-sided confidence intervals for the difference between μ_1 and μ_2 using data from two independent samples. The procedure is similar to the one used for calculating confidence intervals using matched samples. In particular the limits of any confidence interval for the difference between two population means, estimated using data from two independent samples are:

$$(\bar{x}_1 - \bar{x}_2) \pm c \times SE_{(\bar{x}_1 - \bar{x}_2)}$$

where $(\bar{x}_1 - \bar{x}_2)$ is the difference between the two sample means; $SE_{(\bar{x}_1 - \bar{x}_2)}$ is the standard error of the difference between pairs of means; and c is the two-sided critical value for the desired level of significance of the t-distribution with $df = n_1 + n_2 - 2$, where n_1 and n_2 are the sizes of the two independent samples.

Let us apply the above procedure to construct a 95% confidence interval for the biology exam data previously analysed using the independent-samples t-test. In this case we know that $(\bar{x}_1 - \bar{x}_2) = 4.6$, and that $SE_{(\bar{x}_1 - \bar{x}_2)} = 2.0667$. The relevant t-distribution has 118 degrees of freedom (i.e., $df = 60 + 60 - 2$), thus $c = t_{\frac{\alpha}{2}} = 1.98$ (see the t table in the Appendix). Hence:

$$(\bar{x}_1 - \bar{x}_2) \pm c \times SE_{(\bar{x}_1 - \bar{x}_2)} = 4.6 \pm 1.98 \times 2.0667 = 4.6 \pm 4.092 \text{ (to 3 d.p.).}$$

We can conclude that the 95% confidence limits for $(\mu_1 - \mu_2)$ are 0.508 and 8.692, and that the 95% confidence interval is:

$$\text{CI}_{0.95} = 0.508 \leq (\mu_1 - \mu_2) \leq 8.692.$$

Note that this interval does not include the value of $(\mu_1 - \mu_2) = 0$. Hence, the difference between the mean mark of the population of students regularly attending lectures and the mean mark of the population of students who do not regularly attend lectures should be different from zero. This was expected since the independent-samples t-test carried out on the same data was significant at $\alpha = 0.05$. This meant that we accepted the alternative hypothesis stating that our samples were not drawn from the same population. Accordingly, the 95% confidence interval does not include $\mu_1 - \mu_2 = 0$ within its limits. If this value had been included within the 95% confidence interval, then the corresponding t-test, for an alpha level of 0.05, would not have been declared significant.

If, instead of the 95% confidence interval, we had calculated the 99% confidence interval then $c = 2.618$ and the confidence interval would have been:

$$(\bar{x}_1 - \bar{x}_2) \pm c \times SE_{(\bar{x}_1 - \bar{x}_2)} = 4.6 \pm 2.618 \times 2.0667 = 4.6 \pm 5.411$$

with the 99% confidence limits for $(\mu_1 - \mu_2)$ being -0.811 and 10.011, and the 99% confidence interval being:

$$CI_{0.99} = -0.811 \leq (\mu_1 - \mu_2) \leq 10.011.$$

In this case the confidence interval includes zero within its limits. This reflects the fact that we have constructed the interval with more stringent criteria allowing 99 out of 100 intervals, on average, instead of 95 out of 100 as before, to include the true difference between the two populations means μ_1 and μ_2. Similarly, if we had performed an independent-samples t-test on the same data with an alpha level of 0.01, this would not have been significant. As seen in the previous section t was 2.226 while the critical value of the t-distribution ($df = 118$, for an alpha level of 0.01, two tails) is 2.618. Thus, after having reduced the probability of committing a Type I error from 0.05 to 0.01, we cannot reject the null hypothesis stating that $\mu_1 = \mu_2$.

The robustness of the independent-samples t-test

In the section on pages 153–155 we mentioned, albeit briefly, that some assumptions are made in order to correctly apply the independent-samples t-test to test the significance of the difference between two means. The main assumptions are that the observations, other than being independent random samples, need to be drawn from *normally distributed populations with identical variances*, i.e., $\sigma_1^2 = \sigma_2^2$. If these two assumptions are not met, then the outcome of the independent-samples t-test may be biased. This bias is mainly associated with the probability of committing a Type I error. What can happen is that, although the nominal significance level may be set at $p = 0.05$, the violation of some of the underlying assumptions of the t-test may lead to a larger t value than it should really be and hence, to a larger probability of falsely rejecting a true null hypothesis.

Despite the above warning, it is generally acknowledged that the t-test is quite robust to violations of the assumptions of normality and homogeneity of variances. Robustness means that moderate departures from the underlying assumptions leave the outcome of the t-test relatively unaffected. We need to know when to be concerned about these departures from the underlying assumptions, and what the consequences of these deviations are.

The assumption of normality

Let us consider first the assumption about the normality of the distribution of the observations in the two *populations* from which the samples are drawn. Remember that assumptions always refer to the population. For example under the assumption of equal population variances we expect small variations in the estimates of variances obtained using samples drawn from populations with equal variances. Similarly we expect that samples drawn from normal populations will be roughly unimodal, symmetrical and reasonably bell shaped. Generally the distributions of the observations in a population tend to be normal. However, this is not always the case. For example, the distributions of reaction time data tend to be positively skewed. In general, the assumption of normality can be somewhat relaxed without relevant consequences, although it is important that the distributions of the two populations are of comparable shape. So if, for example, they are skewed, they should both be skewed in the same direction.

The application of the *t*-test can lead to biased results if the distributions of the two populations are significantly skewed in opposite directions. In this case it is no longer meaningful to compare means since it is difficult to interpret the outcome of the *t*-test. Its significance could be due to an artefact induced by the different distributions or because of the two experimental conditions being compared. Similarly, the application of the *t*-test to bimodal data is of limited value since means provide a poor summary of bimodal distributions. As a final remark it is important to remember that, since we do not always know the distribution of the entire population, we can use the distribution of the sampled data to gather information about the distribution of the parent population (remember, Chapter 2 provided various techniques that could be employed to describe sets of data).

The assumption of homogeneity of variances

The second assumption underlying the use of the independent-samples *t*-test states that the variances of the populations from which the two samples are drawn are identical, i.e., $\sigma_1^2 = \sigma_2^2$. Since we work with sample data we can calculate point estimates of the population variances, i.e., s_1^2 and s_2^2. As mentioned before, these estimates obtained from sample data may differ numerically even when the two samples are drawn from the same population. Hence we need to know when the discrepancy between these two variance estimates is great enough to be of concern. As a rough rule of thumb, in order to obtain unbiased outcomes of the *t*-test, the larger variance estimate should be no more than three times, and certainly no more than four times, the smaller estimate. If more certainty is required specific tests can be used. The interested reader can consult, for example, Howell (1997). In the example that follows we will show a case where the homogeneity of variance assumption has been violated. We will also show how to deal with this type of problem.

An example of the violation of the assumption of homogeneity of variances

Consider a small fictitious set of observations taken from two samples of 11 young adults and 9 elderly adults (see Table 9.4). Each subject is given a series of 100 anagrams to solve (a maximum of 30 seconds is allowed to solve each anagram), and the dependent variable is the percentage of anagrams correctly completed. Table 9.4 shows the percentage of anagrams solved for each subject in each group, the group means and the estimated variances ($s_1^2 = 16.4$, for the young group; $s_2^2 = 101.50$, for the elderly group). The ratio obtained by dividing the larger variance by the smaller variance is greater than 4. Hence we consider that the variances of the distribution of the percentage of anagrams solved in the populations of young and old adults are different.

Table 9.4 This table shows the percentage of anagrams solved by each subject in each group; the group means and the estimated variances of each sample. The ratio between the largest and the smallest variance estimates is > 4; thus, the homogeneity of variances assumption is considered violated. Finally the standard error of the difference between pairs of means ($SE_{\bar{x}_1-\bar{x}_2}$) used to calculate the *t*-test is given, as well as the value of the modified *t*-test, i.e., *t'*; the degrees of freedom of the appropriate *t*-distribution, and their critical ranges to assess *t'*. A detailed explanation of how to calculate these degrees of freedom is provided in the main text

	Young adults $n_1 = 11$	Elderly adults $n_2 = 9$
	60	42
	61	51
	62	52
	64	54
	65	56
	66	59
	67	63
	68	71
	70	74
	71	
	72	
Mean	66.0	58.0
s_1^2 and s_2^2	16.40	101.50
$\dfrac{s_2^2}{s_1^2} > 4$		

$$SE_{\bar{x}_1-\bar{x}_2} = \sqrt{\frac{s_1^2}{n_1} + \frac{s_2^2}{n_2}} = \sqrt{\frac{16.4}{11} + \frac{101.5}{9}} = 3.573$$

$$t' = \frac{\bar{x}_1 - \bar{x}_2}{\sqrt{\dfrac{s_1^2}{n_1} + \dfrac{s_2^2}{n_2}}} = \frac{66 - 58}{3.573} = 2.239$$

Critical values of *t'* for $df = n_2 - 1 = 9 - 1 = 8$:

±2.306; $\alpha = 0.05$, two tails

$$df' = \frac{\left(\dfrac{s_1^2}{n_1} + \dfrac{s_2^2}{n_2}\right)^2}{\dfrac{\left(\dfrac{s_1^2}{n_1}\right)^2}{n_1 - 1} + \dfrac{\left(\dfrac{s_2^2}{n_2}\right)^2}{n_2 - 1}} \qquad df' = \frac{\left(\dfrac{16.4}{11} + \dfrac{101.5}{9}\right)^2}{\dfrac{\left(\dfrac{16.4}{11}\right)^2}{11 - 1} + \dfrac{\left(\dfrac{101.5}{9}\right)^2}{9 - 1}} = \frac{163.039}{16.121} = 10.114$$

Critical values of *t'* for $df' = 10$: ±2.228

Since the variances in the two populations are considered different, there is no common population variance. So it is not sensible to calculate the pooled variance estimate of the common population variance to estimate the standard error of the difference between pairs of means for use in the *t*-test. When the assumption about the homogeneity of variance is violated, a modified version of the *t*-test, that we will call *t'*, is to be used to assess if the difference between the obtained sample means is significant. *t'* is calculated as:

$$t' = \frac{\bar{x}_1 - \bar{x}_2}{\sqrt{\dfrac{s_1^2}{n_1} + \dfrac{s_2^2}{n_2}}}.$$

(Notice that the formula for *t'* is the same as the one for *t* when samples have the same size.)

In our example we obtain:

$$t' = \frac{66 - 58}{\sqrt{\dfrac{16.4}{11} + \dfrac{101.5}{9}}} = \frac{8}{3.573} = 2.239.$$

The main problem is that *t'* may not be distributed as *t* with $df = n_1 + n_2 - 2$ (i.e., 18 in our example). Hence, we need to find the appropriate number of degrees of freedom of the *t*-distribution to be used to decide whether or not *t'* is significant.

Before showing the method used to calculate the appropriate number of degrees of freedom, it is important to note that this value always lies between the smaller of $n_1 - 1$ and $n_2 - 1$ and $n_1 + n_2 - 2$. If the obtained *t'* lies outside the range of the critical values associated with the *t*-distribution, with *df* being the smaller of the values $n_1 - 1$ and $n_2 - 1$, then there is no need to calculate the precise number of *df*. This value will, most likely, be larger, and therefore, if the result is significant for a smaller number of degrees of freedom, it will necessarily be significant for larger *df*.

In the case of our example, the smaller value between $n_1 - 1$ and $n_2 - 1$ is 8 (i.e., 9 − 1). Hence, let us first inspect if *t'* lies outside the critical range of values of the *t*-distribution with $df = 8$ for an alpha level of 0.05, two-tails. These critical values are ±2.306. Since the calculated *t'* (i.e., 2.239) lies inside this range, we cannot reject the null hypothesis.

Given that we could not reject the null hypothesis for the lowest number of degrees of freedom, we need to accurately calculate the *df* of the *t*-distribution of which *t'* is a member, under the assumption that the null hypothesis underlying the use of the modified *t*-test is true (i.e., $\mu_1 = \mu_2$), and to re-assess the significance of the results. The appropriate number of degrees of freedom to evaluate *t'*, are calculated as the nearest integer to *df'*, which is equal to:

$$df' = \frac{\left(\dfrac{s_1^2}{n_1} + \dfrac{s_2^2}{n_2}\right)^2}{\dfrac{\left(\dfrac{s_1^2}{n_1}\right)^2}{n_1 - 1} + \dfrac{\left(\dfrac{s_2^2}{n_2}\right)^2}{n_2 - 1}}.$$

When this formula is applied to the data in Table 9.4, we find:

$$df' = \frac{\left(\dfrac{16.4}{11} + \dfrac{101.5}{9}\right)^2}{\dfrac{\left(\dfrac{16.4}{11}\right)^2}{11-1} + \dfrac{\left(\dfrac{101.5}{9}\right)^2}{9-1}} = \frac{163.039}{16.121} = 10.114$$

and thus the appropriate t-distribution to be used has $df = 10$. The critical values of this t-distribution, for a two-tailed alpha level of 0.05, are ± 2.228. Since the value of $t' = 2.239$, which lies outside this range, we can reject the null hypothesis and conclude that fewer anagrams, on average, are solved by elderly adults compared to young adults.

If we had, erroneously, used the pooled variance estimate to calculate the t-test to compare the performance of young and elderly in the anagram task, we would have obtained a value of 2.417. This value is inflated by about 8 per cent compared to the value of t', which was calculated using the correct approach when the assumption of homogeneity of variance is violated.

Summarising, if the assumption of homogeneity of variance is violated, then you need to calculate t' instead of t. The significance of the value of t' needs to be assessed using first the t-distribution with df being the smaller of the two values $n_1 - 1$ and $n_2 - 1$. If the test is significant at this number of degrees of freedom, then you stop and the null hypothesis can be rejected. If the test is not significant, then you need to calculate the number of degrees of freedom using the previously described formula for df', and assess t' against the t-distribution with $df = df'$. As a rule of thumb, you may keep in mind that, if the smaller sample has at least 12 observations, then any value of t' larger than 2.25 will lead to the rejection of the null hypothesis (for $\alpha = 0.05$, two tails). Finally, it is important to know that there are alternative tests that do not make any assumption about homogeneity of variances or restrictive assumptions on the shape and spread of the distributions (e.g., normality). These, so-called, *nonparametric* or *distribution-free* statistical tests can be used instead of the t-test when the data collected violate the assumptions underlying the use of the t-test. Some of the most common nonparametric tests and their application will be described in Chapter 10.

Ceiling and floor effects

An important consideration to keep in mind when analysing sets of data is that the outcome of this analysis and its interpretation are strongly associated with the quality of the data collected. In the previous section we saw that the outcome of the independent-samples t-test can be biased if the data do not conform to the boundary conditions for its application. Although it is important to respect the assumptions underlying a statistical test, it is equally important to avoid collecting data that are plagued by ceiling and floor effects. The presence of these effects seriously undermines the interpretation of statistical analyses.

Ceiling effects occur when subjects perform at the top of the possible range of the scores used to measure their performance, while *floor effects* occur when subjects perform at the bottom of this possible range of scores. The presence of ceiling effects indicates that subjects could have obtained higher scores than they did, if the measurement scale had permitted a wider range of scores. Conversely, the presence of floor effects indicates that subjects could potentially have obtained a non-zero score, assuming that zero is the lowest possible attainable score, if the measurement scale had permitted finer measurements at the lowest end of the scale. Ceiling and floor effects indicate that for some subjects we may have a relatively poor measure of their performance, and the outcome of any statistical test may be negatively affected by this fault in the measurement process.

Let us describe an example to demonstrate how ceiling effects can influence the interpretation of results obtained using the independent-samples *t*-test. Table 9.5 provides the data from a fictitious experiment where a sample of 12 first year non-mature university students and a sample of 12 retired elderly adults (who obtained a degree in

Table 9.5 Results of a study comparing the free recall performance of a sample of 12 first year non-mature university students and 12 retired elderly adults in the presence of ceiling effects (Experiment 1; recall of a list of 10 words) and without ceiling effects (Experiment 2; recall of a list of 15 words)

	Experiment 1	$n_1 = n_2 = 12$	Experiment 2	$n_1 = n_2 = 12$
	University students	Retired elderly adults	University students	Retired elderly adults
	10	9	13	11
	10	9	13	10
	9	9	11	9
	9	8	10	9
	8	8	9	9
	8	8	9	8
	8	8	9	8
	8	7	9	7
	7	7	8	7
	7	6	8	6
	6	6	8	6
	6	5	7	5
Mean	8.00	7.50	9.50	7.917
Estimated variance	$s_1^2 = 1.818$	$s_2^2 = 1.727$	$s_1^2 = 3.727$	$s_2^2 = 3.174$

$$s_P^2 = \frac{s_1^2 \times (n_1 - 1) + s_2^2 \times (n_2 - 1)}{n_1 + n_2 - 2} = 1.773 \qquad\qquad s_P^2 = 3.451$$

$$SE_{\bar{x}_1 - \bar{x}_2} = \sqrt{s_P^2 \times \left(\frac{1}{n_1} + \frac{1}{n_2}\right)} = \sqrt{1.773 \times \frac{1}{6}} = 0.544 \qquad SE_{\bar{x}_1 - \bar{x}_2} = \sqrt{3.451 \times \frac{1}{6}} = 0.758$$

Independent-samples *t*-test:

$$t = \frac{\bar{x}_1 - \bar{x}_2}{SE_{\bar{x}_1 - \bar{x}_2}} = \frac{8 - 7.5}{0.544} = 0.920 \qquad\qquad t = \frac{9.5 - 7.917}{0.758} = 2.088$$

$df = 12 \times 2 - 2 = 22$

Critical values of t (22) for $\alpha = 0.05$: ± 2.074

their youth) are asked to memorise a list of 10 words and then to recall as many words as they can in any order they want (Experiment 1). As you can notice, two university students out of twelve recalled all the words, while none of the retired subjects scored perfectly. Therefore, these data suffer from the presence of ceiling effects. The problem is that the score of 10 does not represent the "real" memory performance of the two university students. An artificial ceiling has been imposed on their performance by using a memory task that was too easy. Hence, we have not accurately measured the recall performance of these two students.

The mean performance in the two groups (i.e., 8.0 vs 7.5) did not differ significantly since the obtained independent-samples t-test was 0.92 (see Table 9.5 for the computation details), while the critical values for the t-distribution with $df = 22$ are ±2.074, at the 0.05 two-tailed significance level. This failure to reject the null hypothesis may simply reflect the presence of ceiling effects among young adult students. Imagine that, to avoid ceiling effects, the same subjects had been tested using a longer list of words (e.g., 15), allowing a fair assessment of all the subjects' recall abilities. The data for this fictitious revised Experiment 2 are also displayed in Table 9.5. Now no subject performs at ceiling. These conditions allow a better assessment of the difference in the memory abilities between the university students and the retired elderly adults group. For this second experiment the difference between the groups' means is 1.58. The t-test on this difference is now significant, i.e., $t(df = 22) = 2.088$ (see details in Table 9.5).

In summary, ceiling and floor effects should be avoided (the latter operate in the opposite way to ceiling effects by imposing an artificial floor on subject performance). Their presence makes the interpretation of the results, at best, difficult if not impossible (imagine the case where 50 per cent and 45 per cent of the subjects in two samples obtain a perfect score). To avoid these effects, a small-scale experiment or a small-scale data collection should be done prior to the main data collection phase. If during this pilot study some subjects perform at the maximum possible score in the task they undertake, then you should modify the task. You should then perform a second pilot study using the modified task, and if there is no evidence of floor and/or ceiling effects in the data, you can then start the main data collection phase of your study.

Matched-samples or independent-samples t-test: which of these two tests should be used?

The title of this section may sound a bit strange. You know by now that the matched-samples t-test is used to determine whether the difference between the means from two related samples is significantly different from zero; while the independent-samples t-test is used to assess if the difference between the means from two independent samples is significantly different from zero. This is correct. However, when planning research, you may have the possibility of testing your experimental hypothesis by collecting data using either related samples or independent samples. At this planning stage you should make an informed decision on the type of experimental design you intend to carry out. In some cases there is no choice. For example, if a researcher intends to study a problem-solving skills in young vs elderly adults, then they need to collect data from independent samples (unless the experimenter is prepared to test the same people twice, 30 years apart!). Hence, the independent-samples *t*-test is required to analyse the data. Note, however, that in some very specific circumstances the need for independent samples may be more apparent than real. For example, women's and men's performances are almost certainly related in a study where both members of married couples are asked to rate how satisfied they are about their marriage using a 10-point scale. In this case the matched-samples *t*-test should be the test of choice, to compare the means of the marriage satisfaction scores in the two groups.

In several circumstances, experimental hypotheses can be tested either using matched-samples or independent-samples experimental designs. Which of these options should be used? In general, if the same number of observations is collected, paired samples are more likely to reject a false null hypothesis (i.e., higher statistical power); hence, the use of the matched-samples *t*-test is more appropriate than the independent-samples *t*-test. Moreover, due to the nature of most matched samples, i.e., the same subjects are measured twice, you will need to test fewer subjects than when using independent samples to gather the same number of observations. It seems that you can kill two birds with one stone when using matched instead of independent samples: you have more statistical power while testing fewer subjects. In Chapter 13 we will describe how to calculate statistical power, and how to apply power analysis to the *t*-test. It should then be clear why the matched-samples *t*-test is a more "powerful" tool than the independent-samples *t*-test.

Before using a paired-samples experimental design you should first consider if there is the risk that some carry-over effect may bias the outcome of your study. Carry-over effects are often due to the order in which the experimental conditions are administered. For example, consider a replication of the study described in the section on pages 146–149 about memory for words and pictures. This time words and pictures, instead of being randomly intermixed, are presented in different blocks. Subjects should not always be given, for example, a series of words followed by a series of pictures. Any advantage of pictures over words may simply reflect an order effect (i.e., the items presented last are recalled more easily). It could also happen that subjects develop an efficient learning strategy while committing words to memory. If this strategy can then be refined while studying pictures, these are likely to be remembered better than words. If these types of carry-over effect are a concern, then some form of counterbalancing should be used. Finally, if these effects cannot be adequately dealt with by any counterbalancing procedure, then you should use independent samples in your study (an in-depth analysis of carry-over effects using paired samples, and the associated problems, can be found in Poulton, 1975).

A fundamental conceptual equation in data analysis: Magnitude of a significance test = Size of the effect × Size of the study

We have already met the conceptual equation in the title of this section when we described the Pearson's χ^2 test. In that context, the above relationship between the magnitude of a significance test, the effect size and the size of the study has a very important consequence on the way data analysis should be conducted. Given that:

Magnitude of a significance test = Size of the effect × Size of the study then if the size of the effect studied is non-zero in the population (i.e., the null hypothesis is false), then the magnitude of the significance test will be large enough to warrant the rejection of the null hypothesis provided that a sufficient number of subjects are tested. It then follows that a significant result, provided that the null hypothesis is false, gives us an incomplete picture of the results of an experiment. As seen in the section on pages 119–120, significant tests of the same magnitude can be obtained in studies of different sizes even when the magnitudes of the effects of the variables studied are different. To fully answer our research questions we should not only provide the magnitude of a significant test, but also a measure of the size of the effect of the investigated variables. Hence, we should identify an appropriate effect size index for the t-test. Moreover, we should identify the form of the equation linking the size of the t-test to its effect size and to the size of the study. Given that the t-test is mainly used to compare the means from matched or independent samples, we will focus on these two types of t-test.

The formula to calculate the independent-samples t-test is:

$$t = \frac{(\bar{x}_1 - \bar{x}_2)}{\sqrt{s_P^2 \times \left(\frac{1}{n_1} + \frac{1}{n_2}\right)}}$$

rearranging the elements in the second term we obtain:

$$t = \frac{(\bar{x}_1 - \bar{x}_2)}{s_P} \times \frac{1}{\sqrt{\left(\frac{1}{n_1} + \frac{1}{n_2}\right)}} = \frac{(\bar{x}_1 - \bar{x}_2)}{s_P} \times \frac{1}{\sqrt{\left(\frac{n_1 + n_2}{n_1 \times n_2}\right)}},$$

whence

$$t = \frac{(\bar{x}_1 - \bar{x}_2)}{s_P} \times \sqrt{\left(\frac{n_1 \times n_2}{n_1 + n_2}\right)}$$

where $\dfrac{(\bar{x}_1 - \bar{x}_2)}{s_P}$ is the *effect size*, normally denoted by g (i.e., it is the difference between the sample means that has been standardised using the common pooled estimate of the population standard deviation) and $\sqrt{\left(\dfrac{n_1 \times n_2}{n_1 + n_2}\right)}$ is a function of the *size of the study*.

If $n_1 = n_2 = n$, then $\sqrt{\left(\dfrac{n_1 \times n_2}{n_1 + n_2}\right)} = \sqrt{\left(\dfrac{n \times n}{n + n}\right)} = \sqrt{\left(\dfrac{n \times n}{2n}\right)} = \sqrt{\dfrac{n}{2}}$. Therefore, if the number of observations is the same in the two independent samples we have:

$$t = \frac{(\bar{x}_1 - \bar{x}_2)}{s_P} \times \sqrt{\frac{n}{2}} \quad \text{or equivalently } t = g \times \sqrt{\frac{n}{2}}$$

where g is the effect size, and n is the number of observations in each sample.

If we use the above formula to display the outcome of the *t*-test to analyse the exam results of "good attenders" vs "poor attenders" in Table 9.3 we find:

$$t = g \times \sqrt{\frac{n}{2}} = \frac{59.3 - 54.7}{11.319} \times \sqrt{\frac{60}{2}} = 0.406 \times \sqrt{30} = 2.226$$

and, thus, the standardised difference between good and poor attenders is about 0.4 times the estimated population standard deviation. With this effect size, and the sample size used, it appears that the null hypothesis stating that the effect size in the population is zero can be rejected, since $t = 2.226$ lies outside the ± 1.98 critical interval for the *t* distribution ($df = 118$) for a significance level of 0.05.

The formula for the matched-samples *t*-test is $t = \dfrac{\bar{D} - 0}{\dfrac{s_D}{\sqrt{n}}}$. Rearranging the second term we obtain:

$$t = \frac{\bar{D}}{s_D} \times \sqrt{n}$$

where $\dfrac{\bar{D}}{s_D}$ is the *effect size g* (i.e., it is the mean of the difference scores standardised using the estimate of the population standard deviation of the difference scores), and $\sqrt{n}$ is the *size of the study*.

When this formula is applied to the study assessing memory for pictures and words described in the section on pages 146–149, we obtain:

$$t = g \times \sqrt{n} = \frac{\bar{D}}{s_D} \times \sqrt{n} = \frac{2.048}{1.465} \times \sqrt{21} = 1.398 \times \sqrt{21} = 6.4$$

and thus, the standardised difference between the mean number of pictures and words recalled is about 1.4 times the estimated population standard deviation of the difference scores. With this effect size and the sample size used, the null hypothesis stating that the effect size in the population is zero can be rejected, since $t = 6.4$ lies outside the ± 2.086 critical interval for the *t*-distribution ($df = 20$) for a significance level of 0.05.

As seen in Chapter 5, Type II statistical errors occur when a null hypothesis appears to be false and it is not rejected. A null hypothesis is false if the effect size is different from zero in the population. However, despite the null hypothesis being false (i.e., the effect size is larger than zero), an insufficient number of observations may prevent the rejection of a false null hypothesis (remember that in inferential statistics we always assume that H_0 is true; however, making this assumption does not guarantee its truth). As we saw above, if Magnitude of a significance test = Size of the effect × Size of the study then it should be possible to obtain some indication of the size of the study needed, given an expected non-zero effect size, to be quite confident about rejecting a false null hypothesis. This issue will be developed in Chapter 13 when we describe how to calculate the statistical power for the *t*-test.

Chapter 10

Nonparametric statistical tests

Introduction

In Chapter 9 we showed how to apply the t-test in assessing the probability that two sets of observations, with their observed means, were drawn from the same or different populations. In order to apply the t-test, some assumptions were made with respect to the distributions of the observations in the population, i.e., that the observations were normally distributed with homogeneous variances. In this chapter we will present some useful tests that do not assume that our sampled observations are either normally distributed and/or have homogeneous variances. These tests are part of the family of, so-called, *distribution-free* or *nonparametric* statistical tests. Distribution-free tests do not make specific assumptions about the distributions of the data in the populations from which the observations have been sampled. Since there is not an assumed distribution, then there are no parameters that characterise such a distribution (e.g., mean, variance), hence the name nonparametric tests. Nonparametric tests are attractive because they can be used to perform statistical analyses on data-sets that violate the assumptions underlying the use of the t-test. As stated in Chapter 9, the t-test is fairly robust; hence, violations of the underlying assumptions have a relatively small impact on the precision of the test. Nevertheless, if violations are severe, it may be useful to employ nonparametric tests. We will mainly describe two tests that can be used with matched samples and with independent samples. These are called the Wilcoxon matched-pairs signed-ranks test and the Wilcoxon rank-sum test, respectively. Both tests were devised by Frank Wilcoxon, hence their names.

The Wilcoxon matched-pairs signed-ranks test

In Chapter 4 we described a nonparametric test to be used with matched samples, i.e., the sign test. In applying this test, the difference score for each pair of related observations is calculated, then the number of positive differences and the number of negative differences are recorded. If there is no significant difference between the two conditions being compared, then it is expected that the number of positive differences equals the number of negative differences. A test on this null hypothesis can be carried out using the binomial distribution (as described on pages 75–76). The sign test, unlike the matched-samples t-test, does not take into account the magnitude of the difference scores. By concentrating only on the signs of the difference scores, the application of the sign test implies that some of the information present in the data is lost.

The Wilcoxon matched-pairs signed-ranks test is also a nonparametric analogue of the *t*-test for matched samples. However, this test is based on richer information than the sign test. Not only are the signs of the difference scores considered, but also their ranks. Nevertheless, since the Wilcoxon matched-pairs signed-ranks test is not based on the magnitude of the difference scores, but is based on their ranking, it makes use of less rich information than the *t*-test. Despite this loss of information, it may be usefully applied if the distributions of the two sets of related scores are not normal.

The nonparametric nature of the Wilcoxon matched-pairs signed-ranks test does not imply that it is "assumption free". Some assumptions are still required for its application, but these are less stringent than those underlying the use of the *t*-test. In particular, it is assumed that the populations from which the matched observations are drawn are symmetrical. From this assumption it follows that the *null hypothesis* tested by the Wilcoxon matched-pairs test is that the two sets of paired observations come from populations having the same distribution. The *alternative hypothesis* states that the two sets of paired observations come from populations having different distributions.

The computations and logic involved in the application of the Wilcoxon matched-pairs signed-ranks test are more easily illustrated with an example. Imagine that a group of 16 people with sleeping problems were taught a relaxation technique and that every subject regularly used this technique for the last three months before going to sleep. For each subject the experimenter collected two measurements using a subjective rating of the quality of their sleep. The first measurement occurred at baseline (i.e., before the subjects were introduced to the relaxation technique). The second measurement was taken after subjects had practised the relaxation technique for 90 days. The aim of the experimenter was to decide if practising the relaxation technique improved the quality of the subjects' sleep. Since we have matched samples (i.e., repeated measurements were taken on the same subjects), the Wilcoxon matched-pairs signed-ranks test is a valuable alternative to the matched-samples *t*-test. Table 10.1 provides the subjective rating of each sampled subject, about the quality of their sleep, before and after 90 days of practising the relaxation technique. The rating is based on a 100-point scale where 100 indicates very good sleep and 1 indicates very poor sleep. Below are the steps to follow to apply the Wilcoxon matched-pairs signed-ranks test.

Step 1

The first thing to do is to calculate the difference between the ratings obtained before and after treatment. In this case, for simplicity, we calculated the difference between the rating obtained after having regularly practised the relaxation technique minus the rating at baseline (hence positive scores indicate an overall improvement in the quality of sleep). See the column headed "Difference After – Before" in Table 10.1.

Step 2

The differences obtained should be ordered in terms of their absolute magnitude (i.e., without looking at their sign). Any difference score equal to zero should be discarded. Hence only the non-zero difference scores are ordered. See the column headed "Absolute differences in ascending order" in Table 10.1.

Table 10.1 Data collected in the experiment on the subjective rating of the quality of sleep for a sample of 16 subjects before and after having learned and used a relaxation technique. The steps involved in the computation of the Wilcoxon matched-pairs signed-ranks test are also provided

Subject	Before	After	Difference After − Before	Absolute differences in ascending order	Ranks of absolute differences (with zeros being removed)	Signed ranks of absolute differences
1	67	74	7	0	×	×
2	65	72	7	(−) 3	1	−1
3	48	70	22	(−) 6	2	−2
4	58	65	7	7	4	4
5	52	64	12	7	4	4
6	65	62	−3	7	4	4
7	68	60	−8	(−) 8	6.5	−6.5
8	47	57	10	(−) 8	6.5	−6.5
9	40	56	16	10	8	8
10	29	53	24	12	9	9
11	38	51	13	13	10	10
12	28	49	21	16	11	11
13	55	47	−8	18	12	12
14	27	45	18	21	13	13
15	45	39	−6	22	14	14
16	38	38	0	24	15	15

(R_+) Sum of the positive ranks = 104; (R_-) Sum of the negative ranks = 16

$$z = \frac{R_{large} - \dfrac{n(n+1)}{4}}{\sqrt{\dfrac{n(n+1)(2n+1)}{24}}} \qquad z = \frac{104 - \dfrac{15 \times 16}{4}}{\sqrt{\dfrac{15 \times 16 \times 31}{24}}} = \frac{44}{17.61} = 2.499; \ p < 0.05$$

Remember that n is the number of non-zero difference scores. In this case $n = 15$ since we had one zero difference score

Step 3

A progressive rank is assigned to each ordered non-zero difference score. Note that two difference scores of the same absolute magnitude are assigned their average rank. For example, in Table 10.1 there are three difference scores of 7. These are the third, fourth and fifth smallest absolute difference scores, thus their rank is given by: $\dfrac{3+4+5}{3} = 4$ (see the column headed "Ranks of absolute differences" in Table 10.1).

Step 4

Each rank is signed according to the sign of the difference score. If the difference score is negative, then the rank is negative, otherwise it is positive. See the column headed "Signed ranks" in Table 10.1. If the distributions of the populations from which the matched observations are drawn are identical (i.e., the null hypothesis is true), then it is expected that the distribution of the difference scores will be symmetrical around zero.

Hence, the sum of the ranks with positive sign is not expected to differ from the sum of the ranks with negative signs. The Wilcoxon matched-pairs signed-rank test allows us to decide if the discrepancy between these two sums is too large under the assumption that the null hypothesis is true. If the discrepancy is too large the null hypothesis is rejected.

Step 5

The sum of the ranks of the positive differences (R_+) and the sum of the ranks of the negative differences (R_-) are calculated. Notice that only the absolute totals are considered. Hence, we have $R_+ = 104$ and $R_- = 16$ (see Table 10.1). The largest of the two R values, denoted as R_{large}, is then taken. If the null hypothesis is true then $R_+ = R_-$, in the population.

Step 6

It appears that when $n \geq 15$, the distribution of R_{large} is approximately normal with:

$$\mu = \frac{n(n + 1)}{4}; \quad \sigma^2 = \frac{n(n + 1)(2n + 1)}{24}; \quad \text{and} \quad \sigma = \sqrt{\frac{n(n + 1)(2n + 1)}{24}}$$

and, thus, it is possible to obtain a z score corresponding to R_{large} and to make use of the standard normal distribution in deciding whether or not we can reject the null hypothesis. If z lies outside the range of critical values for the alpha level chosen (as we have already seen in previous examples this is usually 0.05), then the null hypothesis stating that the two sets of matched observations come from the same distribution can be rejected. The value of z is calculated as follows:

$$z = \frac{R_{large} - \frac{n(n + 1)}{4}}{\sqrt{\frac{n(n + 1)(2n + 1)}{24}}}.$$

For the data in Table 10.1, $n = 15$ and $R_{large} = 104$, hence:

$$z = \frac{104 - \frac{15 \times 16}{4}}{\sqrt{\frac{15 \times 16 \times 31}{24}}} = \frac{44}{17.61} = 2.499.$$

Inspecting the z table we see that the value 2.499 lies outside the limits of the range for an alpha level of 0.05, two-tailed (these limits are ± 1.96). Therefore, the null hypothesis is rejected and it is declared that the two sets of observations come from populations with different distributions. The experimenter can then conclude that the subjective rating on the quality of sleep increased with the practising of the recently learnt relaxation technique.

The data shown in Table 10.1 could have been successfully analysed by a matched-samples t-test. The assumptions of normality and homogeneity of variances for these data-sets seems plausible. Hence, in applying the matched-samples t-test to these data we would have declared that the mean of the difference scores was significantly different from zero ($\bar{D} = 8.25$; $SE_{\bar{D}} = 2.681$; $t(df = 15) = \dfrac{\bar{D} - 0}{SE_{\bar{D}}} = \dfrac{8.25}{2.681} = 3.077, p < 0.05$). In general, if the assumptions underlying the use of the t-test are met, then the matched-samples t-test has more power than the nonparametric analogues (e.g., sign test or Wilcoxon matched-pairs signed-rank tests). This means that the matched-samples t-test is more likely to reject a false null hypothesis than the nonparametric analogues. Finally, for more details on the process of hypothesis testing with small samples see Siegel and Castellan (1988).

The Wilcoxon rank-sum test

The Wilcoxon rank-sum test is the nonparametric analogue of the independent-samples t-test. In order to apply the Wilcoxon rank-sum test it is assumed that the populations from which we draw our two independent samples have the same distributions, though they may differ by a constant k (i.e., if a constant k is added to each value of a distribution the shape of the distribution is unchanged, and it is simply shifted by the size of the constant k). If the null hypothesis is true, then the two populations, from which the two sets of observations have been sampled, are identical with the same central tendencies (i.e., it is as if the added constant is zero). If the null hypothesis is false, then the two sets of observations have been sampled from populations with identically shaped distributions that differ by a constant k. This indicates that the two populations differ in their central tendencies. Remember that we are not assuming that the distributions of the observations in the populations are either normal or symmetrical, only that they have the same form. Hence when we stated above that there are differences in central tendencies, this does not necessarily imply differences in the populations' means. When the form of the distribution is left unspecified, a more appropriate index of central tendency is the *median*. Hence, if the null hypothesis underlying the Wilcoxon rank-sum test is false, then it appears that the two sets of observations have been drawn from populations with the same distributions but different medians.

Again, the computations and logic involved in the application of the Wilcoxon rank-sum test can be more easily illustrated with an example. Imagine we are interested in assessing if there are differences between the wages of men and women, of comparable ages, who have recently been employed in the banking sector. A sample of 11 men and a sample of 12 women were asked to provide information on their annual gross salary. To make the two samples more homogeneous, subjects were sampled from students who had just graduated in economics, from the same university, with the same degree class, and had subsequently been employed in the banking sector. Table 10.2 provides the annual gross salaries of each of the 23 sampled subjects. The aim of the experimenter was to investigate if, given comparable backgrounds, women were paid less than men. In order to test this hypothesis the experimenter analysed the data in Table 10.2 using the Wilcoxon rank-sum test. The null hypothesis states that the distributions of the salaries of men and women are identical. The alternative hypothesis states that the

Table 10.2 Data taken from the study assessing whether or not there is a difference between the wages of men and women. The steps involved in calculating the Wilcoxon rank-sum test are also provided

	Salaries £000	Ranked wages	Ranks	
			Men	Women
Men	16.0	13.6		1
(11 subjects)	16.5	14.3		2
	17.3	15.0		3
	17.7	15.7		4
	18.5	16.0		5.5
	19.3	16.0	5.5	
	20.1	16.5	7	
	20.9	17.1		8
	23.0	17.3	9	
	23.5	17.7	10	
	24.2	17.8		11
Women	13.6	18.5		12.5
(12 subjects)	14.3	18.5	12.5	
	15.0	19.2		14
	15.7	19.3	15	
	16.0	19.9		16
	17.1	20.1	17	
	17.8	20.6		18
	18.5	20.8		19
	19.2	20.9	20	
	19.9	23.0	21	
	20.6	23.5	22	
	20.8	24.2	23	

Men's sum of ranks = 162; Women's sum of ranks = 114

$$z = \frac{R_{large} - \dfrac{n_l \times (n_l + n_s + 1)}{2}}{\sqrt{\dfrac{n_l \times n_s \times (n_l + n_s + 1)}{12}}} = \frac{162 - \dfrac{11 \times (11 + 12 + 1)}{2}}{\sqrt{\dfrac{11 \times 12 \times (11 + 12 + 1)}{12}}} = \frac{162 - 132}{16.248} = 1.846$$

n_l = number of subjects in the group having the larger sum of ranks (i.e., 11)

n_s = number of subjects in the group having the smaller sum of ranks (i.e., 12)

two sets of observations were drawn from populations having the same distribution but with different medians. Here are the main steps involved in the calculation of the Wilcoxon rank-sum test.

Step 1

The first thing to do is to rank order, from the smallest to the largest, the salaries of all the subjects involved in the study. See the column headed "Ranked wages" in Table 10.2.

Step 2

A progressive rank is associated to each ordered score. Ordered scores of the same magnitude are assigned their average rank. For example the two salaries of £16,000 have a rank of 5.5, i.e., $\dfrac{5+6}{2}$. See the column headed "Ranks" in Table 10.2. (Note that the ranking starts here with the *lowest* salary in the "Ranked wages" column designated 1.)

Step 3

If the distributions of the populations from which the two samples of observations were drawn are identical, with same median (i.e., the null hypothesis is true), then it is expected that the two groups have identical average ranks. If the null hypothesis is false, then the average ranking of one group should be considerably larger than the average ranking of the other. The Wilcoxon rank-sum test makes use of the largest of the two sums of ranks to decide if the null hypothesis has to be rejected. Hence, the sum of the ranks of each of the two samples has to be calculated. In Table 10.2 the ranks in bold correspond to those of the men's salary, the remaining ones correspond to the women's salaries. The sum of the men's rank is 162, while for the women this sum is 114.

Step 4

The largest sum of ranks is then taken (i.e., 162). If the number of observations in each sample is at least 10, then the distribution of R_{large} is approximately normal with:

$$\mu = \frac{n_l \times (n_l + n_s + 1)}{2}; \quad \sigma^2 = \frac{n_l \times n_s \times (n_l + n_s + 1)}{12}; \quad \text{and}$$

$$\sigma = \sqrt{\frac{n_l \times n_s \times (n_l + n_s + 1)}{12}}$$

where n_l is the number of subjects in the group having the larger sum of ranks (i.e., 11 men here); n_s is the number of subjects in the group having the smaller sum of ranks (i.e., 12 women here).

It is then possible to obtain a z score corresponding to R_{large} and to make use of the standard normal distribution to decide if we can reject the null hypothesis. If z lies outside the range of critical values for the alpha level chosen (i.e., as we have already seen in previous examples this is usually 0.05), then the null hypothesis can be rejected. The value of z is calculated by:

$$z = \frac{R_{\text{large}} - \dfrac{n_l \times (n_l + n_s + 1)}{2}}{\sqrt{\dfrac{n_l \times n_s \times (n_l + n_s + 1)}{12}}}.$$

For the data in Table 10.2 $n_l = 11$, $n_s = 12$ and $R_{large} = 162$, hence:

$$z = \frac{162 - \dfrac{11 \times (11 + 12 + 1)}{2}}{\sqrt{\dfrac{11 \times 12 \times (11 + 12 + 1)}{12}}} = \frac{162 - 132}{16.248} = 1.846.$$

Inspecting the z table we observe that the value 1.846 lies within the critical range for an alpha level of 0.05, two-tailed (the limits are ±1.96). Therefore, the null hypothesis, stating that the distributions of men's and women's salaries do not differ, somewhat surprisingly cannot be rejected.

If the data shown in Table 10.2 had been analysed by an independent-samples t-test, we would have declared that the mean salary for men (i.e., $\bar{x}_{men} = 19.73$, $s = 2.87$) was significantly larger than the mean women's salary (i.e., $\bar{x}_{women} = 17.38$, $s = 2.48$); $t(df = 21) = 2.11$, $p < 0.05$. This example illustrates that in general, if the assumptions underlying the use of the t-test are met, the independent-samples t-test is more powerful than the Wilcoxon rank-sum test. In general, if a set of data does not violate the assumptions underlying the use of the t-test, then you are better off using the t-test instead of its nonparametric analogues. Finally, for more details on the process of hypothesis testing with small samples see Siegel and Castellan (1988).

Chapter 11

Correlation

Introduction

Researchers often need to collect measurements on pairs of variables because they want to study their relationship. For example, in the section on pages 146–149 we described a study where subjects were given words and pictures to commit to memory. It appeared that the mean number of pictures remembered was significantly larger than the mean number of recalled words. Thus, different means corresponded to different levels of the independent variable (i.e., treatments). Looking at this result from a slightly different perspective, we can say that the means were related to the treatments. This example indicates that speaking about differences between treatment means is the same as saying means are related to treatments.

In this chapter we will describe how to calculate indices to measure the strength of the relationship between two variables, where these variables can be measured using different types of numerical scale. In the section on pages 116–119 we have already met one of these indices, i.e., ϕ, which is used to measure the strength of a relationship between two dichotomous variables in 2×2 contingency tables. This chapter will mainly focus on the Pearson product-moment correlation coefficient r and other associated indices. Pearson's r measures the strength of the linear relationship between two continuous variables. In this chapter we will also describe measures of association suitable for ranked data.

Linear relationships between two continuous variables

Consider the case where a researcher collects a series of measurements on two continuous variables X, the mark obtained in the undergraduate degree, and Y, the monthly salary, in pounds, at the end of the third year after graduation, in a sample of former university students now currently employed. This researcher's aim is to investigate if there is a positive linear relationship between grades and salaries. If there is a perfect positive relationship between these variables it is expected that constant increments in monthly salaries (e.g., £25) would correspond to constant increments in degree marks (e.g., 2 points).

A useful starting point to address this issue involves drawing a scatterplot of the data. In this type of diagram the values of the variable X are represented on the abscissa (or x-axis), while the values of the variable Y are represented on the ordinate (or y-axis). Each point in the diagram corresponds to the value attained by each

Table 11.1 Data representing a perfect positive linear relationship between degree mark and monthly salary income

Subject	Degree mark	Monthly salary (£)
1	40	1000
2	44	1050
3	48	1100
4	52	1150
5	56	1200
6	60	1250
7	64	1300
8	68	1350
9	72	1400
10	76	1450
11	80	1500

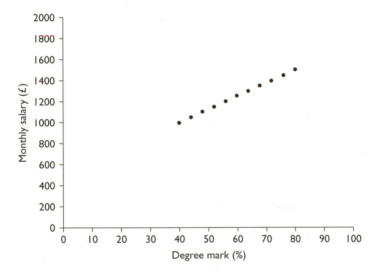

Figure 11.1 Scatterplot of the data from Table 11.1. The diagram shows that the monthly salary increases, in a perfect positive linear relationship, as a function of the degree mark obtained.

subject on the X and Y variables. Imagine that the data from a sample of 11 subjects are shown in Table 11.1. This data-set provides an example of a *perfect positive linear relationship* between degree marks and monthly salaries. When these data are plotted, as in Figure 11.1, they lie on a perfectly straight line. Conversely a *perfect negative linear relationship* is observed when constant *increments* in the value of X correspond to constant *decrements* in the value of Y (see Figure 11.2). If there is no linear relationship between X and Y, then increments in X may correspond to a constant value of Y (e.g., all points in a scattergram would lie on a flat straight line). Notice, however, that the absence of a linear relationship between two variables does not mean that a more complex relationship may not exist (e.g., $y = x^2$, where there is a, so-called, curvilinear relationship between X and Y).

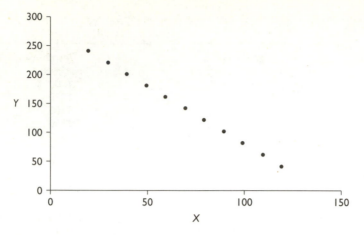

Figure 11.2 Scatterplot displaying a perfect negative linear relationship between two variables X and Y.

It is extremely unlikely to observe perfect linear relationships in real data. We used the above examples to illustrate what it is meant by perfect positive and negative linear relationships, and the absence of a linear relationship between two variables. When two variables are linearly related it is more likely that this relationship will be imperfect. It is therefore important to provide an index that, when applied to a set of empirical data, gives a measure of the magnitude of the linear relationship between two continuous variables. This index is the Pearson product-moment correlation coefficient (*r*). In the next sections we will describe how to calculate it.

More on linear relationships between two variables

Let us now consider the fictitious study aimed at investigating if there is a positive linear relationship between grades and salaries. This time we use a set of data that are more likely to occur in real life. This set consists of the degree marks and the monthly salaries in a sample of 43 former university students, who are in employment three years after graduation. These data are displayed in Tables 11.2 and 11.3, while a scattergram is provided in Figure 11.3. Inspecting the stem-and-leaf displays of the data it appears that both degree marks and monthly salaries are reasonably normally distributed. The first thing to notice in the scattergram is that not all points fall on a tilted straight line; thus, there is not a perfect linear relationship between the two variables. Nevertheless, it appears that there is a certain degree of positive linear relationship between the two variables (i.e., constant increments in degree marks, roughly correspond to constant increments in income). It is possible to capture the presence of this linear relationship by drawing a tilted straight line that provides a relatively good fit of the data (we will see in the next chapter how this, so-called, regression line is obtained). How then can we calculate an index to measure the degree of the linear relationship between these two variables? Let us try to answer this question.

In Figure 11.3 you may have noticed that there are two perpendicular lines (so-called because they form a 90° angle at their intersection). Each line indicates the

Table 11.2 Stem-and-leaf displays of the data collected on degree marks and monthly salaries for a sample of 43 former university students who are in employment three years after graduation. The data collected on each subject are provided on the right

$n = 43$

Degree marks (X)		Monthly salary (Y)	
Stem (tens)	Leaf (units)	Stem (hundreds)	Leaf (tens)
4	023	8	25
4*	589	9	13456
5	0234	10	13336
5*	5678899	11	2223347
6	0012223444	12	1222345667
6*	5677889	13	46667
7	00135	14	267
7*	78	15	277
8	0	16	78
		17	3
$\bar{x} = 60.93$		$\bar{y} = 1225.81$	
$s_x = 9.71$		$s_y = 228.86$	

Mark	Salary	Mark	Salary	Mark	Salary	Mark	Salary
40	820	56	940	62	1340	68	1250
42	930	56	1240	62	1170	69	1030
43	910	57	1130	63	1260	70	1140
45	950	58	1220	64	1370	70	1360
48	850	58	1260	64	1220	71	1470
49	1030	59	1010	64	1570	73	1520
50	1210	59	1060	65	1680	75	1420
52	1120	60	1360	66	1360	77	1730
53	1030	60	960	67	1460	78	1570
54	1120	61	1220	67	1120	80	1670
55	1230	62	1130	68	1270		

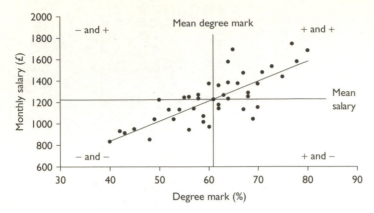

Figure 11.3 Scattergram showing the relationship between degree mark and monthly salary for the observations in Table 11.2. The tilted straight line fitting the points indicates that there is a linear relationship, albeit imperfect, between the variables. The two perpendicular lines in the middle of the scattergram correspond to the mean monthly salary and the mean degree mark for the sample. These lines divide the diagram into 4 quadrants: the bottom left quadrant corresponds to below average scores in both degree mark and salary (i.e., "– and –"); the top right quadrant corresponds to above average scores in both variables (i.e., "+ and +"). The remaining two quadrants include subjects who scored higher than average in one variable, but lower than average in the other variable (i.e., "+ and –" and "– and +").

location of the mean degree mark on the *x*-axis and the location of the mean salary on the *y*-axis. These lines partition the diagram into four quadrants: the bottom left quadrant includes the points corresponding to those subjects who scored below average in both the degree mark and salary (i.e., "– and –"); the top right quadrant includes the points corresponding to those subjects who scored above average in both variables (i.e., "+ and +"); the remaining two quadrants include the points corresponding to those subjects who scored higher than average in one variable, but lower than average in the other (i.e., "+ and –", "– and +").

If there is a strong positive linear relationship between degree mark and salary, then the large majority of subjects should have concordant scores for the two variables. We should observe several data points falling in the concordant quadrants (i.e., "– and –"; "+ and +"), while only a handful of data points should fall in the two remaining "discordant" quadrants ("+ and –"; "– and +").

For weaker positive relationships, the number of data points in the discordant quadrants should increase at the expense of data points in the concordant quadrants. If the two variables are not linearly related we should observe an approximately equal number of data points in the four quadrants. Finally, in the case of negative linear relationships, more data points should fall into the discordant than into the concordant quadrants.

In summary, positive relationships of varying degrees are found when the majority of subjects show *concordant* performances in the two variables being measured. Negative relationships of varying degrees are found when the majority of subjects show *discordant* performances in the two variables. There is no relationship when the number of subjects showing concordant performances is similar to the number of subjects showing discordant performances. To provide a measure of the strength of a linear relationship between two variables, we need a numerical index of the level of concordance (and discordance) of the subjects' performances. This index is called *covariance* and it will be described in the next section.

The covariance between two variables

We saw above that if there is a linear positive relationship between two variables, we expect some degree of concordance between them. Thus the majority of the subjects should score either above or below the mean for both variables, while few subjects should obtain discordant performances in the two variables. To provide a quantitative way to express this, we first need to calculate, for each subject's score on the X and Y variables, the deviation from $\bar{x}$ and $\bar{y}$, i.e., $x - \bar{x}$ and $y - \bar{y}$. Then the product of the deviation scores $(x - \bar{x})(y - \bar{y})$ is calculated. If a subject performs either below the mean, or above the mean, on both variables, then this product is positive. Thus, if there is a positive linear relationship between X and Y, several subjects should have positive deviation scores on one variable which are associated with positive deviation scores on the other variable. Similarly, several subjects should show negative deviation scores on one variable which are associated with negative deviation scores on the other variable. On the other hand, few subjects should show discordant performances in the two variables (in these cases the $(x - \bar{x})(y - \bar{y})$ product is negative).

All the obtained $(x - \bar{x})(y - \bar{y})$ products should then be added up. If there is a positive linear relationship between the two variables X and Y, then the majority of the deviations' products will be positive, thus their sum should also be positive, i.e., $\Sigma(x - \bar{x})(y - \bar{y}) > 0$. On the other hand, if the linear relationship is negative the majority of the deviations' products will be negative, hence their sum will also be negative, i.e., $\Sigma(x - \bar{x})(y - \bar{y}) < 0$. If there is no relationship between X and Y, then positive products will balance out negative products, hence $\Sigma(x - \bar{x})(y - \bar{y})$ should be close to zero. The *covariance* is a measure of the extent to which two variables X and Y vary together. It is defined as the average of the deviations' products between X and Y, and is calculated as:

$$\text{COV}_{xy} = \frac{\Sigma(x - \bar{x})(y - \bar{y})}{n - 1}$$

where $n - 1$ is the number of paired observations (in most cases this corresponds to the number of subjects sampled).

Notice the similarity of the above formula to the formula to calculate the population variance estimated from sample data, $s^2 = \dfrac{\Sigma(x - \bar{x})^2}{n - 1}$. As in the case of the variance, to provide a better estimate of the population covariance using sample data, $n - 1$ is used instead of n as the denominator.

For the data-set presented in Table 11.2 (see also Table 11.3 where computation details are presented) the covariance between degree mark (i.e., X) and monthly salary (i.e., Y) is:

$$\text{COV}_{xy} = \frac{\Sigma(x - \bar{x})(y - \bar{y})}{n - 1} = \frac{72567.44}{42} = 1727.796$$

Table 11.3 Data and computational details for calculating the Pearson correlation coefficient r to measure the strength of the linear relationship between degree mark and monthly income in a sample of 43 graduates

| Degree mark | Salary | | Degree mark | Salary | | Degree mark | Salary | | Degree mark | Salary | |
x	y	$(x - \bar{x})(y - \bar{y})$	x	y	$(x - \bar{x})(y - \bar{y})$	x	y	$(x - \bar{x})(y - \bar{y})$	x	y	$(x - \bar{x})(y - \bar{y})$
40	820	8493.78	56	940	1409.13	62	1340	122.15	68	1250	170.99
42	930	5599.83	56	1240	-69.94	62	1170	-59.71	69	1030	-1580.17
43	910	5662.62	57	1130	376.57	63	1260	70.76	70	1140	-778.31
45	950	4393.78	58	1220	17.04	64	1370	442.62	70	1360	1217.04
48	850	4859.36	58	1260	-100.17	64	1220	-17.85	71	1470	2458.90
49	1030	2336.11	59	1010	416.57	64	1570	1056.57	73	1520	3550.76
50	1210	172.85	59	1060	320.06	65	1680	1848.43	75	1420	2732.15
52	1120	944.94	60	1360	-124.82	66	1360	680.29	77	1730	8102.15
53	1030	1552.85	60	960	247.27	67	1460	1421.45	78	1570	5875.18
54	1120	733.32	61	1220	-0.41	67	1120	-642.27	80	1670	8470.52
55	1230	-24.82	62	1130	-102.50	68	1270	312.39			

$n = 43$; $\bar{x} = 60.930$; $\bar{y} = 1225.81$; $s_y = 228.61$; $s_x = 9.71$; $\sum(x - \bar{x})(y - \bar{y}) = 72567.44$

$$\text{COV}_{xy} = \frac{\sum(x - \bar{x})(y - \bar{y})}{n - 1} = \frac{72567.44}{42} = 1727.796; \quad r_{xy} = \frac{\text{COV}_{xy}}{s_x \times s_y} = \frac{1727.796}{9.71 \times 228.61} = 0.778$$

The Pearson product-moment correlation coefficient *r*

The magnitude of the covariance is a function of the scales used to measure X and Y (i.e., their standard deviations). Hence, the covariance is not appropriate to measure the strength of the relationship between two variables. An absolute covariance of a given size may reflect either a weak relationship, if the standard deviations of the two variables investigated are large, or a strong relationship if the standard deviations of the two variables are small. To avoid this problem we need an index of the strength of the linear relationship between two variables which is independent of the scales used to measure them. To obtain this index the covariance is divided by the product of the standard deviations of the variables. The standardised covariance between two variables is called the Pearson product-moment correlation coefficient *r* and is defined as:

$$r_{xy} = \frac{COV_{xy}}{s_x \times s_y}.$$

In the case of the relationship between degree mark and monthly salary, the correlation coefficient *r* is:

$$r_{xy} = \frac{COV_{xy}}{s_x \times s_y} = \frac{1727.796}{9.71 \times 228.61} = 0.778$$

where s_x is the standard deviation of the degree marks and s_y is the standard deviation of the salaries. Table 11.3 provides, in detail, all the data and the computational steps required to calculate Pearson's *r*.

Since the denominators of COV_{xy}, s_x and s_y all include the common value $n - 1$, these can all be removed, and the following alternative formula for *r* is derived:

$$r_{xy} = \frac{\Sigma(x - \bar{x})(y - \bar{y})}{\sqrt{\Sigma(x - \bar{x})^2 \times \Sigma(y - \bar{y})}}.$$

Pearson *r* ranges from −1 to 1, where −1 corresponds to a perfect negative linear relationship between two variables (see Figure 11.2); 0 indicates that there is no linear relationship; and 1 corresponds to a perfect positive linear relationship (see Figure 11.1).

When the positive correlation is perfect, why does *r* = 1? A perfect linear relationship exists, for example (but not only), when each subject obtains the same score in both variables X and Y, i.e., Y and X are the same number (obviously there are differences in scores across subjects). When this happens then $\Sigma(x - \bar{x})(y - \bar{y}) = \Sigma(x - \bar{x})^2$, and $\Sigma(y - \bar{y})^2 = \Sigma(x - \bar{x})^2$. Therefore $r_{xy} = \dfrac{\Sigma(x - \bar{x})^2}{\sqrt{\Sigma(x - \bar{x})^2 \times \Sigma(x - \bar{x})^2}} = \dfrac{\Sigma(x - \bar{x})^2}{\Sigma(x - \bar{x})^2} = 1.$

Similarly, *r* = −1 when each subject obtains oppositely signed scores for the variables X and Y (e.g., 2 and −2).

Values of *r* between −1 and 0 indicate negatives relationships of varying degrees, with values closer to −1 indicating stronger negative linear relationships. Conversely, values of *r* between 0 and 1 indicate positive linear relationships of varying degrees, with values closer to 1 indicating stronger positive linear relationships. As a rule of thumb, $r = \pm 0.1$ indicates that the linear relationship is weak; $r = \pm 0.3$ indicates that the correlation is of medium strength; and $r = \pm 0.5$ indicates that the correlation is quite strong. In our example, it appears that a strong linear relationship exists between degree mark and monthly salary.

It is important to keep in mind that correlation does not mean causation. In the above study, no variable was manipulated by the experimenter with random allocation of subjects to treatment conditions (i.e., to different degree marks), so no causal inference can be made on the basis of the results. Although higher marks tend to correspond to larger salaries, this does not necessarily mean that higher marks are the cause of larger salaries. For example, a third variable, such as subjects' general intellectual ability, may be associated with both degree mark and salary. If this is true, then the strong relationship between degree mark and salary may simply reflect the presence of a strong relationship between IQ and salary.

Hypothesis testing on the Pearson correlation coefficient r

In calculating r we usually work with samples. It could happen that by chance we obtain a value of r larger (or smaller) than zero, even if in the population there is no linear relationship between the studied variables (i.e., when ρ (rho), the population parameter for r, is zero). It is therefore useful to test if r is significantly different from zero. To perform this test the null hypothesis is H_0: $\rho = 0$. The alternative hypothesis is H_0: $\rho \neq 0$. To test this null hypothesis we need to know the sampling distribution of the correlation coefficient r (and its standard error). This is the distribution of the values of r obtained from all possible samples, of size n, drawn from a population where $\rho = 0$. If n is large (i.e., > 30), then r is approximately normally distributed around zero. Furthermore, let us assume that the population distribution for all possible pairs of observations of the variables X and Y is a bivariate normal distribution. Two variables follow the bivariate normal distribution if, for each value of one variable, the corresponding values of the other variable are normally distributed

(and vice versa). Then it can be shown that the quantity $\dfrac{r}{\sqrt{\dfrac{1 - r^2}{n - 2}}}$ (its denominator

is the standard error of r: $SE_r = \sqrt{\dfrac{1 - r^2}{n - 2}}$) is distributed as t with $n - 2$ degrees of freedom. Thus an appropriate t-test to assess H_0: $\rho = 0$ is the following:

$$t = \frac{r - 0}{\sqrt{\dfrac{1 - r^2}{n - 2}}}$$

where $n - 2$ are the degrees of freedom (i.e., the number of subjects sampled minus two).

Applying this formula to the degree mark and monthly salary study we obtain:

$$t = \frac{0.778}{\sqrt{\dfrac{1 - 0.778^2}{43 - 2}}} = \frac{0.778}{0.098} = 7.924.$$

This value lies outside the critical values, for the 0.05 significance level, of the t-distribution with $df = 41$. We can then reject the null hypothesis and declare that our sample was drawn from a population where degree mark and monthly salary are linearly associated variables, i.e., $\rho \neq 0$.

In some cases the null hypothesis may be of the form $\rho = a$, where $a \neq 0$. For instance, with respect to the correlation between grades and salaries, we may want to see if the sampled data were drawn from a population where $\rho = 0.5$ (i.e., H_0: $\rho = 0.5$ and H_1: $\rho \neq 0.5$). Given that the distribution of r largely departs from a close approximation to normality when $\rho \neq 0$, we cannot use the t-test as above. The solution to this problem consists of transforming r into r_f (better known as Fisher's z; we prefer to use the notation r_f instead of z_f to avoid any confusion with the standard z). This transformation is given by:

$$r_f = 0.5 \times \ln\left|\frac{1+r}{1-r}\right|$$

where $\ln\left|\frac{1+r}{1-r}\right|$ is the natural logarithm of the absolute value of $\frac{1+r}{1-r}$ (you do not have to worry about computing r_f from r using the above formula, and vice versa, since this can easily be done using Table 11.4).

It can be shown that:

$$z = \frac{r_f - \rho_f}{\sqrt{\frac{1}{n-3}}}$$

is a standard normal deviate where r_f and ρ_f are the Fisher's transforms of the observed r, and of the ρ value assumed by the null hypothesis, and n is the number of sampled subjects.

Applying this procedure to the above example with H_0: $\rho = 0.5$, then for $r = 0.778$ the corresponding value of r_f is about 1.04 (by interpolation from Table 11.4), and for $\rho = 0.5$, $\rho_f = 0.549$. Therefore:

$$z = \frac{r_f - \rho_f}{\sqrt{\frac{1}{n-3}}} = \frac{1.04 - 0.549}{\sqrt{\frac{1}{43-3}}} = \frac{0.491}{0.158} = 3.11.$$

This value of z is significant at the 0.05 significance level. Hence, the null hypothesis is rejected and it is declared that the sampled observations were drawn from a population where the correlation between grades and salaries differs from 0.5.

Confidence intervals for the Pearson correlation coefficient

As seen for the sample mean, we do not know how close the sample correlation coefficient r is to the true value of ρ in the population. Therefore, we may want to use

Table 11.4 This table provides the transformation of the Pearson *r* into Fisher's r_f transformed scores and vice versa

r	r_f	*r*	r_f	*r*	r_f	*r*	r_f	*r*	r_f
0	0	0.20	0.203	0.40	0.424	0.60	0.693	0.80	1.099
0.01	0.010	0.21	0.213	0.41	0.436	0.61	0.709	0.81	1.127
0.02	0.020	0.22	0.224	0.42	0.448	0.62	0.725	0.82	1.157
0.03	0.030	0.23	0.234	0.43	0.460	0.63	0.741	0.83	1.188
0.04	0.040	0.24	0.245	0.44	0.472	0.64	0.758	0.84	1.221
0.05	0.050	0.25	0.255	0.45	0.485	0.65	0.775	0.85	1.256
0.06	0.060	0.26	0.266	0.46	0.497	0.66	0.793	0.86	1.293
0.07	0.070	0.27	0.277	0.47	0.510	0.67	0.811	0.87	1.333
0.08	0.080	0.28	0.288	0.48	0.523	0.68	0.829	0.88	1.376
0.09	0.090	0.29	0.299	0.49	0.536	0.69	0.848	0.89	1.422
0.10	0.100	0.30	0.310	0.50	0.549	0.70	0.867	0.90	1.472
0.11	0.110	0.31	0.321	0.51	0.563	0.71	0.887	0.91	1.528
0.12	0.121	0.32	0.332	0.52	0.576	0.72	0.908	0.92	1.589
0.13	0.131	0.33	0.343	0.53	0.590	0.73	0.929	0.93	1.658
0.14	0.141	0.34	0.354	0.54	0.604	0.74	0.950	0.94	1.738
0.15	0.151	0.35	0.365	0.55	0.618	0.75	0.973	0.95	1.832
0.16	0.161	0.36	0.377	0.56	0.633	0.76	0.996	0.96	1.946
0.17	0.172	0.37	0.388	0.57	0.648	0.77	1.020	0.97	2.092
0.18	0.182	0.38	0.400	0.58	0.662	0.78	1.045	0.98	2.298
0.19	0.192	0.39	0.412	0.59	0.678	0.79	1.071	0.99	2.647

sample data to construct confidence intervals which should contain ρ with a given probability. The procedure for calculating the confidence intervals for ρ is similar to the one used for calculating the confidence intervals for the population proportion or the population mean (cf. Chapters 7 and 8).

The calculation of the confidence intervals for ρ is based on the formula $z = \dfrac{r_f - \rho_f}{\sqrt{\dfrac{1}{n-3}}}$.

After rearranging the terms of this formula, and considering that we want to calculate symmetrical confidence intervals, we obtain:

$$\rho_f = r_f \pm c \times \frac{1}{\sqrt{n-3}}$$

where *c* is the two-tailed critical value of *z* for any desired α level (i.e., $z_{\frac{\alpha}{2}}$).

Let us apply this formula to calculate the 99% confidence interval for the population correlation coefficient ρ between grades and salaries. This is denoted as $CI_{99\%}$, with the critical *z* value to be inserted in the above formula being 2.576. Knowing that $r = 0.778$ with a corresponding r_f of about 1.04 we obtain:

$$\rho_f = 1.04 \pm 2.576 \times \frac{1}{\sqrt{40}} = 1.04 \pm 0.407$$

thus the $\text{CI}_{99\%} = 0.633 \le \rho_f \le 1.447$ and the 99% confidence limits for ρ_f are 0.663 and 1.447. We are, however interested in establishing a confidence interval for ρ, so we need to transform the values of ρ_f back into ρ. Using Table 11.4:

$$\text{CI}_{99\%} = 0.56 \le \rho \le 0.895.$$

Testing the significance of the difference between two independent Pearson correlation coefficients r

In some cases researchers are interested in comparing the magnitude of the linear relationship between two variables obtained in two independent samples. A test is required to assess if there is a significant difference between two independent rs. Consider, for example, that a fictitious study (Study-1) found a positive correlation between immediate recall on a digit span task and reading speed, $r = 0.44$, in a sample of 40 10-year-old girls. Another study (i.e., Study-2), conducted on a sample of 50 10-year-old boys, found that the correlation between digit span and reading speed was $r = 0.32$. To test if these two rs differ significantly we need to calculate the quantity:

$$z = \frac{r_{f1} - r_{f2}}{\sqrt{\dfrac{1}{n_1 - 3} + \dfrac{1}{n_2 - 3}}}.$$

This is a standard normal deviate where r_{f1} and r_{f2} are the values of the Fisher's r_f corresponding to the observed rs; and n_1 and n_2 are the sizes of the two independent samples.

Applying this procedure to Study-1 and Study-2, $r_{f1} = 0.472$ and $r_{f2} = 0.332$, thus:

$$z = \frac{0.472 - 0.332}{\sqrt{\dfrac{1}{40 - 3} + \dfrac{1}{50 - 3}}} = \frac{0.14}{0.2198} = 0.639$$

which is not significant at an α level of 0.05. Hence we do not have sufficient evidence to reject the null hypothesis stating that $\rho_1 = \rho_2$, i.e., the difference between the r values is not significant.

The two-sided confidence interval for the difference between two independent correlations can be obtained using the following formula:

$$(r_{f1} - r_{f2}) \pm c \times \sqrt{\frac{1}{n_1 - 3} + \frac{1}{n_2 - 3}}$$

where c is the two-tailed critical value of z for any desired α level (i.e., $z_{\frac{\alpha}{2}}$). The limits of the interval are Fisher's scores, so the values need to be transformed back into ρ values using Table 11.4. For the above example the 95% confidence limits for $\rho_{f1} - \rho_{f2}$ are:

$$(0.472 - 0.332) \pm 1.96 \times \sqrt{\frac{1}{40 - 3} + \frac{1}{50 - 3}}$$, i.e., -0.291 and 0.571. Transforming to ρ

values, the limits of the $\text{CI}_{95\%}$ for $\rho_1 - \rho_2$ are -0.28 and 0.515.

Testing the significance of the difference between two nonindependent Pearson correlation coefficients r

It is common for a researcher to obtain measurements, in the same sample, on three variables X, Y, and Z (where X and Y may be conceptualised as the independent variables and Z as the dependent variable), in order to study the correlation between X and Z and between Y and Z. In cases like this it is possible to test if the correlation between X and Z is significantly different from the correlation between Y and Z. Here the two correlations are not independent since they have been obtained from the same sample, so we need to use a different approach to the one described in the previous section. Consider an extension of the study on the relationship between degree mark and salary, where the researcher also collects the IQ scores for each subject (see Table 11.5). Let us now consider, for example, that "monthly salary" is the dependent variable Z, and that "degree mark" and "IQ" are the independent variables X and Y, respectively. We already know that the correlation between "degree mark" and "monthly salary" is $r_{xz} = 0.778$ in this sample, while the correlation between "IQ" and "monthly salary" turns out to be $r_{yz} = 0.480$. We want to know if the difference between these nonindependent correlation coefficients r is significant.

The test for the significance of these two nonindependent rs is given by the following standard normal deviate (this test was devised by Meng, Rosenthal & Rubin, 1992):

$$z = (r_{f(xz)} - r_{f(yz)}) \times \sqrt{\frac{n-3}{2 \times (1 - r_{xy}) \times h}}$$

where $r_{f(xz)}$ and $r_{f(yz)}$ are the values of the Fisher's r_f corresponding to r_{xz} and r_{yz}, respectively; n is the sample size; r_{xy} is the correlation between the two independent variables; while h is calculated using:

$$h = \frac{1 - (g \times \bar{r}^2)}{1 - \bar{r}^2}$$

where $\bar{r}^2 = \dfrac{r_{xz}^2 + r_{yz}^2}{2}$ and $g = \dfrac{1 - r_{xy}}{2 \times (1 - \bar{r}^2)}$. The value of g has to be ≤ 1. If it turns out that $g > 1$, then g is set equal to 1.

To test if there is a significant difference between the correlation between "degree mark" and "monthly salary", i.e., $r_{xz} = 0.778$, and the correlation between "IQ" and "monthly salary", i.e., $r_{yz} = 0.480$, we need to carry out some background calculations. First we need to know the corresponding Fisher's r_f scores for r_{xz} and r_{yz}. Inspecting Table 11.5 we find that $r_{f(xz)} = 1.04$ and that $r_{f(yz)} = 0.523$. We then need the correlation between X and Y (i.e., "degree mark" and "IQ"). This turns out to be $r_{xy} = 0.66$. Furthermore,

$$\bar{r}^2 = \frac{r_{xz}^2 + r_{yz}^2}{2} = \frac{0.778^2 + 0.48^2}{2} = 0.418 \quad \text{and}$$

$$g = \frac{1 - r_{xy}}{2 \times (1 - \bar{r}^2)} = \frac{1 - 0.66}{2 \times (1 - 0.418)} = 0.292.$$

Table 11.5 Sample data used to calculate the values of r between "degree mark" and "monthly salary", i.e., $r_{xz} = 0.778$; between "IQ" and "monthly salary", i.e., $r_{yz} = 0.480$; and between "degree mark" and "IQ", i.e., $r_{xy} = 0.660$

Degree X	Salary Z	IQ Y	Degree X	Salary Z	IQ Y	Degree X	Salary Z	IQ Y	Degree X	Salary Z	IQ Y
40	820	97	56	940	110	62	1340	99	68	1250	118
42	930	92	56	1240	106	62	1170	107	69	1030	112
43	910	110	57	1130	117	63	1260	115	70	1140	113
45	950	95	58	1220	108	64	1370	111	70	1360	106
48	850	98	58	1260	124	64	1220	108	71	1470	123
49	1030	110	59	1010	107	64	1570	114	73	1520	124
50	1210	95	59	1060	125	65	1680	105	75	1420	133
52	1120	102	60	1360	118	66	1360	114	77	1730	110
53	1030	103	60	960	107	67	1460	102	78	1570	122
54	1120	108	61	1220	104	67	1120	108	80	1670	130
55	1230	105	62	1130	106	68	1270	117			

Therefore:

$$h = \frac{1 - (g \times \bar{r}^2)}{1 - \bar{r}^2} = \frac{1 - (0.292 \times 0.418)}{1 - 0.418} = 1.508,$$

and thus,

$$z = (r_{f(xz)} - r_{f(yz)}) \times \sqrt{\frac{n - 3}{2 \times (1 - r_{xy}) \times h}}$$

$$= (1.04 - 0.523) \times \sqrt{\frac{43 - 3}{2 \times (1 - 0.66) \times 1.508}} = 3.231.$$

Since this value lies outside the ±1.96 critical region of the z-distribution, for an α level of 0.05, it is concluded that the correlation between degree and salary is significantly larger than the correlation between IQ and salary. The steps required to compute the above test are fairly intricate, so be careful not to make mistakes in the intermediate computations.

The two-sided confidence intervals for the difference between two nonindependent correlations $\rho_{xz} - \rho_{yz}$ can be obtained using the following formula:

$$(r_{f(xz)} - r_{f(yz)}) \pm c \times \sqrt{\frac{2 \times (1 - r_{xy}) \times h}{n - 3}}$$

where c is the two-tailed critical value of z for any desired α level (i.e., $z_{\frac{\alpha}{2}}$). The limits of the obtained interval are in Fisher's scores; thus, these values need to be transformed back into ρ values using Table 11.4. For the study we examined above, the limits of the 95% confidence interval for $\rho_{f(xz)} - \rho_{f(yz)}$ are:

$$(1.04 - 0.523) \pm 1.96 \times \sqrt{\frac{2 \times (1 - 0.66) \times 1.508}{43 - 3}} \text{ , i.e., } 0.203 \text{ and } 0.831.$$

Transforming these values back to ρ values, the limits of the $\text{CI}_{95\%}$ for $\rho_{xz} - \rho_{yz}$ are 0.20 and 0.68.

Partial correlation

From the analyses presented in the earlier sections of this chapter it appeared that there was a fairly strong correlation between degree mark and monthly salary. Inspecting the data from the previous section it also appeared that IQ was strongly correlated with both "degree mark" and "monthly salary". Given this scenario we may become suspicious of the strong relationship between degree mark and salary. This relationship may simply be an artefact of the following more "complex" relationships: Intelligent people do well at university and they also earn a good salary. Therefore, to assess whether or not the relationship between degree mark and monthly salary is genuine, we need a technique that "purifies" the relationship between degree mark and monthly salary from the influence of the IQ variable. This can be achieved by calculating the *partial correlation* between degree mark (i.e., X) and monthly salary (i.e., Z) where the linear influence of IQ (i.e., Y) has been removed from the relationships between X and Z. The partial correlation between two variables X and Z, denoted as $r_{xz \cdot y}$, where Y is the variable partialled out, is:

$$r_{xz \cdot y} = \frac{r_{xz} - (r_{xy} \times r_{yz})}{\sqrt{(1 - r_{xy}^2) \times (1 - r_{yz}^2)}}.$$

In our example the correlation between degree mark and monthly salary is $r_{xz} = 0.778$; the correlation between IQ and monthly salary is $r_{yz} = 0.480$; and the correlation between degree mark and IQ is $r_{xy} = 0.660$. Therefore, the partial correlation between degree mark (i.e., X) and monthly salary (i.e., Z), with the effect of IQ (i.e., Y) being partialled out of both variables is:

$$r_{xz \cdot y} = \frac{0.778 - (0.66 \times 0.48)}{\sqrt{(1 - 0.66^2) \times (1 - 0.48^2)}} = 0.699.$$

It therefore appears that there is still a strong correlation between degree mark and monthly salary after the linear influence of IQ has been removed from the relationship between degree mark and monthly salary.

The test for the significance of partial correlations is calculated as:

$$z = \frac{r_{f(xz \cdot y)} - \rho_{f(xz \cdot y)}}{\sqrt{\dfrac{1}{n - 4}}}$$

Table 11.6 Artificial data-set to demonstrate what happens when the effect of one variable (i.e., Y) is partialled out of the correlation between two variables X and Z. See pages 191–192 for details

X	Z	Y
10	270	30
11	250	30
12	230	30
13	210	30
14	300	40
15	280	40
16	270	40
17	240	40
18	340	60
19	320	60
20	300	60
21	290	60
$r_{xz} = 0.584$	$r_{yz} = 0.808$	$r_{xy} = 0.929$

$$r_{xz \cdot y} = \frac{r_{xz} - (r_{xy} \times r_{yz})}{\sqrt{(1 - r_{xy}^2) \times (1 - r_{yz}^2)}}$$

$$= \frac{0.584 - (0.929 \times 0.808)}{\sqrt{(1 - 0.929^2) \times (1 - 0.808^2)}} = -0.764$$

where $r_{f(xz \cdot y)}$ and $\rho_{f(xz \cdot y)}$ are the corresponding Fisher's r_f scores for $r_{xz \cdot y}$ and $\rho_{xz \cdot y}$. In our example the test of H_0: $\rho_{xz \cdot y} = 0$ is based on the following standard normal deviate:

$$z = \frac{0.867 - 0}{\sqrt{\dfrac{1}{43 - 4}}} = 5.414$$

which is significant at an α level of 0.05. Thus, we reject the null hypothesis.

Let us look a bit more closely at what it is meant by "to control for" (or "partial out" or "remove", these terms are all equivalent) the linear influence of a third variable Y on the relationship between variables X and Z. This corresponds to calculating the correlation between X and Z while holding Y constant. Consider the artificial data-set in Table 11.6. As you can see, there is a *positive* correlation between the variables X and Z, $r_{xz} = 0.584$ (notice that r_{xy} and r_{yz} are also positive). On the other hand, the partial correlation between X and Z, when Y is partialled out of both variables is *negative*, i.e., $r_{xz \cdot y} = -0.764$.

To appreciate why this happens you should look at the relationship between X and Z when, for example, Y is kept constant at 30. For this value of Y, it appears that while the values that X takes increase, the values of Z decrease. The same occurs when the value of Y is kept constant at 40 and at 60. This example demonstrates that the partial correlation between two variables X and Z, with Y being partialled out, corresponds to the correlation between X and Z when Y is held constant.

Finally, notice that controlling for a third variable does not mean carrying out the computation of the correlation between X and Z as if Y does not exist. In fact, we saw in this case that r_{xz} is positive (i.e., 0.584), yet, when the effect of Y is controlled for, $r_{xz \cdot y}$ is negative (i.e., −0.764).

Factors affecting the Pearson correlation coefficient r

There are some factors that can have a relatively strong influence on the size of the correlation coefficient obtained from sampled data. This section will examine these factors.

Range effects

In correlational studies, sometimes the range of scores in either one or both studied variables may be restricted compared to the range of scores in the population. These restrictions may be due to the sampling procedure, or to some limitation of the instruments used to measure the variables. For example, the range of IQ scores for university students is more likely to be restricted than the range of IQ scores for the general population (i.e., it should be relatively unlikely to find university students with an IQ lower than the average population IQ). Similarly, if a test used to measure a variable is too easy, we will have ceiling effects, restricting the range of test scores (the same problem will be present if the test is too difficult). For example, if a test is too easy everybody may score at least 80 per cent correct, while with a slightly more difficult test the correct scores could range from 30 per cent to 90 per cent. The main consequences of restricted ranges are either a reduction or an increment in the size of the correlation coefficient r. In general, the size of r tends to be *deflated* if range restrictions *reduce* the standard deviation of the distribution of scores on one or both variables. Conversely, the size of r tends to be *inflated* if range restrictions *increase* the standard deviation of the distribution of scores on one or both variables.

For example, in the section on pages 181–182 we saw that the correlation between degree mark and monthly salary, in a sample of 43 subjects, was $r = 0.778$. Imagine that we restrict the range of scores by considering only the subjects with a degree mark greater than 54, but smaller than 65 (i.e., we roughly select the subjects with a degree mark within half a standard deviation from the mean degree mark for the total sample of 43 subjects). With this range restriction the standard deviation of the degree mark variable is smaller than in the original sample (i.e., 2.9 vs 9.7). The consequence of this is that the shape of the scatterplot of degree mark and monthly salary is more circular than the original one (see Figure 11.3). Hence, the size of r between degree mark and monthly salary in this sub-set of subjects is *smaller* than in the full sample, i.e., 0.467 vs 0.778. Conversely, if we select only those subjects with relatively extreme degree marks, i.e., lower than 55 and greater than 64, the standard deviation of the degree mark variable is larger than in the original sample (i.e., 12.6 vs 9.7). This range restriction makes the elliptical shape of the scatterplot between degree mark and monthly salary slightly more elongated than in the full sample. Hence, the size of r between these variables in this sub-set of subjects is *larger* than in the full sample, i.e., 0.834 vs 0.778.

In summary, range restrictions, either due to the sampling procedure or to the limitations of the instruments used to measure the variables, can affect the size of the observed correlation between two variables in a sample, compared to the correlation present in the population. Therefore, range restrictions should be avoided by using sampling procedures that do not affect the range of the scores in the investigated variables, and by using appropriate measurement instruments (i.e., those that do not induce either floor or ceiling effects).

Outliers

An outlier is an observation that greatly differs from the other observations. Imagine, for example, that in the scatterplot shown in Figure 11.3, the subject with a degree mark of 80 earns £800 per month, instead of £1,670. This would certainly be an observation that greatly differs from the others (i.e., the highest degree mark in the sample is associated with the lowest salary). Depending on their location, outlier(s) tend to increase or decrease the correlation coefficient. With the above outlier substituted for the original data, the correlation between degree mark and monthly salary becomes 0.605 instead of 0.778.

Often outliers simply reflect errors in data recording. For example, a salary of £1,420 corresponding to a degree mark of 75 could be wrongly recorded as a monthly salary of £4,120! In other cases outliers may be genuine. To avoid a single observation in a data-set dictating the size of the correlation (or of the difference between means), it is recommended that a large number of observations are collected when possible.

Reliability

We want the instruments of measurement we use to be *valid* (i.e., they should really measure what they intend to measure). Moreover, they should be *reliable* (i.e., measurements of the same variable, using the same instrument, should be stable over time). For example, we do not want IQ test scores to fluctuate between two administrations of the same IQ test on the same sample of subjects. An index of reliability of a test is the correlation coefficient r for the scores between two administrations of the test (i.e., test–retest correlation). In general, a well designed and reliable psychological test should have a test–retest correlation coefficient r of at least 0.75.

The correlation of a test with itself sets a limit for the correlation of this test with any others. If the test–retest correlation of Test-A with itself is, for example, 0.78, and the test–retest correlation of Test-B with itself is 0.83, we cannot expect the correlation between Test-A and Test-B to be greater than 0.78. A variable cannot correlate more strongly with another variable than with itself!

Nonlinear relationships

A very low and non-significant linear correlation between two variables may occur even if the variables are associated. This can happen in cases where two variables are related in a nonlinear manner (e.g., $y = x^2$, where there is a curvilinear relationship between X and Y). It is therefore important to keep in mind that if there is no association between two variables, their linear correlation should be 0. Nevertheless,

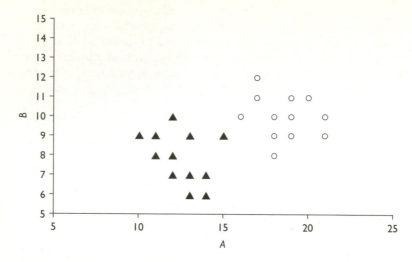

Figure 11.4 Effect of heterogeneous sub-samples on correlation. The data from Sample-1 are the black triangles; those from Sample-2 are the unfilled circles. The correlation between variables A and B is negative in both samples ($r = -0.36$ and $r = -0.21$, respectively). However, when the samples are combined into one larger sample, the correlation between these variables is positive, $r = 0.51$.

if two variables are not linearly related this does not necessarily mean that there is no relationship between these variables. The treatment of nonlinear correlations is outside the scope of this textbook (see however the section on pages 198–200).

Heterogeneous sub-samples

In carrying out correlational analyses (as well as regression analyses, see Chapter 12), it is important to be aware that when heterogeneous sub-samples are pooled together, correlations between two variables may be biased. Consider the abstract example presented in Figure 11.4. Here it appears that the correlation between variables A and B in both Sample-1 and Sample-2 is *negative* (hence the correlation between variables A and B is negative). However, when the two samples are combined into one larger sample, the correlation between these variables is *positive*. This spurious positive correlation between variables A and B mainly reflects the fact that subjects in Sample-2 scored higher than subjects in Sample-1 on both variables A and B. To avoid spurious correlations, it is advisable to calculate relevant correlations on individual sub-samples, and not on the grouped data which combine the heterogeneous sub-samples.

The point biserial correlation r_{pb}

In the previous sections we showed how to calculate the Pearson correlation coefficient r between two continuous variables. In some cases we may want to calculate the correlation between a dichotomous variable and a continuous variable (remember that the correlation between two dichotomous variables can also be calculated as shown in the section on pages 116–119). For example, in Chapter 9 (Table 9.5), we described

Table 11.7 Results of a study comparing the performance of a sample of 12 first year non-mature university students and 12 retired elderly adults in the free recall of a list of 15 words. The relevant quantities required for the computation of the point biserial correlation r_{pb}, between age (i.e., X) and number of items recalled (Y), are given. The steps required to compute r_{pb} are also provided

X = Age (Students = 0 Elderly = 1)	Y = Number of items recalled	$(x - \bar{x})(y - \bar{y})$
0	13	−2.145833
0	13	−2.145833
0	11	−1.145833
0	10	−0.645833
0	9	−0.145833
0	9	−0.145833
0	9	−0.145833
0	9	−0.145833
0	8	0.354167
0	8	0.354167
0	8	0.354167
0	7	0.854167
1	11	1.145833
1	10	0.645833
1	9	0.145833
1	9	0.145833
1	9	0.145833
1	8	−0.354167
1	8	−0.354167
1	7	−0.854167
1	7	−0.854167
1	6	−1.354167
1	6	−1.354167
1	5	−1.854167
$\bar{x} = 0.500$ $s_x = 0.511$	$\bar{y} = 8.7083$ $s_y = 1.989$	$\Sigma(x - \bar{x})(y - \bar{y}) = -9.500$

$$COV_{xy} = \frac{\Sigma(x - \bar{x})(y - \bar{y})}{n - 1} = \frac{-9.5}{23} = -0.413$$

$$r_{pb} = \frac{COV_{xy}}{s_x \times s_y} = \frac{-0.413}{0.511 \times 1.989} = -0.407$$

a study to assess if a group of first year non-mature university students recalled, on average, more items than a sample of retired elderly subjects (who obtained a degree in their youth). Instead of assessing the effect of groups on the average number of items recalled, as we did in Chapter 9, we could assess if the number of items recalled correlates with the group variable. In this case free recall performance is a continuous variable. The group variable, on the other hand, was considered a dichotomous variable that could take the following values: first year non-mature university students = 0; retired elderly adults = 1 (see Table 11.7). In Chapter 9 we saw that elderly subjects recalled significantly fewer items than young university students; hence, we should find a negative correlation between the group variable and number of items recalled (i.e., when "age" increases recall decreases).

The index measuring the strength of the relationship between a dichotomous and a continuous variable is called point biserial correlation, and it is denoted as r_{pb}. Its calculation is carried out as for the Pearson correlation coefficient r (see Table 11.7). When the point biserial correlation is calculated from the data in Table 11.7, it appears, as expected, that there is a negative correlation between age and the number of items recalled (i.e., $r_{pb} = -0.407$). This example highlights the fact that speaking about differences between two treatments' means, is the equivalent of saying that means are related to treatments. As an addendum, notice that the selection of values assigned to the levels of the dichotomous variable is arbitrary. For example, if we had chosen the following values: elderly adults = 0; young adults = 1, we would have obtained a positive point biserial correlation between age and number of items recalled, i.e., $r_{pb} = 0.407$. This is the equivalent of saying that young adults recalled more items than elderly adults. Accordingly, from the computations shown in the section on pages 162–164, it appears that the mean number of items recalled by young adults, i.e., 9.5, was larger than the mean number of items recalled by the elderly sample, i.e., 7.92. A t-test on these data showed the difference to be significant, t ($df = 22$) = 2.088, $p < 0.05$.

Moreover, notice this important relationship between t and r_{pb}. It can be proved that:

$$r_{pb} = \sqrt{\frac{t^2}{t^2 + df}}$$

where, with respect to our example, r_{pb} is the point biserial correlation between age and the number of items recalled; t^2 is the square of the t-test assessing the significance of the difference between the number of items recalled by the young and the elderly sample; and df is the degrees of freedom associated with the t-test.

Applying the above formula to the relationship between age and free recall we obtain that:

$$r_{pb} = \sqrt{\frac{2.088^2}{2.088^2 + 22}} = 0.407.$$

Assuming that H_0: $\rho_{pb} = 0$, the significance of r_{pb}, is given, as in the case of Pearson's r, by:

$$t = \frac{r_{pb} - 0}{\sqrt{\dfrac{1 - r_{pb}^2}{df}}} \quad \text{where } df = n - 2.$$

Applying the above formula to the relationship between age and free recall:

$$t = \frac{0.407 - 0}{\sqrt{\dfrac{1 - 0.407^2}{24 - 2}}} = 2.088.$$

(This is the same value as that obtained in the *t*-test when assessing the significance of the difference in the mean number of items recalled by young and elderly adults.)

These last formulae further highlight the fact that, stating that there is a significant difference between pairs of means, is the same as saying that there is a significant correlation between a dichotomous and a continuous variable (e.g., age and number of items recalled). Furthermore, rearranging the formula for the significance of r_{pb} it appears, again, that:

Magnitude of a significance test = Size of the effect × Size of the study

i.e., $t = \dfrac{r_{pb}}{\sqrt{1 - r_{pb}^2}} \times \sqrt{df}$

where $\dfrac{r_{pb}}{\sqrt{1 - r_{pb}^2}}$ is an index of the size of the effect of the dichotomous variable on the continuous variable, and $\sqrt{df}$ is a measure of the size of the study.

The formulae linking r_{pb} and t also apply to the matched-samples *t*-test. However, in this case r_{pb} *does not* correspond to the correlation between the two sets of matched pairs of scores. Table 11.8 provides an artificial data-set for the number of errors made by a sample of subjects on a video-game, before and after receiving training (reduced scores indicate improvements). In our example, the point biserial correlation obtained by applying the formula:

$r_{pb} = \sqrt{\dfrac{t^2}{t^2 + df}}$ where df = number of subjects − 1,

is the point biserial correlation between the training dichotomous variable (i.e., Before = 1 and After = 0), and the number of errors before and after training, after subtracting the average performance of each subject in the two conditions (i.e., Before − $\dfrac{\text{Before} + \text{After}}{2}$ and After − $\dfrac{\text{Before} + \text{After}}{2}$; these values are the "Individual differences from the mean" in Table 11.8). For the data in Table 11.8 the point biserial correlation between training and number of errors is:

$r_{pb} = \sqrt{\dfrac{5.715^2}{5.715^2 + 4}} = 0.944.$

Finally, the point biserial correlation should be used to calculate the correlation between a genuine dichotomous variable and a continuum variable. Genuine dichotomous variables are those where a subject is clearly in one of the two categories used, and for which it is difficult to consider that there is some sort of underlying continuum between the two categories (e.g., male vs female). If the dichotomous variable has been created artificially, as for example by dividing subjects into two groups as a function of an arbitrary dividing point along an underlying continuum scale (and provided that this underlying continuum is normally distributed), then the point biserial correlation may not be appropriate to estimate the correlation in the population (i.e., ρ) between

Table 11.8 Relationship between point biserial correlation and *t*-test in the case of matched samples. See the section on pages 194–198 for a description of the details of the data-set

Subject	Before training	After training	Mean	Before – After (B – A)		Individual differences from the mean	Before = 1 After = 0
1	6	2	4	4	Subject1 Before	2	1
2	5	3	4	2	Subject2 Before	1	1
3	6	4	5	2	Subject3 Before	1	1
4	8	6	7	2	Subject4 Before	1	1
5	11	7	9	4	Subject5 Before	2	1
Mean$_{B-A}$	$\bar{x} = 2.8$				Subject1 After	−2	0
Standard Deviation	$s = 1.095$				Subject2 After	−1	0
Standard error	$SE = 0.490$				Subject3 After	−1	0
Paired *t*-test (i.e., Mean/SE)	$t = 5.715$ $df = 4$				Subject4 After	−1	0
					Subject5 After	−2	0

$$r_{pb} = \sqrt{\frac{t^2}{t^2 + df}} = \sqrt{\frac{5.715^2}{5.715^2 + 4}} = 0.944$$

the "artificial" dichotomous variable and a continuous variable. The biserial correlation (denoted as r_b) is generally considered to be give a more accurate estimate of ρ. Thus, for example, if we divide subjects into two groups depending on their IQ scores being either above or below some cut-off point, i.e., high IQ vs low IQ individuals, we have created an artificial dichotomous variable from an underlying continuum of normally distributed observations (i.e., IQ scores). Thus, if we want to estimate the correlation in the population between this dichotomous variable and any continuous variable, using sampled data, we should then use the biserial correlation. However, it has been pointed out that the biserial correlation may, under some specific conditions, exceed the value of 1 (Howell, 1997). Thus this feature makes this test unappealing. In practice the biserial correlation is rarely used. The point biserial correlation could be used to provide an approximated estimate of the correlation in the population between an artificial dichotomous variable having an underlying normally distributed continuum, and a continuous variable (for details about the computation of the biserial correlation see Howell, 1997).

The Spearman Rank correlation coefficient

In some circumstances we may need to calculate the correlation between two sets of ranks. For example, two judges are asked to rank the pleasantness of 10 pictures and we want to assess if the judges tend to agree in their opinions (see Table 11.9). If there

Table 11.9 Example of the application of the Pearson correlation coefficient r to ranks (i.e., this corresponds to the Spearman r_s). See text for details

Picture	A	B	C	D	E	F	G	H	I	J	Mean	Standard Deviation
Ranking by Judge 1 (i.e., X)	3	2	4	6	7	8	5	1	10	9	5.5	3.028
Ranking by Judge 2 (i.e., Y)	4	5	2	6	7	9	3	1	8	10	5.5	3.028
$(x - \bar{x})(y - \bar{y})$	3.75	1.75	5.25	0.25	2.25	8.75	1.25	20.25	11.25	15.75	$\Sigma(x - \bar{x})(y - \bar{y}) = 70.5$ $n = 10$ (i.e., number of pictures)	

$$COV_{xy} = \frac{\Sigma(x - \bar{x})(y - \bar{y})}{n - 1} = \frac{70.5}{9} = 7.83 \qquad r_s = = \frac{COV_{xy}}{s_x \times s_y} = \frac{7.83}{3.028 \times 3.028} = 0.855$$

is perfect agreement, both judges should give the same ranking to the 10 pictures. If there is complete disagreement, we would expect the ranking of one judge to be the opposite of the ranking of the second judge. One of the most common tests used to calculate the correlation between ranks is the Spearman rank correlation coefficient, denoted as r_s. Several textbooks provide a special formula to compute r_s which is based on the difference between the ranks given by the two judges for each particular item. However, this formula is just a simplification of the ordinary formula used to calculate the Pearson correlation coefficient r. To obtain the Spearman rank correlation coefficient r_s, it is enough to calculate the Pearson correlation coefficient r on the ranks. Table 11.9 shows the details of this computation on the correlation for the ranking of 10 pictures by two different judges. Since $r_s = 0.855$, this indicates that the two judges strongly agree in their ranking of the pleasantness of the 10 pictures.

Provided that $n \geq 10$ a rough indication of the significance of r_s (for H_0: $\rho = 0$) can be computed as for Pearson r (i.e., $t = \dfrac{r - 0}{\sqrt{\dfrac{1 - r^2}{n - 2}}}$). Notice that if $n < 10$, r_s can only be significantly different from 0, at an α level of 0.05 two-tailed, if n is larger than 5 (i.e., the critical values of r_s for $n = 6$, $n = 7$, $n = 8$, $n = 9$ are: ± 0.886, ± 0.786, ± 0.738 and ± 0.7, respectively).

An alternative and equivalent test to Spearman's r_s is Kendall's Tau coefficient. Given that these two tests are comparable, Kendall's Tau coefficient will not be described in this text (for details see Siegel and Castellan, 1988).

Finally, Spearman's test can be used to assess increasing or decreasing associations including nonlinear ones. For example, we could have that the values of the X variable are 2, 4, 5, 7, 9 and 11, and the associated values of the Y variables are 8, 64, 125, 343, 729, 1331. In this case we have that $y = x^3$. If r is calculated on this data we obtain a value of 0.94, thus despite the fact there is a perfect (nonlinear) relationship in our data, Pearson's r cannot detect it (remember that Pearson's r is an index of the strength of linear associations). On the other hand, if Spearman's r_s had been calculated on these data (after they are ranked) we would have obtained a value of 1 (this is because in all cases where x increased y increased as well). In all cases where one variable increases as the second variable decreases $r_s = -1$ (obviously intermediate values would indicate different strengths of the association between two variable). For further details on the use of Spearman's r_s in dealing with nonlinear associations see, e.g., Upton and Cook (1997).

Kendall's coefficient of concordance W

If instead of two judges, we have three or more judges ranking a set of objects, we cannot use the Spearman rank correlation coefficient to measure the degree of agreement between judges. In theory, we could calculate the rank correlation between all possible pairs of judges, and then calculate their average. Unfortunately, unless the number of judges is relatively small, this procedure would be very tedious and time consuming. An alternative approach consists of calculating the Kendall's coefficient of concordance W. This index ranges from 0 (i.e., complete disagreement among judges) to 1 (i.e., perfect agreement). The calculation of W is given in Table 11.10. This table

Table 11.10 Example of the application of the Kendall's coefficient of concordance *W* to ranks. See text for details

	Picture									
	A	B	C	D	E	F	G	H	I	J
Ranking by Judge 1	3	2	4	6	7	8	5	1	10	9
Ranking by Judge 2	4	5	2	6	7	9	3	1	8	10
Ranking by Judge 3	3	4	5	7	6	8	1	2	9	10
Sum of ranks (i.e., T_j)	10	11	11	19	20	25	9	4	27	29
Squared sum of ranks	100	121	121	361	400	625	81	16	729	841

$$W = \frac{12 \sum T_i^2 - 3k^2 n(n+1)^2}{k^2 n(n^2 - 1)} = \frac{12 \times 3395 - 3 \times 3^2 \times 10 \times (10+1)^2}{3^2 \times 10 \times (10^2 - 1)} = \frac{8070}{8910} = 0.906 \text{ (to 3 d.p.)}$$

provides an extension of the example described in the last section. Here three judges, instead of two, have been asked to rate the pleasantness of 10 pictures.

W is calculated as:

$$W = \frac{12 \sum T_i^2 - 3k^2 n(n+1)^2}{k^2 n(n^2 - 1)}$$

where $\sum T_i^2$ is the sum of the squared sum of ranks for each of the *n* individuals or objects being ranked; *n* is the number of objects being ranked; and *k* is the number of judges. As seen in Table 11.10, *W* = 0.906, indicating that there is a substantial agreement in the ranking of the pleasantness of the 10 pictures between the three judges.

Tests on the significance of *W* have been proposed, but they are outside the scope of this text (see Siegel & Castellan, 1988). However it is worth noticing that *W* is only calculated to check if there is substantial agreement between the rankings of different judges. As a rule of thumb, if *W* is less than 0.5 there is no substantial agreement between judges.

Given *W*, it is possible to calculate the average rank correlation of *n* objects between all possible pairs of judges. This average(r_s) is calculated as:

$$\text{average}(r_s) = \frac{kW - 1}{k - 1}$$

where *k* is the number of judges. In our example the average(r_s) = $\dfrac{3 \times 0.906 - 1}{3 - 1} = 0.859$.

Chapter 12

Regression

Introduction

In some cases researchers are not only interested in assessing the strength of the linear relationship between two continuous variables X and Y, but they would also like to predict the values of Y, on the basis of their knowledge about the X variable. In this case, the appropriate statistical tool is linear regression analysis. The main aim of this analysis is to estimate a linear equation of the form $y = a + bx$ so that the relationship between X and Y can be plotted as a straight line (called a regression line), and the values of the dependent variable Y can be predicted using the values of the independent variable X. This chapter will describe how to perform a simple linear regression analysis on two continuous variables.

Notice that linear regression analyses can be conducted using more than one independent variable to predict the value of the dependent variable. This type of statistical tool is called multiple linear regression analysis and it is outside the scope of this book (for an introduction to multiple regression see, for example, Allison, 1999).

The regression line

In Chapter 11 we described how to calculate the linear correlation between two variables (i.e., Pearson's r). This was demonstrated with a data-set of degree marks (i.e., the independent variable X) and monthly income (i.e., the dependent variable Y) gathered from a sample of 43 graduates. We saw that there was a strong positive linear correlation between these variables (i.e., $r = 0.778$). We also saw that the presence of a linear relationship between these two variables was captured by the tilted straight line that provided a relatively good fit of the data shown in Figure 11.3. This is called a regression line and it provides, for any given value of X, the predicted value of Y. Before describing how to obtain a regression line, it is useful to review how a straight line can be mathematically represented by an equation.

All points forming a straight line can be identified by an equation of the form:

$$y = a + bx$$

where the xs are the values of the independent variable X; b is the parameter that specifies the slope of the straight line (i.e., the rate of increment of Y as a function of unit increments in X); a is the parameter that specifies the intercept, i.e., the value of

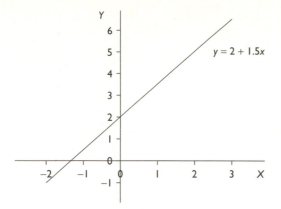

Figure 12.1 Graph of the equation y = 2 + 1.5x.

the dependent variable Y when $x = 0$; and the ys are the values of the dependent variable Y associated with the values of the independent variable X.

Figure 12.1 shows a section of the graph of the equation $y = 2 + 1.5x$. It can be noticed that when the value $x = 0$ is entered into this equation we obtain $y = 2$ (i.e., the intercept of the straight line with the y-axis). In this equation $b = 1.5$, thus the slope of the straight line is 1.5. The slope indicates the rate of change in the value of the variable Y as a function of increments in the value of the independent variable X (hence steeper slopes correspond to larger absolute values of b). This means that when we increase the value of the variable X by 1 unit the corresponding value of the variable Y increases by 1.5 units. For example, if we select $x = 1$ and $x = 2$, the corresponding values for the Y variable are $y = 3.5$ and $y = 5$. Negative slopes indicate that when the values of the variable X increase, the values of the variable Y decrease.

The regression line superimposed on the data in Figure 11.3 intended to provide the best-fitting straight line of the scattered data. The next step is to show how the a and b parameters, that characterise the regression line, are obtained using the sampled data. The calculation of the regression line will be shown on a new set of data presented in Table 12.1. This table shows the age (in years) and the reaction times (in milliseconds) in a detection task for each of the subjects in a sample of 24 people. These data are also displayed in the scattergram in Figure 12.2. The regression line superimposed on the data in this figure aims to predict the reaction times (i.e., the dependent variable Y) on the basis of the age of the subjects (i.e., the independent variable X). Usually the predicted values of the dependent variable Y are indicated as $\hat{y}$s, hence the equation representing the regression line is of the form $\hat{y} = a + bx$.

The a and b parameters of the regression line are obtained so that, given the values of the independent variable X (i.e., the xs), the corresponding predicted values of the dependent variable Y lying on the regression line (i.e., the $\hat{y}$s) are as close as possible to the observed values of Y (i.e., the ys). This is achieved by selecting those values of a and b so that the sum of the squared error of prediction (or residual) is minimal. The error of prediction for each of the ys is $y - \hat{y}$ (shown in Figure 12.2 for two data points). Thus the appropriate estimate of the a and b parameters of the regression line is calculated so that the $\sum(y - \hat{y})^2$ around the regression line is minimal. The so-called

Table 12.1 Age and reaction times (RT) recorded in a simple reaction time task where subjects have to press a button as soon as a predetermined stimulus appears on the computer screen. The values of the quantities $(x − \bar{x})(y − \bar{y})$, $(x − \bar{x})$, $(x − \bar{x})^2$, $\hat{y}$ and $(y − \bar{y})^2$ are given for each subject. Details of how to calculate the regression line to predict RT, given the age of the subjects, are provided. Finally, the Pearson's correlation coefficient r between RT and age is also reported

Subject	Age (X)	RT (Y)	$(x − \bar{x})(y − \bar{y})$	$(x − \bar{x})^2$	$(y − \bar{y})^2$	$\hat{y} = 161.433 + 2x$	$(y − \hat{y})^2$
1	38.4	241.0	771.542	413.783	1438.622	238.233	7.656
2	41.3	246.4	567.363	304.212	1058.147	244.033	5.603
3	42.9	258.0	331.553	250.958	438.030	247.233	115.928
4	45.2	264.4	196.749	183.377	211.097	251.833	157.929
5	46.9	272.5	76.132	140.225	41.334	255.233	298.149
6	47.8	254.6	266.202	119.720	591.908	257.033	5.919
7	48.9	245.4	329.983	96.858	1124.205	259.233	191.352
8	50.2	251.3	235.999	72.960	763.371	261.833	110.944
9	51.7	244.0	245.960	49.585	1220.047	264.833	434.014
10	52.0	258.1	140.423	45.450	433.854	265.433	53.773
11	55.3	266.5	42.777	11.845	154.484	272.033	30.614
12	56.2	280.1	−2.976	6.460	1.371	273.833	39.275
13	58.5	261.1	4.309	0.058	317.879	278.433	300.433
14	61.0	284.0	11.452	5.100	25.713	283.433	0.321
15	62.5	307.5	107.379	14.125	816.293	286.433	443.818
16	64.0	292.6	71.886	27.650	186.892	289.433	10.030
17	66.2	274.4	−33.780	55.627	20.513	293.833	377.641
18	67.8	291.1	110.247	82.053	148.129	297.033	35.200
19	70.5	324.1	531.134	138.258	2040.404	302.433	469.459
20	72.5	309.7	423.355	189.292	946.844	306.433	10.673
21	75.3	321.2	699.935	274.178	1786.823	312.033	84.034
22	77.2	332.0	979.599	340.710	2816.513	315.833	261.372
23	78.0	298.6	378.827	370.883	386.942	317.433	354.682
24	79.5	315.7	763.301	430.908	1352.094	320.433	22.401
Means	58.742	278.929	Totals 7249.351	3624.278	18321.51		3821.224

$$b = \frac{\sum(x − \bar{x})(y − \bar{y})}{\sum(x − \bar{x})^2} = \frac{7249.351}{3624.278} = 2.000 \text{ to 3 d.p.}$$

$$a = \bar{y} − b\bar{x} = 278.929 − 2 \times 58.742 = 161.433 \text{ to 3 d.p.}$$

Hence the equation for the regression line is: $\hat{y} = a + bx = 161.433 + 2x$

$$r_{xy} = \frac{\sum(x − \bar{x})(y − \bar{y})}{\sqrt{\sum(x − \bar{x})^2 \times \sum(y − \bar{y})^2}} = \frac{7249.351}{\sqrt{3624.278 \times 18321.51}} = 0.890$$

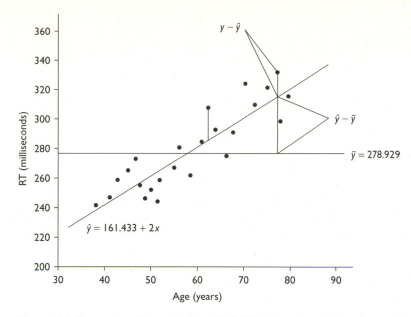

Figure 12.2 Scatterplot of the data from Table 12.1. Superimposed on the graph is the regression line used to predict reaction times (i.e., RT) on the basis of age. The distance between the height of each data point y and its predicted value ŷ lying on the regression line, is the residual or error of prediction (i.e., $y - \hat{y}$). As an example the error of prediction is shown for two data points of the scatterplot. Moreover, for one data point both the error of prediction, i.e., $(y - \hat{y})$, and $(\hat{y} - \bar{y})$ are shown.

Method of Least Square Estimation, leading to the calculation of the parameters of the regression line, is outside the scope of this book. Here it is sufficient to say that the appropriate values of the *a* and *b* parameters that minimise the $\sum (y - \hat{y})^2$ are obtained as:

$$b = \frac{COV_{xy}}{s_x^2} \quad \text{(or equivalently } b = \frac{\sum(x - \bar{x})(y - \bar{y})}{\sum(x - \bar{x})^2}) \quad \text{and} \quad a = \bar{y} - b\bar{x},$$

where COV_{xy} is the covariance between the variables *X* and *Y*; $\bar{x}$ is the mean of the independent variable; and $\bar{y}$ is the mean of the dependent variable.

Applying these formulae to the data shown in Table 12.1 it appears that:

$$b = \frac{\sum(x - \bar{x})(y - \bar{y})}{\sum(x - \bar{x})^2} = \frac{7249.351}{3624.278} = 2.000 \text{ to 3 d.p.}$$

or equivalently,

$$b = \frac{COV_{xy}}{s_x^2} = \frac{\dfrac{\sum(x - \bar{x})(y - \bar{y})}{n - 1}}{\dfrac{\sum(x - \bar{x})^2}{n - 1}} = \frac{\dfrac{7249.351}{23}}{\dfrac{3624.278}{23}} = 2.000$$

and that:

$a = \bar{y} - b\bar{x} = 278.929 - 2 \times 58.742 = 161.433$ to 3 d.p.

Thus the equation for the regression line for the variable Y on the variable X is:

$\hat{y} = 161.433 + 2x.$

Interpretation of the regression equation

The slope of the regression line measures the rate of change in the predicted values of the dependent variable ($\hat{y}$) as a function of one-unit increments in the value of the independent variable X. Thus, the outcome of the above regression analysis indicates that when age is increased by 1 year the predicted reaction time increases by 2 milliseconds. The intercept gives the value of $\hat{y}$ when $x = 0$. In this case it would appear that the subjects at age 0 are expected to have a reaction time of about 161.4 milliseconds. Often, as for example in the above case, there is no interesting interpretation of the intercept. It is often unlikely that 0 is within the range of values of the independent variable X. In these cases the intercept only provides an extreme extrapolation from the obtained data that has either little or no interesting interpretation.

Remember that despite being able to predict the value of the dependent variable as a function of the independent variable, this does not mean that increments (or decrements) in the dependent variable are caused by changes in the values of the independent variable. Whenever the independent variable is not under the control of the experimenter, causal inferences are not warranted. Since in regression analyses the independent variable is unlikely to be manipulated by the experimenter, no causal interpretation of the effect of the independent on the dependent variable should be provided.

Regressing the variable X on the variable Y

Notice that it is also possible to calculate the regression equation of the regression line for the variable X on the variable Y. In the case of our example, the independent variable would then become "reaction time", and "age" would be the dependent variable. In this case $b = \dfrac{\Sigma(x - \bar{x})(y - \bar{y})}{\Sigma(y - \bar{y})^2}$ or equivalently $b = \dfrac{\text{COV}_{xy}}{s_y^2}$ and $a = \bar{x} - b\bar{y}$. Thus, knowing that $\Sigma(y - \bar{y})^2 = 18321.51$ in our sample, the following regression parameters would be obtained to predict age from reaction times:

$$b = \frac{\Sigma(x - \bar{x})(y - \bar{y})}{\Sigma(y - \bar{y})^2} = \frac{7249.351}{18321.51} = 0.396$$

and $a = \bar{x} - b\bar{y} = 58.742 - 0.396 \times 278.929 = -51.623$, and the regression equation would be $\hat{x} = -51.623 + 0.396y$. The two regression lines of Y on X, and of X on Y are different because minimising the error of prediction for reaction times given age is not the same as minimising the error of prediction for age given reaction times. The only case in which the two regression lines coincide is when the linear correlation between the variables X and Y is perfect (i.e., when r is either 1 or -1). Regardless of the correlation between X and Y, the two regression lines always intersect at the point $(\bar{x}, \bar{y})$.

Linear regression and correlation

Pearson's correlation coefficient r provides a measure of the strength of the linear relationship between two continuous variables. The slope of the regression line b provides an index of the linear increment in the predicted values of a continuous dependent variable as a function of unit changes in the value of a continuous independent variable. Since both correlation and regression deal with the linear association between two continuous variables, we would expect r and b to be somehow related.

We know that $r = \dfrac{\text{COV}_{xy}}{s_x \times s_y}$ and that $b = \dfrac{\text{COV}_{xy}}{s_x^2}$. The two formulae only differ in the denominator. For r this is the product of the standard deviations of variables X and Y, while for b this is the variance of the independent variable X. Now, instead of having the dependent and the independent variables measured in their original units, we could standardise them, to express them in z scores. In this case we would have $s_x^2 = s_x = s_y = 1$ and $r = b$. It therefore appears that the correlation coefficient measured on standardised data and the standardised regression coefficient (i.e., the slope obtained on standardised data) are identical.

Hypothesis testing on the slope b

In estimating the slope b we usually work with samples. It is possible that, by chance, we obtain a value of b larger (or smaller) than zero, even if the slope obtained by regressing variable Y on X in the population, i.e., β, is zero (if $\beta = 0$ it means that in the population there are no linear increments (or decrements) in the dependent variable as a function of increments in the independent variable). Hence, like the correlation coefficient r, it is useful to test whether the value of b is significantly different from zero.

Consider also that if it is true that X and Y are linearly correlated, then it should also be true that the slope of the regression line obtained by regressing Y on X is different from zero. Moreover, we saw that r and b are strictly related since both their formulae have the covariance between X and Y as their numerator. It then follows that if this covariance is zero, $r = b = 0$. Hence, testing for the significance of b is equivalent to testing for the significance of r.

In testing the significance of b we assume that the following null hypothesis is true: H_0: $\beta = 0$ (where β indicates the slope in the population). The alternative hypothesis is H_1: $\beta \neq 0$. To test this null hypothesis we need to know the standard error of b. Assuming that in the population, for each value of the variable X, the marginal distributions of the values of the variable Y, around the regression line, are normal with homogeneous

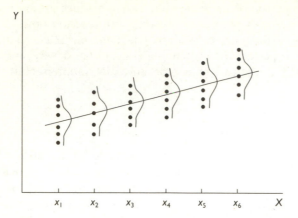

Figure 12.3 Scattergram illustrating the regression assumptions. For each value of the variable X, the marginal distributions of the values of the variable Y, around the regression line in the population, are assumed to be normal with homogeneous variances.

variances (see Figure 12.3). Then it can be shown that the quantity $\dfrac{b}{\dfrac{s_y}{s_x} \times \sqrt{\dfrac{1-r^2}{n-2}}}$ (its

denominator is the standard error of b: $SE_b = \dfrac{s_y}{s_x} \times \sqrt{\dfrac{1-r^2}{n-2}}$) is distributed as t with

$n-2$ degrees of freedom. Thus an appropriate t-test to assess H_0: $\beta = 0$ is the following:

$$t = \dfrac{b-0}{\dfrac{s_y}{s_x} \times \sqrt{\dfrac{1-r^2}{n-2}}}$$

where b is the regression slope estimated from sampled observations; s_y and s_x are the standard deviations of the dependent and the independent variables, respectively; r^2 is the correlation between X and Y in the sampled observations; and $n-2$ is the degrees of freedom (i.e., the number of subjects sampled minus two).

Applying this formula to the regression slope obtained by regressing reaction times on age, and noting that from Table 12.1, $r_{xy} = 0.890$ to 3 d.p., we have:

$$t = \dfrac{b-0}{\dfrac{s_y}{s_x} \times \sqrt{\dfrac{1-r^2}{n-2}}} = \dfrac{2-0}{\dfrac{278.929}{58.742} \times \sqrt{\dfrac{1-0.89^2}{24-2}}} = 4.33.$$

This value lies outside the critical values of the t-distribution with $df = 22$, for the 0.05 significance level. We can then reject the null hypothesis and declare that our sample was drawn from a population where increasing age leads to increments in predicted reaction times.

We have just said that testing for the significance of b is equivalent to testing for the significance of r. Although the formulae for the t-test for the significance of b and r look different, that is:

$$t = \frac{b}{\frac{s_y}{s_x} \times \sqrt{\frac{1 - r^2}{n - 2}}} \quad \text{and} \quad t = \frac{r}{\sqrt{\frac{1 - r^2}{n - 2}}},$$

this difference is more apparent than real. In fact, we know that $b = \frac{COV_{xy}}{s_x^2}$, so let us substitute $\frac{COV_{xy}}{s_x^2}$ for b in the above equation for the t-test of the significance of b. Thus we obtain:

$$t = \frac{b}{\frac{s_y}{s_x} \times \sqrt{\frac{1 - r^2}{n - 2}}} = \frac{\dfrac{COV_{xy}}{s_x^2}}{\frac{s_y}{s_x} \times \sqrt{\frac{1 - r^2}{n - 2}}},$$

then rearranging the last term and simplifying:

$$\frac{\dfrac{COV_{xy}}{s_x^2} \times \dfrac{s_x}{s_y}}{\sqrt{\dfrac{1 - r^2}{n - 2}}} = \frac{\dfrac{COV_{xy}}{s_x \times s_y}}{\sqrt{\dfrac{1 - r^2}{n - 2}}}$$

and since $r = \dfrac{COV_{xy}}{s_x \times s_y}$, after substitution we obtain:

$$t = \frac{r}{\sqrt{\dfrac{1 - r^2}{n - 2}}}.$$

Hence, the tests for the significance of b and r are equivalent.

Confidence intervals for the population regression slope β

As seen in the case of the correlation coefficient r for sampled observations, we do not know how close the estimated b is to the true value of β in the population. Therefore, we may want to use sample data to construct confidence intervals that should contain β with a given probability. The general formula for confidence intervals for β is:

$$b \pm c \times \left(\frac{s_y}{s_x} \times \sqrt{\frac{1 - r^2}{n - 2}} \right)$$

where c is the two-tailed critical value for the desired level of significance of the t-distribution with $df = n - 2$.

Applying this formula to calculate the 95% confidence interval for the population regression slope β between age and reaction times:

$$2 \pm 2.07 \times \left(\frac{s_y}{s_x} \times \sqrt{\frac{1 - r^2}{n - 2}} \right) = 2 \pm 2.07 \times 0.462$$

and, thus, the 95% confidence limits for β are 1.043 and 2.957, and the 95% confidence interval is:

$$\text{CI}_{0.95} = 1.043 \leq \beta \leq 2.957.$$

Further on the relationship between linear regression and Pearson's r: r^2 as a measure of effect size

We know that the total variability in the values of the dependent variable Y is given by the quantity $\Sigma(y - \bar{y})^2$. We also saw that the parameters of the regression line are selected to minimise $\Sigma(y - \hat{y})^2$. Since each $y - \hat{y}$ corresponds to the error in the prediction of each value of the dependent variable Y, $\Sigma(y - \hat{y})^2$ expresses the sum of squares residual (i.e., the total variability in the dependent variable not accounted for by the independent variable X). Moreover, it can be shown that the quantity $\Sigma(y - \bar{y})^2 - \Sigma(y - \hat{y})^2$ corresponds to the part of the variability in Y that is associated with the variable X, i.e., $\Sigma(\hat{y} - \bar{y})^2$.

Interestingly it can be shown that:

$$r^2 = \frac{\Sigma(y - \bar{y})^2 - \Sigma(y - \hat{y})^2}{\Sigma(y - \bar{y})^2}, \quad \text{or equivalently that} \quad r^2 = \frac{\Sigma(\hat{y} - \bar{y})^2}{\Sigma(y - \bar{y})^2}$$

and, thus, $r^2 = \dfrac{\text{Variability in } Y \text{ explained by the regression}}{\text{Total variability in } Y}$. Hence, r^2 as a measure of the effect size, can be interpreted as the proportion of the variability of the dependent variable that is predictable, given our knowledge of the independent variable.

Let us consider this interpretation of r^2 with respect to our study on predicting reaction times given age. In this study we have variability in the following values taken from Table 12.1:

1) the age of subjects, $\Sigma(x - \bar{x})^2 = 3624.278$;
2) the reactions times, $\Sigma(y - \bar{y})^2 = 18321.51$;
3) the reaction times *not* associated with the variability in the independent variable, $\Sigma(y - \hat{y})^2 = 3821.224$;
4) the reaction times associated with the variability in the independent variable, $\Sigma(\hat{y} - \bar{y})^2 = 14550.286$ (i.e., $\Sigma(y - \bar{y})^2 - \Sigma(y - \hat{y})^2$).

In this example $r^2 = \dfrac{\Sigma(\hat{y} - \bar{y})^2}{\Sigma(y - \bar{y})^2} = \dfrac{14550.286}{18321.51} = 0.791$. It then appears that 79.1 per cent of the variability in reaction times is predicted (or equivalently "accounted for") by the variability in the age of the subjects tested. Remember that, as said earlier, unless the independent variable is directly manipulated by the experimenter, the above statement does not mean that age is the cause of increased reaction times. For example, reduced muscle elasticity is associated with ageing. If reaction times were measured when subjects pressed a button on the keyboard, muscle elasticity could be one of the factors responsible for slower reaction times in older adults.

Further on the error of prediction

We saw that the quantity $\Sigma(y - \hat{y})^2$ is the sum of squares error or residual (i.e., the total variability in the dependent variable Y not accounted for by the independent variable X). If this quantity is divided by $n - 2$ (two degrees of freedom are lost because, to obtain the $\hat{y}$s, both the a and b parameters of the regression line are estimated from sampled data) we obtain the estimated error variance:

$$s_{y \cdot x}^2 = \frac{\Sigma(y - \hat{y})^2}{n - 2}.$$

The square root of this estimated error variance, i.e., $s_{y \cdot x} = \sqrt{\dfrac{\Sigma(y - \hat{y})^2}{n - 2}}$, is known as the *standard error of estimate*. This provides a measure of the overall error of prediction. However, the standard error of estimate does not provide a good estimate of the error in predicting the value of Y for an individual value of the independent variable X.

The appropriate measure of the standard error for the prediction of individual values of Y is:

$$s_{y \cdot x} \times \sqrt{\frac{n + 1}{n} + \frac{(x_i - \bar{x})^2}{\Sigma(x - \bar{x})^2}}.$$

This quantity can be used to set up confidence intervals for the predicted value of Y, given a specific value of the independent variable X (i.e., x_i). The general formula for this type of confidence interval is:

$$\hat{y}_i \pm c \times \left(s_{y \cdot x} \times \sqrt{\frac{n + 1}{n} + \frac{(x_i - \bar{x})^2}{\Sigma(x - \bar{x})^2}} \right)$$

where $\hat{y}_i$ is the predicted value of Y calculated by inserting x_i in the estimated regression equation, and c is the two-tailed critical value for the desired level of significance of the t-distribution with $df = n - 2$.

For example, the 95% confidence interval for the predicted reaction time for a person aged 50.2 is:

$$\hat{y}_i \pm c \times \left(s_{y \cdot x} \times \sqrt{\frac{n+1}{n} + \frac{(x_i - \bar{x})^2}{\Sigma(x - \bar{x})^2}} \right)$$

$$= 261.833 \pm 2.07 \times \sqrt{\frac{3821.224}{22}} \times \sqrt{\frac{24+1}{24} + \frac{(50.2 - 58.742)^2}{3624.278}}$$

$$= 261.833 \pm 2.07 \times 13.179 \times 1.03.$$

Thus, the 95% confidence limits for the predicted reaction time of a person aged 50.2 years are 233.722 and 289.944 milliseconds, and the 95% confidence interval is: $CI_{0.95} = 233.722 \le RT \le 289.944$.

Finally notice that the value of X does not necessarily have to be taken from one of the values being sampled. For example, we could find the 95% confidence interval for the predicted value of Y, for a person aged 70. The predicted value of Y estimated using the regression equation is:

$$\hat{y}_i = 161.433 + 2 \times 70 = 301.448$$

and, thus, the 95% confidence interval for the predicted reaction time of a person aged 70 is:

$$301.448 \pm 2.07 \times \sqrt{\frac{3821.224}{22}} \times \sqrt{\frac{24+1}{24} + \frac{(70 - 58.742)^2}{3624.278}}$$

$$= 301.448 \pm 2.07 \times 13.179 \times 1.038.$$

Hence, the limits of the 95% confidence interval for the reaction times are 273.141 and 329.755.

Why the term regression?

Historically, the term regression is due to Frances Galton (1888). Studying the relationships between the height of parents and offspring, he noted that offspring of extreme parents also tended to be extreme, but not as extreme as the parents. Thus the height of offspring tended to *regress* toward the mean height of the population.

Consider, for example, the case where the mean height of men in the population is 175 cm (with $\sigma = 6$), and that the correlation in the population between the standardised heights of fathers and sons is $r = 0.8$ (to be more precise we should have used the symbol ρ and not r since we are dealing with a population parameter). As seen in the section on page 207, *when variables are standardised r = b*, thus when the height of sons is regressed to the height of fathers the regression slope is 0.8 (because the mean of standardised variables is zero, the intercept is always zero). It then follows that if the height of a father is, let us say, one standard deviation *above* the mean (181 cm), the predicted height of his son will be only 0.8 standard deviations above the mean

(179.8 cm), i.e., $\hat{y} = 0.8 \times 1$. Similarly, if the height of a father is one standard deviation *below* the mean (169 cm), the predicted height of his son will be 0.8 standard deviation below the mean (170.2), i.e., $\hat{y} = 0.8 \times (-1)$.

In general if the correlation between two variables is not perfect (i.e., $r \neq \pm 1$, thus the slope of standardised variables is larger than -1 and smaller than 1) then extreme values of the independent variable tend to be associated with less extreme predicted values of the dependent variable. This phenomenon is called *regression to the mean*. Moreover, the lower the correlation, the greater the regression to the mean. Assuming that the correlation in the population between the standardised heights of fathers and sons is $r = 0.5$, thus $b = 0.5$, if the height of a father is, let us say, one standard deviation *above* the mean (181 cm), the predicted height of his son will be 0.5 standard deviations above the mean (178 cm), i.e., $\hat{y} = 0.5 \times 1$. Similarly, if the height of a father is one standard deviation *below* the mean (169 cm), the predicted height of his son will be 0.5 standard deviations below the mean (172), i.e., $\hat{y} = 0.5 \times (-1)$.

Regression to the mean is so pervasive that it often provides the most parsimonious explanation of empirical phenomena. For example, very intellectually gifted parents tend to have, on average, less intellectually gifted children. Since the correlation between the IQ of parents and their children is not perfect, regression to the mean IQ of the population provides a simple explanation of the above phenomenon.

Chapter 13

Introduction to power analysis

Introduction

In the section on pages 89–93 we saw that when statistical tests are performed there is the possibility of committing one of two types of error: Type I or Type II. *Type I errors* occur when H_0 *is true*, but it is rejected. The probability of making this error is given by the α level selected. For example, if $\alpha = 0.05$ and H_0 is true, the probability of committing a Type I error is 0.05. If H_0 is true and we fail to reject it, we make a correct statistical decision. The probability of this correct decision is $1 - \alpha$.

It is important to keep in mind that failing to reject H_0 should not be taken as evidence that the null hypothesis is true. This conclusion may be incorrect: absence of evidence is not evidence for the absence. It could be the case that H_0 *is false*, but the empirical results do not lead to its rejection, thus we commit a *Type II error*. The probability of making a Type II error is equal to β. Unlike α, β is not immediately quantifiable since it depends on various parameters, i.e., α, the number of subjects tested and the effect size. On the other hand, if H_0 is false and we reject it we make a correct statistical decision. The probability of correctly rejecting a false H_0 is called *power* and it is equal to $1 - \beta$. Table 13.1, reproduced from Chapter 5, provides a summary of the types of correct and incorrect decisions, with their probabilities, that can be reached in statistical inference.

Historically, the main emphasis in the process of statistical inference has been on the Type I error. It is however important to keep in mind that there are risks associated with failing to reject a false null hypothesis. Consider the case where H_0 states that a new anti-cancer drug is no better than a previous drug, but it is in fact *false* (i.e., the new drug is better than the old one). If the experimenters fail to reject the null hypothesis they will be blind to the potentially beneficial effect that the new drug can have on cancer patients. Power analysis would provide the tools required to set up empirical studies which, assuming that H_1 is true and H_0 is false, should be able to reject this false H_0 with a relatively large probability (e.g., 0.8). The aim of this chapter is to describe the logic of power analysis and its application. We will describe in detail the logic and the application of power analysis to the *t*-test. We will also briefly outline how to calculate power for the various versions of the correlation coefficient (i.e., r, the point biserial correlation, Spearman's r_s, and ϕ); for the difference between two independent rs; for the test on a single proportion; and for the test on the difference between two independent proportions.

Table 13.1 Summary table of the possible outcomes, and probabilities, for the process of statistical inference

Statistical decision	True state of the world	
	H_0 True	H_0 False
Reject H_0	Type I error $p = \alpha$	Correct decision $p = 1 - \beta$ (i.e., Power)
Do not reject H_0	Correct decision $p = 1 - \alpha$	Type II error $p = \beta$

Effect size and power

If H_0 *is true*, it means that *the size of the effect* exerted by the independent variable on the dependent variable *is zero in the population*. Even when the effect size in the population is zero, random variations in the sampling process may lead to a non-zero effect size in the sample. Since we know that:

Magnitude of a significance test = Size of the effect × Size of the study

it follows that, *given a non-zero effect size in the sample*, if a large enough sample of subjects has been selected, we could obtain a significant result by chance. In this case we would commit a Type I error.

On the other hand if H_0 *is false*, it means that *the size of the effect* exerted by the independent variable on the dependent variable *is non-zero in the population*. Thus, assuming that the effect size in the sampled data is also non-zero, we should be able to reject H_0, provided enough subjects have been tested. However, if the number of subjects is not large enough we may fail to reject a false H_0 because the magnitude of the statistical test will not be large enough to be significant (i.e., we will commit a Type II error). This abstract example demonstrates that, to correctly reject a false H_0, it is not enough to have a non-zero effect size in the sample and in the population. A relatively large number of subjects also have to be tested. In the following sections we will illustrate how to calculate the power of an experiment and how many subjects are required to secure a relatively high probability of rejecting a false null hypothesis, i.e., to have a high level of power. This will mainly be illustrated for the statistical analyses intended to compare means, i.e., the different types of *t*-test.

Factors affecting the power of a statistical test

Power depends on various parameters. These are α, i.e., the probability of committing a Type I error; the number of subjects tested; and the true alternative hypothesis (H_1). This last parameter is in essence the effect size (i.e., the effect size is a measure of the degree to which H_0 is false). In the section on pages 89–93 we briefly illustrated how the above factors, apart from sample size, influenced the probability of committing a Type II error. Then we described a study aimed at deciding whether on not individually tested children could be classified as having some form of reading disorder. We will now show how these factors influence power in the context of the comparison between means.

As seen in Chapters 8 and 9, when comparing means we first need to consider the standard distribution of the means of samples of n subjects drawn from the population assumed by H_0. We know that, according to the Central Limit Theorem (see the section on pages 134–136), for a population of values with mean μ and variance σ^2, the sampling distribution of the mean will be approximately normal with mean equal to μ, and standard error $\sigma_{\bar{x}} = \dfrac{\sigma}{\sqrt{n}}$, where n is the sample size. To see how α, the number of subjects tested, and the true alternative hypothesis (H_1) can affect power we are going to reconsider the study described in the section on pages 134–136. In that study we wanted to test whether a crash course in speed reading improved reading speed. We saw that the 36 people who took the course read an average of 218 words per minute in a standardised test measuring reading speed. To decide if the course was effective we needed to see if we could reject the null hypothesis, stating that our sample was drawn from the population of normal readers. We know that in the population of normal readers the distribution of the scores in the reading test is normal with $\mu_0 = 200$ words per minute and $\sigma = 30$. Thus the null hypothesis is H_0: $\mu = 200$ and H_1: $\mu \neq 200$. If the course is effective, then it would be extremely unlikely to see the mean reading score from our sample among the sampling distribution of the means of samples of 36 subjects who did not take the speed reading course. Performing the appropriate z-test clarifies the issue:

$$z = \frac{\bar{x} - \mu_0}{\dfrac{\sigma}{\sqrt{n}}} = \frac{218 - 200}{\dfrac{30}{\sqrt{36}}} = \frac{18}{5} = 3.6.$$

The z-value was outside the ± 1.96 range. Hence the null hypothesis is rejected and we can conclude that the reading speed of the subjects who attended the reading course was significantly different (faster) than the average performance expected from samples of normal readers.

Now imagine that we know the distribution of the reading test scores in the population of people who took the course in speed reading is not centred at $\mu_0 = 200$, but at $\mu_1 = 215$ with $\sigma = 30$. Consider the case where another sample of 36 people, who took the course, are given the reading test and the mean reading test score turns out to be a relatively poor 205. Since we have drawn this sample from a population with a larger mean than the one for normal readers, we should reject the null hypothesis because this is false. However, performing a z-test we obtain:

$$z = \frac{\bar{x} - \mu_0}{\dfrac{\sigma}{\sqrt{n}}} = \frac{205 - 200}{\dfrac{30}{\sqrt{36}}} = \frac{5}{5} = 1$$

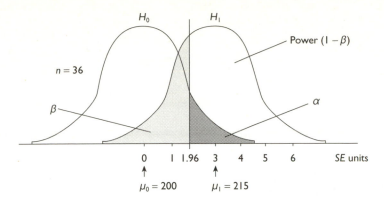

Figure 13.1 Reading test: sampling distributions of the mean of samples of 36 observations under the null hypothesis (H_0: $\mu_0 = 200$) and under the alternative hypothesis (H_1: $\mu_1 = 215$). The points on the x-axis indicate the distance from μ_0 in standard error units. One standard error unit corresponds to 5 points in the reading test, i.e., $\dfrac{\sigma}{\sqrt{n}} = \dfrac{30}{\sqrt{36}} = 5$.

(remembering that any statistical test assumes that H_0 is true; hence, in the above test we subtracted $\mu_0 = 200$ from the sample mean of 205). Thus, although H_0 is false (we sampled the subjects from a population with $\mu_1 = 215$ and not from a population with $\mu_0 = 200$), in this case we failed to reject it (1 lies within the ±1.96 range). Hence we committed a Type II error. Why did we make this error?

Figure 13.1 illustrates why we committed this error. This figure shows the sampling distribution of the mean under H_0 (from samples of 36 observations), and under H_1. Whenever a statistical test is performed on a sample mean, it is assumed that the sample was drawn from the population specified by the null hypothesis. Thus the null hypothesis is rejected when the mean of the sampled data, in terms of standard error units from the mean assumed by H_0, is either equal to or larger than 1.96, or equal to or smaller than −1.96 (for simplicity we showed only the criterion placed at 1.96). These values are those corresponding to a two-tailed α value of 0.05. As shown in Figure 13.1, there is a large overlap of the distribution of the sample means under H_0 and H_1. Several means of the distribution centred at $\mu_1 = 215$, when expressed in standard error units, fall to the left of the significance criterion set at 1.96. For all these means, we cannot reject the null hypothesis, thus we commit a Type II error. The light grey area in Figure 13.1 gives the probability of committing this error (i.e., β). Power corresponds to the area of the H_1 distribution to the right of the significance criterion (i.e., $1 - \beta$).

Power as a function of α

Figure 13.1 illustrates why power is a function of α. If we allow a more lenient level of significance, while keeping everything else constant, α is increased. Therefore β decreases, and power (i.e., $1 - \beta$) increases. Conversely if α is decreased, power decreases too.

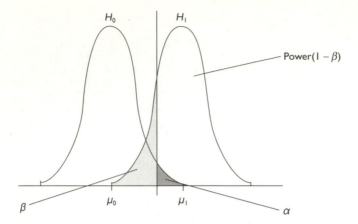

Figure 13.2 Effect on power of decreasing the standard error of the mean.

Power as a function of H_1

If the distance between μ_0 and μ_1 in Figure 13.1 is increased, while keeping everything else constant, the overlap between the two distributions decreases, thus power increases. Conversely if the overlap between these distributions increases, power decreases.

Power as a function of the sample size

From the Central Limit Theorem we know that the standard error of the mean is equal to $\dfrac{\sigma}{\sqrt{n}}$, where σ is the standard deviation of the distribution of the individual observations in the population and n is the sample size. Thus, if n is increased the standard error of the mean is reduced. Hence, keeping everything else constant, the overlap between the two distributions in Figure 13.1 will be reduced, and power will increase. This effect is schematically shown in Figure 13.2 where the sampling distributions of the means under H_0 and H_1 are shown for large sample sizes.

How to manipulate power in an experiment

As seen above power can be increased by either increasing α, increasing the distance between μ_0 and μ_1, or by increasing the number of subjects sampled. Increasing α is not recommended since this would increase the probability of making a Type I error. The use of one-tailed tests could be a legitimate way to increase α, and thus power. However, remember that one-tailed tests are rarely recommended (see discussion in the section on pages 93–95).

Increasing the distance between μ_0 and μ_1 leads to increased power. The distance between μ_0 and μ_1 depends on the strength of the effect of the independent variable. Unfortunately, it is not always possible to increase the distance between μ_0 and μ_1. If a study intends to assess whether 3-year-old children name more pictures than 4-year-old children, it would be difficult to tamper with the distance between μ_0 and μ_1, i.e., the mean number of pictures named by the populations of 3- and 4-year-old children. On the other hand, consider a study intended to assess the effect of study time on the retention of a list of words. In the baseline condition subjects study words at a rate of one word per second (this is the condition associated with μ_0). In two experimental conditions subjects are allowed to study each word for either 10 s or 2 s (these conditions refer to different options for μ_1). It seems reasonable to assume that the distance between μ_0 and μ_1 is larger when comparing the baseline with the 10 s study condition, than with the 2 s condition.

Increasing n increases power. Having large samples of subjects is the simplest way to increase power. In the next sections we will show how to calculate power when comparing means using the t-test. In doing this we will also elaborate on the issue of effect size.

Power calculations for the one-sample t-test

The method used to calculate power for the various types of t-test is based on a simplified approach suggested by Welkowitz, Ewen, and Cohen (1991). This technique provides an approximation to the true power of a test (because it is based on the z-distribution rather than the t-distribution). However, when calculating power we do not need extreme precision, since we mainly want to know if a study has a relatively large power or not (as a rule of thumb, if $(1 - \beta)$ is roughly 0.8 or larger, then power is relatively large). Notice also that the remaining techniques described in this chapter provide an approximation to the true power of a test.

In order to calculate the power of the t-test we need to have an estimate of the size of the effect of the independent variable (i.e., the extent to which the null hypothesis is false). As seen in the previous section, the overlap between the distribution of the sample means under H_0 and H_1 depends on the difference between μ_0 and μ_1, and the standard error of the mean. Therefore an appropriate effect size could be obtained by dividing $\mu_1 - \mu_0$ by the standard error of the mean. The problem with this type of effect size is that it depends on the sample size (remember the standard error is obtained as $\frac{\sigma}{\sqrt{n}}$). Since we usually want to know how many subjects are needed to obtain a particular level of power, or the power associated with a study for a given sample size, it is more useful to adopt a measure of the effect size that does not include the sample size in its formula. For this purpose, an appropriate effect size is Cohen's d:

$$d = \frac{\mu_1 - \mu_0}{\sigma}$$

where $\mu_1 - \mu_0$ is the difference between the population means assumed under H_1 and H_0; and σ is the common standard deviation of the population of individual observations. Thus d is a measure of the standardised difference between population means.

As stated earlier, when *planning* an experiment power analysis is of paramount importance. Before running an experiment, experimenters should have an estimate of the extent to which the null hypothesis is false, i.e., they should have an estimate of the effect size d exerted by the independent variable. Given an expected non-zero effect size d, it is possible to calculate how many subjects are needed to reject a false null hypothesis with a given probability (note that H_0 is retained as false because the effect size is non-zero). Generally, the standard acceptable probability of committing a Type II error is $\beta = 0.20$. This corresponds to a statistical power of 0.80. As a precaution, power analysis should always be used to avoid running sloppy experiments. Remember that, assuming the alternative hypothesis is true, if a planned experiment appears to have a power of 0.25, the null hypothesis will be rejected on only one occasion out of four. Power analysis provides the tool for planning experiments with a much higher probability of rejecting H_0 when H_1 is true. Power analysis is also useful to assess the statistical power of previous studies.

When carrying out research, it is not always clear how to estimate the effect size. In which case, previous studies, relevant to the one being planned, could help. By inspecting the sample means and the estimated population standard deviations in these studies it is possible to obtain an informed estimate of the approximate value of d for the planned study. An alternative way to estimate the extent to which H_0 is false, especially when a priori data are not available, is to use conventional values for d. In these cases, it may be useful to specify conventional values corresponding to small, medium, and large effect sizes. As suggested by Cohen (1988) these are: $d = 0.2$, $d = 0.5$ and $d = 0.8$ for small, medium and large effect sizes, respectively.

Given the above premises, in order to calculate the power for the one-sample t-test we first need to calculate the value of δ (delta), an index that combines effect size and sample size. The power corresponding to δ can then be read from Table 13.2. In the case of the one-sample t-test δ is defined as:

$$\delta = d\sqrt{n}$$

where n is the sample size.

Let us see an application of the above formula. Imagine that a researcher is interested in studying the effect of caffeine on state anxiety. A standardised test is used to measure state anxiety. According to normative data on this anxiety test, the mean state anxiety score, in the population from which the studied sample is going to be drawn, is 50 and the standard deviation is 10. The experimenters intend to give the subjects a dose of caffeine (e.g., 300 mg) and they expect a 5-point difference in state anxiety between the normal population and the population of people taking 300 mg of caffeine. Since they intend to test 16 subjects, what power does this study have to reject H_0 given an $\alpha = 0.05$ (two-tailed)?

The *first step* to calculate power is to calculate d. We know that the experimenter expects the treatment to increase the state anxiety level by about 5 points above the population mean of 50 (i.e., that assumed by H_0) thus $\mu_1 = 55$. Since $\sigma = 10$ then

$$d = \frac{\mu_1 - \mu_0}{\sigma} = \frac{55 - 50}{10} = 0.5.$$

The *second step* involves calculating δ. Since the experimenter intends to test 16 subjects:

$$\delta = d\sqrt{n} = 0.5 \times \sqrt{16} = 2.$$

Table 13.2 Power table: The entries in the table below provide the statistical power (i.e., $1 - \beta$) as a function of δ and the α level (both one- and two-tailed)

δ	$\alpha = 0.10$ two-tailed	$\alpha = 0.05$ two-tailed	$\alpha = 0.01$ two-tailed	δ	$\alpha = 0.10$ two-tailed	$\alpha = 0.05$ two-tailed	$\alpha = 0.01$ two-tailed
0.8	0.20	0.12	0.04	2.7	0.85	0.77	0.55
0.9	0.23	0.15	0.05	2.8	0.88	0.80	0.59
1.0	0.26	0.17	0.06	2.9	0.90	0.83	0.63
1.1	0.29	0.20	0.07	3.0	0.91	0.85	0.67
1.2	0.33	0.22	0.09	3.1	0.93	0.87	0.70
1.3	0.37	0.26	0.10	3.2	0.94	0.89	0.73
1.4	0.40	0.29	0.12	3.3	0.95	0.91	0.77
1.5	0.44	0.32	0.14	3.4	0.96	0.93	0.80
1.6	0.48	0.36	0.17	3.5	0.97	0.94	0.82
1.7	0.52	0.40	0.19	3.6	0.98	0.95	0.85
1.8	0.56	0.44	0.22	3.7	0.98	0.96	0.87
1.9	0.60	0.48	0.25	3.8	0.98	0.97	0.89
2.0	0.64	0.52	0.28	3.9	0.988	0.97	0.91
2.1	0.68	0.56	0.32	4.0	0.991	0.98	0.92
2.2	0.71	0.60	0.35	4.2	0.995	0.987	0.95
2.3	0.74	0.63	0.39	4.4	0.997	0.993	0.97
2.4	0.78	0.67	0.43	4.6	0.998	0.996	0.98
2.5	0.80	0.71	0.47	4.8	0.999	0.998	0.987
2.6	0.83	0.74	0.51	5.0	0.999	0.999	0.992
	$\alpha = 0.05$ one-tailed	$\alpha = 0.025$ one-tailed	$\alpha = 0.005$ one-tailed		$\alpha = 0.05$ one-tailed	$\alpha = 0.025$ one-tailed	$\alpha = 0.005$ one-tailed

The *third step* evaluates the power corresponding to $\delta = 2$ for an $\alpha = 0.05$ (two-tailed) by using Table 13.2. Inspecting this table it appears that power is 0.52. Thus, if H_0 is false and $\mu_1 = 55$, then the project has only a 52 per cent chance of rejecting H_0.

Sample size determination

Let us assume that the experimenter is not happy with this level of power and wants to increase it to 0.80. How many subjects are needed to attain this level of power?

The *first step* calculates the number of subjects required to obtain the value of δ corresponding to a power of 0.8, for an $\alpha = 0.05$ (two-tailed), using Table 13.2. From the table it appears that $\delta = 2.8$.

The *second step* enters the appropriate values of δ and d in the formula for δ, and solves the equation for n. Since $\delta = d\sqrt{n}$ then:

$$n = \frac{\delta^2}{d^2}.$$

In our example we know that $d = 0.5$ and that the required δ for a power of 0.8 is 2.8. Hence, substituting these values in the formula above:

$$n = \frac{\delta^2}{d^2} = \frac{2.8^2}{0.5^2} = 31.36.$$

Thus, if H_0 is false and $\mu_1 = 55$, then with 31 subjects tested the project has 80 per cent chance of rejecting H_0.

Power calculations for the independent-samples t-test

The independent-samples t-test is employed to test if the difference between the means from two independent samples is significant. To calculate the power of this test we need to calculate δ. For the independent-samples t-test, δ is defined as:

$$\delta = d\sqrt{\frac{n}{2}}$$

where n is the *size of each sample* (assuming that the two samples have the same number of subjects), and not the total number of subjects tested.

For the independent-samples t-test the effect size d is:

$$d = \frac{\mu_1 - \mu_2}{\sigma}.$$

The null hypothesis for this test states that $\mu_1 - \mu_2 = 0$. Hence the numerator of d is the non-zero difference between the population means assumed by H_1, while σ is the standard deviation of the population. (Remember that for the independent-samples t-test it is assumed that $\sigma_1 = \sigma_2 = \sigma$.)

Imagine that the previous experimenters also intended to compare the effect of two different doses of caffeine on state anxiety (e.g., 150 mg vs 450 mg; roughly the difference between drinking one cup of espresso vs three cups). They expect a 5-point difference in the state anxiety index between the population of people taking 150 mg of caffeine, and the population of people taking 450 mg of caffeine. Moreover, they intended to test 18 subjects in each group using an α value of 0.01 (two-tailed). Using this information we can then calculate d:

$$d = \frac{\mu_1 - \mu_2}{\sigma} = \frac{5}{10} = 0.5.$$

(Remember that, as seen in the previous section, the standard deviation of the state anxiety test in the population is 10.)

The next step consists of calculating δ:

$$\delta = d\sqrt{\frac{n}{2}} = 0.5 \times \sqrt{\frac{18}{2}} = 1.5. \quad \text{(Remember that } n \text{ is the size of each sample!)}$$

The power for $\delta = 1.5$ is then read from Table 13.2. From the reading, it appears that power = 0.14. (Notice that if the experimenter had been more lenient toward the risk of committing a Type I error, by choosing an α level of 0.05 (two-tailed) instead of 0.01, then power would have been 0.32.)

Since 0.14 is an unsatisfactory level of power, the experimenter wants to find out how many subjects are needed to secure a power of 0.8. To find this out we need the value of δ corresponding to a power of 0.8, for an $\alpha = 0.01$ (two-tailed). Using Table 13.2 it appears that $\delta = 3.4$.

The next step consists of entering the required values of δ and d in the formula for δ and solving the equation to find n. Since $\delta = d\sqrt{\dfrac{n}{2}}$, then

$$n = 2 \times \frac{\delta^2}{d^2}.$$

In our example we know that $d = 0.5$ and that the required δ for a power of 0.8 is 3.4. Hence, substituting these values in the above formula we obtain:

$$n = 2 \times \frac{3.4^2}{0.5^2} = 92.48.$$

Thus, if H_0 is false and $\mu_1 - \mu_2 = 5$, and 92 subjects are tested in *each* group, the project has an 80 per cent chance of rejecting H_0 (for $\alpha = 0.01$, two tails).

Notice that with the independent-samples t-test, to obtain a relatively high level of power (i.e., at least around 0.8) with medium effect sizes (i.e., for values of d around 0.5), it is necessary to test quite a large number of subjects in each condition.

The above formula to calculate power can also be applied when different numbers of subjects are tested in each sample. However, in the case of samples of different sizes, the value of n, to be used in the formula to calculate δ, is given by the harmonic mean of the two sample sizes n_1 and n_2, i.e., $n = \dfrac{2n_1 n_2}{n_1 + n_2}$.

Finally, we stated on pages 219–220 that previous studies relevant to the one being planned could help to estimate the expected effect size d. Unfortunately, sample means and the estimated population standard deviations are not always reported, making it difficult to obtain an informed estimate of the value of d for the planned study. In these cases not everything is lost. Provided that the value of the independent-samples t-test is reported in the study, an approximated value of d can be calculated as follows:

$\dfrac{2t}{\sqrt{n_1 + n_2}}$ (notice that this is g as shown in the section on pages 165–167).

Power calculations for the matched-samples t-test

The matched-samples t-test is used to compare pairs of means from two sets of related scores (these two sets are assumed to have been drawn from normally distributed populations with equal standard deviations, i.e., $\sigma_1 = \sigma_2 = \sigma$). For each subject a difference score is calculated between the two conditions in which they were tested. The matched-samples t-statistic is obtained by dividing the mean of these difference scores by their standard error. The standard error of the difference scores is calculated by dividing the standard deviation of the difference scores by the number of paired observations in the sample.

For the matched-samples t-test the effect size d is defined as:

$$d = \frac{\mu_1 - \mu_2}{\sigma_D}$$

where $\mu_1 - \mu_2$ is the non-zero difference between the population means assumed by H_1, while σ_D is the standard deviation of the population of difference scores (i.e., the difference between pairs of individual observations x_1 and x_2, where the first observation is taken from Population-1 and the second from Population-2). Remember that, as for the independent-samples t-test, it is assumed that $\sigma_1 = \sigma_2 = \sigma$. In the case of difference scores for related populations, it can be shown that:

$$\sigma_D = \sigma\sqrt{2(1 - \rho)}$$

where ρ is the absolute value of the correlation between the individual observations x_1 and x_2 in the two populations (where the observations labelled x_1 and x_2 are drawn from Population-1 and Population-2, respectively). In the case of the matched-samples t-test $\rho > 0$.

For the matched-samples t-test, δ is defined as:

$$\delta = d\sqrt{n}$$

where n is the number of paired observations. As you will notice, the formula to calculate power is identical for the matched-samples t-test and the one-sample t-test. For the matched-samples t-test a difficulty arises in calculating d because we need to know the size of ρ, i.e., the correlation in the two related populations between the individual observations x_1 and x_2. If the dependent variable is the performance in a standardised test, then ρ is the test–retest reliability index. Hence knowing the test–retest reliability value we can compute d, and so the power of the matched-samples t-test. In general, for any standardised psychometric test the correlation measuring the test–retest reliability is provided.

As an example of power analysis for the matched-samples t-test, once again imagine that our experimenters compare the effect of two different doses of caffeine on state anxiety (150 mg vs 450 mg), testing the same subjects in the two conditions. As before they expect $\mu_1 - \mu_2$ to be 5 points on the state anxiety index. We already know that $\sigma = 10$, and let us assume that the test–retest reliability of the state anxiety test is $\rho = 0.9$. The experimenters want to know the power of a matched-samples t-test when testing 18 subjects with an α value of 0.01 (two-tailed).

To calculate d we first need to calculate σ_D:

$$\sigma_D = \sigma\sqrt{2(1 - \rho)} = 10 \times \sqrt{2 \times (1 - 0.9)} = 10 \times \sqrt{0.2} = 4.472 \text{ to 3 d.p.}$$

Then d is found from:

$$d = \frac{\mu_1 - \mu_2}{\sigma_D} = \frac{5}{4.472} = 1.118.$$

Thus, δ is given by:

$$\delta = d\sqrt{n} = 1.118 \times \sqrt{18} = 4.74.$$

Inspecting Table 13.2 it appears that power >0.98, for $\alpha = 0.01$, two tails.

Notice that power for matched-samples t-tests is usually greater than for the independent-samples t-test. The reason is that, everything else being equal, d is greater in the case of the matched-samples t-test than in the independent-samples case. This is because when $\rho > 0$, the denominator of d for the matched-samples case is smaller than the denominator of d for the independent-samples case (i.e., when $\rho = 0$).

To illustrate this, reconsider the example above with a test–retest reliability of zero. If $\rho = 0$ then $\sigma_D = \sigma\sqrt{2(1-0)} = 10 \times \sqrt{2} = 14.14$, thus $d = \dfrac{\mu_1 - \mu_2}{\sigma_D} = \dfrac{5}{14.14} = 0.35$, and $\delta = d\sqrt{n} = 0.35 \times \sqrt{18} = 1.5$, power = 0.14 (for $\alpha = 0.01$, two tails). This example shows that the presence of a non-zero correlation between observations in two populations can heavily affect power. Thus if the use of matched pairs is feasible, i.e., no carry-over effects are suspected, then these studies are usually more powerful than those using independent samples.

As stated above, previous studies relevant to the one being planned could help to estimate the expected effect size d. Unfortunately, sample means, estimated population standard deviations, and the size of ρ are not always reported, making it difficult to obtain an informed estimate of the value of d. Once again, not everything is lost. Provided that the value of the matched-samples t-test is reported in the study, an approximated value of d can be calculated as: $\dfrac{t}{\sqrt{n}}$, where n is the number of paired observations (notice that this is g as shown in the section on pages 165–167).

Finally, the calculation of the sample size required to achieve a desired level of power is carried out as in the one-sample t-test case.

Power calculation for correlation coefficients

The following approach to calculate the power for correlation coefficients applies to Pearson's r, to the point biserial correlation, to Spearman's r_s, and to ϕ. In Chapter 11 we saw that, apart from the case of ϕ, although these correlation coefficients have different names and are applied to different types of data, they are all calculated using the same formula; the one used to calculate Pearson's r.

As seen in the section on pages 116–119, ϕ measures the strength of the relationship between two dichotomous variables. This index is, in fact, a Pearson's r. Consider the mini data-set shown in Table 13.3 where there are two dichotomous variables: X, i.e., sex (Male = 0; Female = 1), and Y, i.e., smoking behaviour (Non-smoker = 0; Smoker = 1). The example in Table 13.3 demonstrates that ϕ and r are equivalent indices.

The effect size d, used to calculate the power of r, is the non-zero value of ρ_1 specified by the alternative hypothesis (H_1). Therefore,

$$d = \rho_1$$

and δ is defined as: $\delta = d\sqrt{n-1}$.

Table 13.3 Example showing that the calculations for the ϕ coefficient are identical to those used to compute Pearson's r. For completeness, the data are also displayed in a 2 × 2 contingency table with the Pearson's χ^2 value provided

X: Sex (Male = 0; Female = 1)	Y: Smoking behaviour (Non-smoker = 0; Smoker = 1)	$(x - \bar{x})(y - \bar{y})$
0	0	0.25
0	0	0.25
0	0	0.25
0	0	0.25
0	1	−0.25
0	1	−0.25
1	0	−0.25
1	0	−0.25
1	1	0.25
1	1	0.25
1	1	0.25
1	1	0.25
$\bar{x} = 0.5$	$\bar{y} = 0.5$	$\Sigma(x - \bar{x})(y - \bar{y}) = 1$
$s_x = 0.522$	$s_y = 0.522$	$n = 12$

$$COV_{xy} = \frac{\Sigma(x - \bar{x})(y - \bar{y})}{n - 1} = \frac{1}{11} = 0.091$$

$$\phi = r = \frac{COV_{xy}}{s_x \times s_y} = \frac{0.091}{0.522 \times 0.522} = 0.334$$

	Non-smoker	Smoker	
Male	4	2	$\chi^2 = 1.336;\ \phi = \sqrt{\dfrac{\chi^2}{n}}$
Female	2	4	$\phi = \sqrt{\dfrac{1.336}{12}} = 0.334$

Imagine experimenters predict that, in the population, the Pearson's correlation coefficient between the weekly time spent doing aerobic exercise and a measure of psychological well-being is $\rho_1 = 0.2$. If they study the correlation between the above variables in a sample size of 65 subjects, then

$$\delta = d\sqrt{n - 1} = 0.2 \times \sqrt{65 - 1} = 1.6.$$

Inspecting Table 13.2 it appears that, for $\alpha = 0.05$, two tails; power = 0.36.

The formula to calculate the sample size required for a given level of power is:

$$n = \frac{\delta^2}{d^2} + 1.$$

To obtain a power of 0.8 in the above case $\delta = 2.8$. Therefore, substituting the values of d and δ in the above formula we obtain:

$$n = \frac{2.8^2}{0.2^2} + 1 = \frac{7.84}{0.04} + 1 = 197.$$

Hence if $\rho_1 = 0.2$, the experimenter needs to test 197 subjects to have a 0.8 chance of finding that the sample correlation coefficient r is significantly different from zero.

In the case of the correlation coefficient, conventional values corresponding to small, medium and large effect sizes are: $d = 0.1$, $d = 0.3$ and $d = 0.5$, respectively. Remember that the above procedure to calculate power applies to Pearson's r, to the point biserial correlation, to Spearman's r_s, and to ϕ, the index of the association between two dichotomous variables.

Power calculation for the difference between two independent Pearson correlation coefficients r

The effect size to be used for the power calculation for the difference between two independent Pearson r-values is called q, and it corresponds to the difference between the Fisher's z_f transformed scores (i.e., r_f) associated to the population values, ρ_1 and ρ_2, assumed by H_1. Therefore:

$$q = \rho_{f1} - \rho_{f2}.$$

We saw in Chapter 11, that Table 11.4 provides the Fisher's z_f transformed scores associated with specific values of Pearson's correlation coefficient.

Imagine a researcher expects the correlation between perceived and actual body size to be $\rho_1 = 0.67$ in the male population, and $\rho_2 = 0.39$ among females. If the experimenters intend to compare the correlations between perceived and actual body size in two samples of 30 males and 30 females, what is the probability that they can reject H_0: $\rho_1 = \rho_2$, (for $\alpha = 0.05$, two tails) assuming that H_1: $\rho_1 - \rho_2 = 0.67 - 0.39 = 0.28$ is true?

The first step consists of reading the Fisher's z_f transformed scores for $\rho_1 = 0.67$ and $\rho_2 = 0.39$. Using Table 11.4 it appears that $\rho_{f1} = 0.811$ and $\rho_{f2} = 0.412$. Thus

$$q = \rho_{f1} - \rho_{f2} = 0.811 - 0.412 = 0.399.$$

Since the experimenter intends to test 30 subjects in each group, it appears, using Table 13.4, that power $= 0.31$. For a power of 0.8, the experimenter would need to test about 100 subjects in each group.

In the case of the difference between correlation coefficients, conventional values corresponding to small, medium and large effect sizes are: $q = 0.1$, $q = 0.3$, and $q = 0.5$, respectively. If different number of subjects are tested in each sample, then the harmonic mean of the two sample sizes n_1 and n_2, i.e., $n = \dfrac{2n_1n_2}{n_1 + n_2}$, needs to be entered as the value for n. Finally, for the values not present in Table 13.4, approximate levels of power can be obtained by interpolation.

Table 13.4 Table to calculate the power for the difference between two independent correlation coefficients *r* (for $\alpha = 0.05$, two tails). The value of power can be read out for various sample sizes, and various magnitudes of the effect size $q = \rho_{f1} - \rho_{f2}$, ranging from 0.1 to 1.4. *n* is the size for *each* of the two samples, assumed to have identical size: hence, the total number of subjects that need to be sampled is 2*n*

n in each sample	Effect size													
	0.1	0.2	0.3	0.4	0.5	0.6	0.7	0.8	0.9	1.0	1.1	1.2	1.3	1.4
20	0.05	0.08	0.14	0.21	0.31	0.42	0.53	0.65	0.75	0.83	0.89	0.94	0.97	0.98
25	0.05	0.10	0.17	0.26	0.38	0.51	0.64	0.76	0.85	0.91	0.95	0.98	–	–
30	0.06	0.11	0.20	0.31	0.45	0.60	0.73	0.84	0.91	0.96	0.98	–	–	–
35	0.06	0.12	0.22	0.36	0.52	0.67	0.80	0.89	0.95	0.98	–	–	–	–
40	0.06	0.14	0.25	0.41	0.58	0.73	0.85	0.93	0.97	–	–	–	–	–
45	0.07	0.15	0.28	0.45	0.63	0.79	0.89	0.96	0.98	–	–	–	–	–
50	0.07	0.16	0.31	0.49	0.68	0.83	0.92	0.97	–	–	–	–	–	–
60	0.08	0.19	0.36	0.57	0.76	0.89	0.96	–	–	–	–	–	–	–
70	0.08	0.21	0.41	0.64	0.82	0.93	0.98	–	–	–	–	–	–	–
80	0.09	0.24	0.46	0.70	0.87	0.96	–	–	–	–	–	–	–	–
90	0.10	0.26	0.51	0.75	0.91	0.98	–	–	–	–	–	–	–	–
100	0.10	0.29	0.55	0.80	0.94	–	–	–	–	–	–	–	–	–
120	0.12	0.33	0.63	0.86	0.97	–	–	–	–	–	–	–	–	–
140	0.13	0.38	0.70	0.91	–	–	–	–	–	–	–	–	–	–
160	0.14	0.43	0.76	0.94	–	–	–	–	–	–	–	–	–	–
200	0.17	0.51	0.85	0.98	–	–	–	–	–	–	–	–	–	–
300	0.23	0.68	0.96	–	–	–	–	–	–	–	–	–	–	–
400	0.29	0.80	–	–	–	–	–	–	–	–	–	–	–	–
500	0.35	0.88	–	–	–	–	–	–	–	–	–	–	–	–
1000	0.61	–	–	–	–	–	–	–	–	–	–	–	–	–

Notes: Effects size, $q = \rho_{f1} - \rho_{f2}$.
$\alpha = 0.05$, two tails.
– Power ≥ 0.99 to 2 d.p.

Power calculation for a single proportion

Imagine the case where a new improved psychotherapeutic treatment to cure phobics' fear of flying has been devised, and an experimenter expects 80 per cent of the treated patients in the population to be free from their problem after this new treatment. This contrasts with a 60 per cent recovery rate with the standard most successful treatment (cf. the binomial test in Chapter 4). Thus, the researchers expect the new treatment to be better than the old one. Moreover, they expect that for people treated with the new approach, H_0: $p_0 = 0.6$ is false, while H_1: $p_1 = 0.8$ is true. Thus a 20 per cent difference is expected between the population proportions under H_0 (the proportion of patients recovered following the standard treatment) and H_1 (the proportion of patients recovered following the new treatment). Given that the experimenter intends to assess if there is a significant difference, with $\alpha = 0.05$, two tails, between the proportion of recovered patients in a sample of 49 patients treated with the new approach and H_0: $p_0 = 0.6$, what is the statistical power of this test?

The first thing to do to solve this problem is to calculate the appropriate effect size d for the test of a single proportion. In this case d is:

$$d = \frac{p_1 - p_0}{\sqrt{p_0 \times (1 - p_0)}}$$

where p_1 and p_0 are the population proportion of successes assumed by H_1 and H_0, respectively, and δ is defined as: $\delta = d\sqrt{n}$.
Therefore, for the above example,

$$d = \frac{p_1 - p_0}{\sqrt{p_0 \times (1 - p_0)}} = \frac{0.8 - 0.6}{\sqrt{0.8 \times 0.6}} = 0.289 \quad \text{and} \quad \delta = d\sqrt{n} = 0.289\sqrt{49} = 2.021.$$

Inspecting Table 13.2 it appears that, for $\alpha = 0.05$, two tails, power $= 0.6$. Thus, if the rate of recovery in the population due to the new treatment is 80 per cent, then the above study has a 60 per cent chance of rejecting H_0.

The formula to calculate the sample size required for a given level of power is: $n = \dfrac{\delta^2}{d^2}$. To obtain a power of 0.8 in the above case, then $\delta = 2.8$. Therefore, substituting the values of d and δ in the above formula:

$$n = \frac{2.8^2}{0.289^2} = 93.87.$$

Hence, if $p_1 = 0.8$, the experimenter needs to test about 94 subjects to have a 0.8 chance of rejecting H_0: $p_0 = 0.6$.

Conventional values corresponding to small, medium and large effect sizes are: $d = 0.1$, $d = 0.3$ and $d = 0.5$, respectively.

Power calculation for the difference between two independent proportions

The effect size for the power calculation for the difference between two independent proportions is denoted as d and is calculated as:

$$d = \sqrt{\frac{2 \times \left[p_1 - \left(\dfrac{p_1 + p_2}{2} \right) \right]^2}{\dfrac{p_1 + p_2}{2} \times \left(1 - \dfrac{p_1 + p_2}{2} \right)}} = \frac{\sqrt{2} \times \left[p_1 - \left(\dfrac{p_1 + p_2}{2} \right) \right]}{\sqrt{\dfrac{p_1 + p_2}{2} \times \left(1 - \dfrac{p_1 + p_2}{2} \right)}}$$

where p_1 and p_2 correspond to the population proportions assumed by H_1 (remember that H_0 assumes that is $p_1 - p_2 = 0$, while for H_1 $p_1 - p_2 \neq 0$). For convenience the proportion labelled p_1 is the larger of the two proportions. Recall that δ is defined as:

$$\delta = d\sqrt{n}$$

where n is the number of subjects in *each* of the two samples (considered to be of equal size).

Imagine that in the population of British females (aged between 20 and 50) the expected proportion of smokers is $p_1 = 0.43$, while among British males this is $p_2 = 0.32$. If an experimenter intends to compare the proportions of smokers in two samples of 100 females and 100 males, what is the probability that he or she can reject H_0: $p_1 = p_2$, (for $\alpha = 0.01$, two tails) assuming that H_1: $p_1 - p_2 = 0.43 - 0.32 = 0.11$ is true?

The first step consists of calculating the effect size d according to H_1:

$$d = \frac{\sqrt{2} \times \left[p_1 - \left(\frac{p_1 + p_2}{2} \right) \right]}{\sqrt{\frac{p_1 + p_2}{2} \times \left(1 - \frac{p_1 + p_2}{2} \right)}} = \frac{\sqrt{2} \times \left[0.43 - \left(\frac{0.43 + 0.32}{2} \right) \right]}{\sqrt{\frac{0.43 + 0.32}{2} \times \left(1 - \frac{0.43 + 0.32}{2} \right)}}$$

$$= \frac{\sqrt{2} \times (0.43 - 0.375)}{\sqrt{0.375 \times (1 - 0.375)}} = \frac{\sqrt{2} \times 0.055}{\sqrt{0.375 \times 0.625}} = 0.161 \text{ to 3 d.p.}$$

Since the experimenter intends to test 100 subjects in each group, then δ is:

$$\delta = d\sqrt{n} = 0.161 \times \sqrt{100} = 1.61.$$

Then, using Table 13.2, it appears that for $\alpha = 0.01$, two tails, power is about 0.17.

The formula to calculate the size of *each* of the two samples required for a given level of power is:

$$n = \frac{\delta^2}{d^2}.$$

For a power of 0.8, for $\alpha = 0.01$, two tails, $\delta = 3.4$. Thus entering the appropriate values in the above equation:

$$n = \frac{\delta^2}{d^2} = \frac{3.4^2}{0.161^2} = 447.8.$$

Hence, to attain a power of 0.8 in the above study, the experimenter would need to test about 448 subjects in each group.

If different numbers of subjects are tested in each sample, then the harmonic mean of the two sample sizes n_1 and n_2, i.e., $n = \dfrac{2n_1 n_2}{n_1 + n_2}$ for n.

Appendix

Z table

χ^2 table

t table

Main formulae used in the text

Z table The table below gives the cumulative probability values for normal Z standard deviation scores. The cumulative probability attached to each Z score is equivalent to the area underneath the normal curve from minus infinity to each Z score. The critical values of Z for a significant level of $p = 0.05$ (two-tailed) are -1.96 and $+1.96$. The critical values of Z for a significant level of $p = 0.01$ (two-tailed) are -2.576 and $+2.576$

z	Cumulative p-value	z	Cumulative p-value	z	Cumulative p-value	z	Cumulative p-value
-4.0	0.00003	-1.82	0.03438	0.1	0.53983	1.84	0.96712
-3.9	0.00005	-1.81	0.03515	0.2	0.57926	1.85	0.96784
-3.8	0.00007	-1.80	0.03593	0.3	0.61791	1.86	0.96856
-3.7	0.00011	-1.79	0.03673	0.4	0.65542	1.87	0.96926
-3.6	0.00016	-1.78	0.03754	0.5	0.69146	1.88	0.96995
-3.5	0.00023	-1.77	0.03836	0.6	0.72575	1.89	0.97062
-3.4	0.00034	-1.76	0.03920	0.7	0.75804	1.90	0.97128
-3.3	0.00048	-1.75	0.04006	0.8	0.78814	1.91	0.97193
-3.2	0.00069	-1.74	0.04093	0.9	0.81594	1.92	0.97257
-3.1	0.00097	-1.73	0.04182	1.0	0.84134	1.93	0.97320
-3.0	0.00135	-1.72	0.04272	1.1	0.86433	1.94	0.97381
-2.95	0.00159	-1.71	0.04363	1.2	0.88493	1.95	0.97441
-2.90	0.00187	-1.70	0.04457	1.3	0.90320	1.96	0.97500
-2.85	0.00219	-1.69	0.04551	1.4	0.91924	1.97	0.97558
-2.80	0.00256	-1.68	0.04648	1.5	0.93319	1.98	0.97615
-2.75	0.00298	-1.67	0.04746	1.51	0.93448	1.99	0.97670
-2.70	0.00347	-1.66	0.04846	1.52	0.93574	2.00	0.97725
-2.65	0.00402	-1.65	0.04947	1.53	0.93699	2.05	0.97982
-2.60	0.00466	-1.64	0.05050	1.54	0.93822	2.10	0.98214
-2.55	0.00539	-1.63	0.05155	1.55	0.93943	2.15	0.98422
-2.50	0.00621	-1.62	0.05262	1.56	0.94062	2.20	0.98610
-2.45	0.00714	-1.61	0.05370	1.57	0.94179	2.25	0.98778
-2.40	0.00820	-1.60	0.05480	1.58	0.94295	2.30	0.98928
-2.35	0.00939	-1.59	0.05592	1.59	0.94408	2.35	0.99061
-2.30	0.01072	-1.58	0.05705	1.60	0.94520	2.40	0.99180
-2.25	0.01222	-1.57	0.05821	1.61	0.94630	2.45	0.99286
-2.20	0.01390	-1.56	0.05938	1.62	0.94738	2.50	0.99379
-2.15	0.01578	-1.55	0.06057	1.63	0.94845	2.55	0.99461
-2.10	0.01786	-1.54	0.06178	1.64	0.94950	2.60	0.99534
-2.05	0.02018	-1.53	0.06301	1.65	0.95053	2.65	0.99598
-2.00	0.02275	-1.52	0.06426	1.66	0.95154	2.70	0.99653
-1.99	0.02330	-1.51	0.06552	1.67	0.95254	2.75	0.99702
-1.98	0.02385	-1.5	0.06681	1.68	0.95352	2.80	0.99744
-1.97	0.02442	-1.4	0.08076	1.69	0.95449	2.85	0.99781
-1.96	0.02500	-1.3	0.09680	1.70	0.95543	2.90	0.99813
-1.95	0.02559	-1.2	0.11507	1.71	0.95637	2.95	0.99841
-1.94	0.02619	-1.1	0.13567	1.72	0.95728	3.0	0.99865
-1.93	0.02680	-1.0	0.15866	1.73	0.95818	3.1	0.99903
-1.92	0.02743	-0.9	0.18406	1.74	0.95907	3.2	0.99931
-1.91	0.02807	-0.8	0.21186	1.75	0.95994	3.3	0.99952
-1.90	0.02872	-0.7	0.24196	1.76	0.96080	3.4	0.99966
-1.89	0.02938	-0.6	0.27425	1.77	0.96164	3.5	0.99977
-1.88	0.03005	-0.5	0.30854	1.78	0.96246	3.6	0.99984
-1.87	0.03074	-0.4	0.34458	1.79	0.96327	3.7	0.99989
-1.86	0.03144	-0.3	0.38209	1.80	0.96407	3.8	0.99993
-1.85	0.03216	-0.2	0.42074	1.81	0.96485	3.9	0.99995
-1.84	0.03288	-0.1	0.46017	1.82	0.96562	4.0	0.99997
-1.83	0.03362	0.0	0.50000	1.83	0.96638		

Note: The values entered in this table were computed by the author.

χ^2 **table**   The table below gives the critical χ^2 scores for significance levels of $p =$ 0.05 and $p = 0.01$. The null hypothesis is rejected if the obtained χ^2 score is larger than the critical one for the appropriate number of degrees of freedom

df	p = 0.05	p = 0.01	df	p = 0.05	p = 0.01
1	3.84	6.63	21	32.67	38.93
2	5.99	9.21	22	33.92	40.29
3	7.81	11.34	23	35.17	41.64
4	9.49	13.28	24	36.42	42.98
5	11.07	15.09	25	37.65	44.31
6	12.59	16.81	26	38.89	45.64
7	14.07	18.48	27	40.11	46.96
8	15.51	20.09	28	41.34	48.28
9	16.92	21.67	29	42.56	49.59
10	18.31	23.21	30	43.77	50.89
11	19.68	24.73	31	44.99	52.19
12	21.03	26.22	32	46.19	53.49
13	22.36	27.69	33	47.40	54.78
14	23.68	29.14	34	48.60	56.06
15	25.00	30.58	35	49.80	57.34
16	26.30	32.00	36	51.00	58.62
17	27.59	33.41	37	52.19	59.89
18	28.87	34.81	38	53.38	61.16
19	30.14	36.19	39	54.57	62.43
20	31.41	37.57	40	55.76	63.69

Note: The values entered in this table were computed by the author.

t table   The table below gives the critical values of *t* for various significance levels (one tail or two tails). The null hypothesis is rejected if the obtained *t* score is larger than the critical one for the appropriate number of degrees of freedom. Degrees of freedom are displayed in the first column on the left hand side

df	p = 0.05 (one tail) p = 0.10 (two tails)	p = 0.025 (one tail) p = 0.05 (two tails)	p = 0.0125 (one tail) p = 0.025 (two tails)	p = 0.005 (one tail) p = 0.01 (two tails)
1	6.31	12.71	25.45	63.66
2	2.92	4.30	6.21	9.92
3	2.35	3.18	4.18	5.84
4	2.13	2.78	3.50	4.60
5	2.02	2.57	3.16	4.03
6	1.94	2.45	2.97	3.71
7	1.89	2.36	2.84	3.50
8	1.86	2.31	2.75	3.36
9	1.83	2.26	2.69	3.25
10	1.81	2.23	2.63	3.17
11	1.80	2.20	2.59	3.11
12	1.78	2.18	2.56	3.05
13	1.77	2.16	2.53	3.01
14	1.76	2.14	2.51	2.98
15	1.75	2.13	2.49	2.95
16	1.75	2.12	2.47	2.92
17	1.74	2.11	2.46	2.90
18	1.73	2.10	2.45	2.88
19	1.73	2.09	2.43	2.86
20	1.72	2.09	2.42	2.85
21	1.72	2.08	2.41	2.83
22	1.72	2.07	2.41	2.82
23	1.71	2.07	2.40	2.81
24	1.71	2.06	2.39	2.80
25	1.71	2.06	2.38	2.79
26	1.71	2.06	2.38	2.78
27	1.70	2.05	2.37	2.77
28	1.70	2.05	2.37	2.76
29	1.70	2.05	2.36	2.76
30	1.70	2.04	2.36	2.75
31	1.70	2.04	2.36	2.74
33	1.69	2.03	2.35	2.73
35	1.69	2.03	2.34	2.72
37	1.69	2.03	2.34	2.72
40	1.68	2.02	2.33	2.70
45	1.68	2.01	2.32	2.69
50	1.68	2.01	2.31	2.68
55	1.67	2.00	2.30	2.67
60	1.67	2.00	2.30	2.66
65	1.67	2.00	2.29	2.65
70	1.67	1.99	2.29	2.65
75	1.67	1.99	2.29	2.64
80	1.66	1.99	2.28	2.64
85	1.66	1.99	2.28	2.63
90	1.66	1.99	2.28	2.63
95	1.66	1.99	2.28	2.63
100	1.66	1.98	2.28	2.63
120	1.66	1.98	2.27	2.62
140	1.66	1.98	2.27	2.61
160	1.65	1.97	2.26	2.61
180	1.65	1.97	2.26	2.60
200	1.65	1.97	2.26	2.60
300	1.65	1.97	2.25	2.59
1000	1.65	1.96	2.24	2.58

Note: The values entered in this table were computed by the author.

Main formulae used in the text

Statistics obtained using sample data

Sample mean: $\bar{x} = \dfrac{\Sigma x}{n}$ Sum of squares: $\Sigma(x - \bar{x})^2$

Population variance estimated using sampled observations: $s^2 = \dfrac{\Sigma(x - \bar{x})^2}{n - 1}$

Population standard deviation estimated using sampled observations: $s = \sqrt{\dfrac{\Sigma(x - \bar{x})^2}{n - 1}}$

Standard error of the mean estimated using s: $SE_{\bar{x}} = \dfrac{s}{\sqrt{n}}$

Standardised scores: $z = \dfrac{x - \bar{x}}{s}$

Chi-square analysis

Pearson's chi-square test: $\chi^2 = \Sigma \dfrac{(O - E)^2}{E}$

$\phi = \sqrt{\dfrac{\chi^2}{N}}$ $\phi_c = \sqrt{\dfrac{\chi^2}{N(k - 1)}}$ (Cramer's phi)

Tests on proportions

Test on a single proportion: $z = \dfrac{p_{obs} - p}{\sqrt{\dfrac{pq}{n}}}$ (where p is the population proportion)

Confidence interval on a single population proportion: $P_{obs} \pm c \times s_p$

where $s_p = \sqrt{\dfrac{p_{obs} \times (1 - p_{obs})}{n}}$ and $c = z_{\frac{\alpha}{2}}$

Test on the difference between two independent proportions:

$z = \dfrac{p_{obs1} - p_{obs2}}{s_{p_1 - p_2}} = \dfrac{p_{obs1} - p_{obs2}}{\sqrt{\dfrac{\hat{p}\hat{q}}{n_1} + \dfrac{\hat{p}\hat{q}}{n_2}}}$

where $\hat{p} = \dfrac{n_1 \times p_{obs1} + n_2 \times p_{obs2}}{n_1 + n_2}$; $\hat{q} = 1 - \hat{p}$; and n_1 and n_2 are the sample sizes

Tests on means when the population standard deviation is estimated from sampled data

Single-sample t-test: $t = \dfrac{\bar{x} - \mu}{SE_{\bar{x}}} = \dfrac{\bar{x} - \mu}{\dfrac{s}{\sqrt{n}}}$

Confidence interval on a single population mean: $\bar{x} \pm c \times SE_{\bar{x}}$ (where $c = t_{\frac{\alpha}{2}}$)

Matched-samples t-test: $t = \dfrac{\bar{D} - 0}{SE_{\bar{D}}} = \dfrac{\bar{D} - 0}{\dfrac{s_D}{\sqrt{n}}}$

where $\bar{D}$ and s_D are the mean and the standard deviation of the difference scores, respectively, n is the number of difference scores, and $SE_{\bar{D}}$ is the standard error of the mean of the difference scores

Confidence interval for μ_D: $\bar{D} \pm c \times SE_{\bar{D}}$ (where $c = t_{\frac{\alpha}{2}}$)

Independent-samples t-test:

$$t = \dfrac{(\bar{x}_1 - \bar{x}_2)}{SE_{\bar{x}_1 - \bar{x}_2}} = \dfrac{(\bar{x}_1 - \bar{x}_2)}{\sqrt{s_P^2 \times \left(\dfrac{1}{n_1} + \dfrac{1}{n^2}\right)}}$$

where $s_P^2 = \dfrac{s_1^2 \times (n_1 - 1) + s_2^2 \times (n_2 - 1)}{n_1 + n_2 - 2}$

Confidence intervals for the difference between two (independent) population means: $(\bar{x}_1 - \bar{x}_2) \pm c \times SE_{(\bar{x}_1 - \bar{x}_2)}$ (where $c = t_{\frac{\alpha}{2}}$)

Nonparametric statistical tests

Wilcoxon matched-pairs signed-ranks test (nonparametric analogue of the matched-samples t-test): $z = \dfrac{R_{large} - \dfrac{n(n + 1)}{4}}{\sqrt{\dfrac{n(n + 1)(2n + 1)}{24}}}$ (where R_{large} is the greater sum of ranks between R_+ and R_-)

Wilcoxon rank-sum test (nonparametric analogue of the independent-samples t-test):

$z = \dfrac{R_{large} - \dfrac{n_l \times (n_l + n_s + 1)}{2}}{\sqrt{\dfrac{n_l \times n_s \times (n_l + n_s + 1)}{12}}}$ (where R_{large} is the greatest of the two sums of ranks)

Correlation and regression

$$COV_{xy} = \frac{\Sigma(x - \bar{x})(y - \bar{y})}{n - 1}$$

$$r_{xy} = \frac{COV_{xy}}{s_x \times s_y} \quad \text{or equivalently } r_{xy} = \frac{\Sigma(x - \bar{x})(y - \bar{y})}{\sqrt{\Sigma(x - \bar{x})^2 \times \Sigma(y - \bar{y})^2}}$$

partial correlation: $r_{xz \cdot y} = \dfrac{r_{xz} - (r_{xy} \times r_{yz})}{\sqrt{(1 - r_{xy}^2) \times (1 - r_{yz}^2)}}$

$$b = \frac{COV_{xy}}{s_x^2} \quad \text{(or equivalently } b = \frac{\Sigma(x - \bar{x})(y - \bar{y})}{\Sigma(x - \bar{x})^2})$$

$$a = \bar{y} - b\bar{x}$$

Statistical power

One-sample t-test: $\delta = d\sqrt{n}$ (where $d = \dfrac{\mu_1 - \mu_0}{\sigma}$)

Independent-samples t-test: $\delta = d\sqrt{\dfrac{n}{2}}$ (where $d = \dfrac{\mu_1 - \mu_2}{\sigma}$ and n is the size of each sample)

Matched-samples t-test: $\delta = d\sqrt{n}$ (where $d = \dfrac{\mu_1 - \mu_2}{\sigma_D}$; $\sigma\sqrt{2(1 - \rho)}$)

Power for Pearson's r, for the point biserial correlation, for Spearman's r_s, and for ϕ: $\delta = d\sqrt{n - 1}$ (where $d = \rho_1$, i.e., the non-zero value of ρ_1 specified by the alternative hypothesis)

References

Abelson, R. P. (1995). *Statistics as Principled Argument*. Hillsdale: Erlbaum.

Allison, P. D. (1999). *Multiple Regression: A Primer*. Thousand Oaks: Pine Forge Press.

Cochran, W. G. (1952). The χ^2 test of goodness of fit. *Annals of Mathematical Statistics, 23*, 315–345.

Cohen, J. (1988). *Statistical Power Analysis for the Behavioral Sciences* (2nd ed.). Hillsdale: Erlbaum.

Galton, F. (1888). Co-relations and their measurement, chiefly from anthropometric data. *Proceedings of the Royal Society, 45*, 135–145.

Howell, D. C. (1997). *Statistical Methods for Psychology* (4th ed.). Belmont, CA: Duxbury Press.

Kirk, R. E. (1991). *Experimental Design: Procedures for the Behavioral Science* (3rd ed.). Pacific Grove, CA: Brooks/Cole.

Lord, F. M. (1953). On the statistical treatment of football numbers. *American Psychologist, 8*, 750–751.

Meng, X. L., Rosenthal, R., & Rubin, D. B. (1992). Comparing correlated correlation-coefficients. *Psychological Bulletin, 111*, 172–175.

Miller, S. (1974). *Experimental Design and Statistics*. London: Methuen.

Poulton, E. C. (1975). Range effects in experiments on people. *American Journal of Psychology, 88*, 3–32.

Roberts, M. J. & Russo, R. (1999). *A Student's Guide to Analysis of Variance*. London: Routledge.

Siegel, S. & Castellan N. J. Jr (1988). *Nonparametric Statistics for the Behavioral Sciences* (2nd ed.). New York: McGraw-Hill.

Spielberger, C. D., Gorusch, R., Lushene, R., Vagg, P. R., & Jacobs, G. A. (1983). *Manual for the State-Trait Anxiety Inventory*. Palo Alto, CA: Consulting Psychology Press.

Sutherland, N. S. (1994). *Irrationality: The Enemy Within*. London: Penguin.

Upton, G. J. G. & Cook, I. T. (1997). *Understanding Statistics*. Oxford: Oxford University Press.

Welkowitz, J., Ewen, R. B., & Cohen, J. (1991). *Introductory Statistics for the Behavioral Sciences* (4th ed.). Fort Worth: HBJ.

Yates, F. (1934). Contingency tables involving small numbers and the χ^2 test. *Journal of the Royal Statistical Society (Series B), 1*, 217–235.

Index

addition rule of probability 47–8
anxiety inventory 8, 11

Bayes's theorem 54–6
Bernoulli distribution 59
Bernoulli trials process 60, 63, 68, 70, 71, 74
bimodal distributions 21
binomial distribution 57–8, 66–9; Bernoulli trials process 60, 63, 68, 70, 71, 74; combinations 66; discrete random variables 57–8; hypothesis testing 57, 70–75, 76–7; mean 70; orderings (permutations) 63–6; sign test 75–6; variance 70; *see also* normal distribution; probability distributions
boxplot 27–8

ceiling effects 162–4
central limit theorem 134–6
central tendency: estimators of 36–8; measures of 20, 21–6; *see also* mean; median; mode
chi-square/squared (χ^2) distribution 100–101; *see also* Pearson's test
chi-square/squared (χ^2) table 233
"classical music study" example 1–6, 10–12, 42
combinations 66
conceptual equations 165–7
conditional probability 50–53; and independence 53–4
confidence intervals: difference between two population means 157–8; for population proportion 124–7; for two independent populations proportions 129–30; two-sided, for a population mean 141–5, 149–50
contingency tables 53; measuring association strength 116–19; nonoccurrences in 120–22; R × C contingency tables 114–15; 2 × 2 contingency tables 110–13

continuous random variables: distribution of 78–81; representation by histograms 80–81; treatment as discrete 79; *see also* chi-square distribution; normal distribution
continuous variables 7
correlation 176–201; formula 236–7; Kendall's coefficient of concordance W 200–202; linear relationships between two variables 176–82; Spearman rank 198–200; *see also* Pearson product-moment correlation coefficient r
correlational studies 11–12
counterbalancing 150–51
covariance between two variables 181–2
cumulative frequency distribution 15–18

data: organising 14; qualitative 7; quantitative 7
decision tree for statistical test selection xiii
dependent variables 10
descriptive statistics 9–10, 14–41
discrete random variables 57–8
discrete variables 7, 57–8
discrete uniform distributions 58
dispersion, measures of 27–32
distribution-free tests *see* nonparametric tests

empirical studies 10, 11
error: inferential statistics 90; regression 211–12; type I/II 89–93, 214
estimators of central tendency 36–8; efficient 36; sufficient 36; unbiased 37
events, simple 43
experiments, defining 10–13
external validity 3

floor effects 162–4
freedom, degrees of 38
frequency distribution tables 14, 15, 18; cumulative 15–18; grouped 15–17

frequency histograms 14, 16
frequency polygons 17, 18

Galton, Frances 212
goodness of fit test 103–8
grouped data 15–17

homogeneity of variances, assumption of
  159; violation of 159–62
hypothesis testing: binomial distribution 57,
  70–77; inferential statistics in 87, 93;
  Pearson product-moment correlation
  coefficient r 184–5; power analysis 92–3;
  regression 207–9; Wilcoxon matched-pairs
  signed-ranks test 169; Wilcoxon rank-sum
  test 172–3
hypothesis testing for normal distribution
  87–95; alternative hypothesis 88; external
  validity 87; internal validity 87; lopsided
  tests 94, 98; null hypothesis 88, 93; one/
  two-tailed tests 93–5; research hypothesis
  87; type I/II errors 89–93
hypothesis testing for sampling distribution
  of the mean 134; when standard deviation
  is known 136–7; when standard deviation
  is unknown 137–41

independent-samples t-test 153–5;
  application of 155–7; assumption of
  homogeneity of variances 159–62;
  assumption of normality 158–9; formula
  236; power analysis for 222–3; robustness
  of 158; use of 164–5
independent variables 10
inferential statistics 5, 6, 10; error in 90; in
  hypothesis testing 87, 93; probability in
  42
internal validity 2
interquartile range 27
interval measurement scales 7, 8

Kendall's coefficient of concordance W
  200–202

least squares estimation 205
linear regression: and correlation 207;
  Pearson's r 210–11
linear relationships between two variables
  176–82; concordance/discordance 180;
  covariance between two variables 181–2;
  perfect negative 177; perfect positive 177

McNemar test 130–33
magnitude of a significance test 165–7
matched-samples t-test 146–9; formula 236;
  power analysis for 223–5; uses of 164–5

mean 23–6, 33–5; absolute average
  deviation from 29; average deviation
  from 28–9; binomial distribution 70;
  calculating 60–62; combined 35–6;
  comparing pair of 146–67; confidence
  intervals for population mean 149–50;
  confidence interval for difference between
  two population means 157–8; formula
  236; of linearly transformed data 38–41;
  sampling distribution of differences
  151–3; see also independent-samples t-test;
  matched-samples t-test; sampling
  distribution of the mean
measurement scales 6–9; interval 7, 8;
  nominal 7; ordinal 7–8; ratio 7, 8
median 21–6
method of least square estimation 205
mode 21, 23–6
multiplication rule of probability 48

nominal measurement scales 7
nonindependent-samples t-test 146–9; use of
  164–5
nonparametric tests 168–75; formula 236;
  see also Wilcoxon matched-pairs signed-
  ranks test; Wilcoxon rank-sum test
normal distribution 81–3; to approximate
  binomial distribution 95–9; standard
  84–7; Z scores table 85; see also
  hypothesis testing for normal distribution

observational studies 11
one-sample t-test 137–41, 219–21
orderings (permutations) 63–6
ordinal measurement scales 7–8

paired-samples t-test 146–9; use of 164–5
parameters, indexes of 10
Pearson correlation coefficients r, power
  analysis for independent 227–8
Pearson product-moment correlation
  coefficient r 176, 183–4; confidence
  intervals 185–7; heterogeneous sub-
  samples 194; hypothesis testing 184–5;
  linear regression 210–11; non-linear
  relationships 193–4; outliers 193; partial
  correlation 190–92; point biserial
  correlation 194–8; range effects 192–3;
  reliability 193; significant differences
  between independent samples 187;
  significant differences between
  nonindependent samples 188–90
Pearson's chi-square/squared (χ^2) test 54,
  101–3, 165; assumptions underlying
  108–10; degrees of freedom 113–14;
  formula 235; goodness of fit test 103–8;